Pressure Groups in the Global System

The Transnational Relations of Issue-Orientated Non-Governmental Organizations

Edited by
Peter Willetts

St. Martin's Press, New York

All rights reserved. For information, write:
St. Martin's Press, Inc., 175 Fifth Avenue, New York, NY 10010
Printed in Great Britain
First published in the United States of America in 1982

ISBN 0–312–64162–1

Library of Congress Cataloging in Publication Data
Main entry under title:

Pressure groups in the global system.

(Global politics ; v. 2)
Bibliography: p.
1. Pressure groups.   2. International organization.
3. World politics.   I. Willetts, Peter.   II. Series.
JF529.P72 1982   322.4'3   81–47979
ISBN 0–312–64162–1   AACR2

Contents

Preface and Acknowledgements

The aim of the Global Politics Series of books is to move away from the idea that international relations is simply concerned with the diplomatic and military relations between 'states'. The series will promote work on transnationalism (that is the relations between non-governmental organizations from different countries) and on the concept of interdependence. Greater emphasis than has been traditional in the past will be given to the effect on global politics both of international organizations and of politics within individual countries. In all these four respects a book on *Pressure Groups in the Global System* belongs in the series.

The idea of putting together this book grew out of a discussion at the British International Studies Association annual conference in December 1979. It was felt those who were interested in international organizations had a wide selection of materials available on the structure of institutions, but very little on what happens with respect to particular issues. It seemed that those who were best qualified to explore such questions were the leaders of pressure groups, who work full-time trying to achieve progress in a certain direction on a specific issue. As the editorial work progressed it became apparent that very little had been written about the international activities of pressure groups. The exception is a reasonably extensive coverage of multi-national companies, but there is virtually nothing on issue-orientated pressure groups. The result is that the original idea was modified to lay more emphasis on the structure of pressure groups and how they may relate to other elements in the global system. Fortunately, two of the forthcoming volumes in the Global Politics Series will explore how specific issues have been pursued by two very different actors. Andy Chetley of War on Want will analyse the remarkable story of how a pressure group, the International Baby Foods Action Network, put an issue on the global agenda and successfully isolated and embarassed some multi-national companies and the American government. Along a very different issue dimension, Steve Smith will analyse the attempts by the American government and other international actors to obtain the release of the United States' diplomats who had in November 1979 been taken hostage in their embassy in Teheran.

The editor is very grateful to all the contributors who agreed to give their spare time to produce their chapters for little return other than the satisfaction of making the work of their organizations more widely known. Their tolerance towards the badgering of a strong-minded and ill-informed editor was generous. Thanks go to the Barrow and Geraldine Cadbury Trust who kindly made a grant available so that the contributors could meet together and receive copies of each other's first drafts. This meant that the chapters were not solely the work of the individual authors and in particular the first and last chapters benefited from comments and corrections made by the other contributors. Nevertheless, the responsibility for the final contents and any opinions expressed remains with each respective author.

The editor would like to record his appreciation to John Groom and William Wallace for their encouragement in the early stages of the project, to the British International Studies Association for allowing three of the first drafts of chapters to be presented in a series of sessions at their 1980 annual conference, to the BISA Theory Group for further more detailed discussion and to the Political Studies Association Women's Group for discussion of the first draft of Chapter 7. Two of the chapters have already appeared elsewhere and thanks are expressed for permission to include them in this volume. Chapter 2 by Abdul S. Minty appeared in an earlier version as 'Utilising the System: A Non-Governmental Perspective' in P. Taylor and A. J. R. Groom, *International Organisation. A Conceptual Approach* (Frances Pinter, London, 1978) and Chapter 9 by Gilbert Jaeger appeared in an earlier version with the same title in *International Associations* No. 3, 1980, having been delivered as a paper at the World Forum organized by the Union of International Associations at Brussels in June 1980. Numerous organisations were most helpful in responding to requests for information, but special recognition must be given to Pat Farquhar and Eva Schmoll of the United Nations Information Centre in London for their diligent and meticulous assistance. Last but not least I am grateful to my colleagues at The City University. This study was started during a sabbatical year during which they undertook my normal teaching and administrative work, leaving me free to do research.

While preparing the book, it was heartening that there was a great deal of interest in the subject from people who saw early drafts of the various chapters. However, the clearest reaction was that far more questions remain to be tackled than those which are raised here and that far more sophistication is needed in the analysis. These points are accepted, as this is more an empirical than a theoretical work. Many other people, who were not consulted, will dismiss pressure groups as being irrelevant to the 'really important' issues in international politics, such as East–West relations. (How, one wonders, do such sceptics assess the recent rise of the European Nuclear Disarmament movement?) Thirty years ago, facing the sceptics of his time, David Truman in the Preface to *The Governmental Process* (Alfred Knopf, New York, 1951) argued the case for the systematic study of pressure groups in order to understand American politics.

Without some working conception of the political role of interest groups, their functions, and the ways in which their powers are exercised, we shall not be able adequately to understand the nature of the political process. Descriptions of that process that treat the nonparty group peripherally and merely anecdotally are not sufficient. The puzzle cannot be solved if some of the pieces are virtually ignored.

Those words apply with equal force today to the study of global politics. The puzzle of how to understand the processes of diplomacy cannot be solved if the non-governmental pieces, the pressure groups, are virtually ignored. This study is an initial attempt to examine the shape of a few of the pieces.

London,
December 1981   Peter Willetts

Notes on Contributors

Georgina Ashworth is a graduate in History, who went successively into teaching, Further Education and then university administration for two and a half years in Kenya. Back in Britain again she worked for five years with the Minority Rights Group, as Research Officer and later Assistant Director. After a brief spell as General Secretary of the Fawcett Society, she established *CHANGE International Reports*, to produe a series of studies on the conditions of women in different countries. In July 1980 she was a representative of the Fawcett Society at the Copenhagen *United Nations Decade for Women Conference* and is now co-convenor of the Decade Network in Britain.

Tom Burke is a graduate in Philosophy, who went into Further Education and started working for Merseyside *Friends of the Earth* as their Co-ordinator, before moving full-time in 1973 to the central FOE London office as their Local Groups Co-ordinator. In 1975 he joined the Board of Directors and in 1979 became their International Consultant. In 1980 he was Vice-Chairman of FOE in Britain. Currently he is Press Officer for the *European Environment Bureau*.

Olle Dahlén is a graduate in Political Science, who after the Second World War had a long career in Swedish politics, as an administrator in the Liberal Party and as a member of parliament, specialising in foreign affairs. Since 1973 he has been *Swedish Ambassador to Non-Governmental Organisations*. He has also been the Chairman of the World Council of Churches, Commission of the Churches on International Affairs.

Martin Ennals is a graduate in International Relations, who worked for UNESCO in the 1950s. From 1960 to 1966 he was General Secretary of the *National Council for Civil Liberties* in Britain and then until 1968 was Information Officer for the National Committee for Commonwealth Immigrants, when he resigned in protest at the 1968 Immigration Act. From July 1968 to June 1980 he was Secretary-General of *Amnesty International*.

David Gilmour is a graduate in Modern History, who has worked for several years in the Middle East, initially at the Institute of Palestine Studies, Beirut, during the first year of the Lebanese civil-war and then as a journalist in Cairo.

From April 1978 to mid-1979 he was with the *Council for the Advancement of Arab-British Understanding*, becoming Deputy Director, and then for two years was Assistant Editor of *Middle East International*. He is the author of *Dispossessed: the Ordeal of the Palestinians 1917–1980*.

Gilbert Jaeger is a graduate in Economics, who had a career in finance and banking from 1941 to 1952 in Belgium. Then he joined the *United Nations High Commission for Refugees* and served with them until his retirement in 1979. He occupied a series of senior positions, including Director of Assistance from 1972 to 1977 and Director of Protection from 1977 to 1979. Throughout his work he was involved in co-operation with voluntary agencies both in material assistance programmes and in international legal protection for refugees.

Abdul S. Minty was born in South Africa, but because of the apartheid system left the country in 1958 to complete his education, obtaining a degree in International Relations from London University. He was a founder member of the *Anti-Apartheid Movement* in Britain and started work with them while still a student. Since 1963 he has been Honorary Secretary of the Movement. In 1979 he also became Director of the new specialist group, the *World Campaign against Military and Nuclear Collaboration with South Africa*, which is based in Oslo.

Elizabeth Stamp is a graduate in Economics and Political Science, who initially worked in market research for several years. She has been the Information Officer for *Oxfam* since 1963 and has visited the Middle East, India, East Africa and Central America to see some of Oxfam's work at firsthand. She has written a book on the Third World for school children, *The Hungry World*, and edited a book on the agricultural aspects of development, *Growing out of Poverty*.

Peter Willetts is a graduate in International Relations, who has taught for one year in a secondary school in Nigeria and for three years at Makerere University, Uganda. Since 1973 he has been a Lecturer in International Relations in the Department of Systems Science at The City University and has specialized on the Third World and on the United Nations. His publications have included two books, *The Non-Aligned Movement* and *The Non-Aligned in Havana*.

Introduction

Journalists, academics and members of the general public who follow politics usually make a strong distinction between the politics of their own country and international politics. The newspapers are divided into separate pages for 'Home News' and 'Overseas News'; university departments offer courses on individual countries or on 'Comparative Government' and separate courses on 'International Relations'; legislatures have specialist foreign affairs committees and set aside particular days for foreign affairs debates. Yet we are in such an interdependent world that these distinctions are artificial.

When we consider particular political issues, the boundary between domestic and international politics can sometimes seem to be relatively insignificant. Issues within one country, such as the role of trades unions within Polish society, Islamic consciousness in Iran or the assassination of an Archbishop in El Salvador, can easily and rapidly become global issues. Even when governments want to isolate an issue from foreign interference, they are often unable to do so. The British government found that a hunger-strike by Irish republican prisoners in a Northern Ireland jail involved them in dealings with the European Commission for Human Rights, the Irish Commission for Justice and Peace, the International Committee of the Red Cross, United States Congressmen and a personal representative of the Pope. Thus, events within countries can produce activity at the international level. Equally, change can come from the other direction, from the international level to the domestic. The NATO decision in December 1979 to instal Cruise and Pershing missiles in Western Europe has caused turmoil in Belgian, British, Dutch and West German politics. In the British case, through the Labour Party going 'unilateralist', the NATO decision helped to create the Social Democratic Party, which is mounting a major challenge to the two parties which have dominated British politics since 1945. At a less dramatic level, the proclamation by the United Nations of a series of campaigns, such as the International Year for Disabled Persons, has had an impact throughout the world.

So a major problem when trying to understand politics is finding out how issues arise and especially what takes issues across the boundaries of different countries with the result that they enter international politics. One thing that all the issues mentioned above do have in common is the intense involvement of highly organised interest groups or promotional pressure groups. It has long been accepted that pressure groups are essential to an understanding of politics within individual countries. However, most people concentrate overwhelmingly on pressure group activities within one single country trying to influence the government's policy. On the other hand, those people focussing on international politics tend to ignore the activities of pressure groups. As a result the study of pressure groups has been unbalanced, because it has been affected markedly by the artificial distinction between domestic and international politics. This book, *Pressure Groups in the Global System*, is aimed at opening up a new subject and helping to challenge the still-dominant assumption that there is a distinct realm of inter-state relations. It is not possible in this introductory study to reach general conclusions on how issues are put on the global agenda, but it has been possible to show that the day to day work of many pressure groups frequently transcends international boundaries. On some of the major issues of contemporary world politics pressure groups are having a significant impact through their contact with their own and foreign governments, with the United Nations and other intergovernmental organisations, with the world's media, and with international non-governmental organizations.

The first chapter aims to show how pressure groups fit into the structure of the global political system. In the traditional approach to international relations, now usually known as 'Realism', the separation of domestic from international politics is a central assumption. Academics who challenge Realism have created the new word 'transnational' to refer to groups which have contact with more than one country without involving governments. A second new word, 'interdependence', has entered into everyday language, to refer to the idea that communications and economic relations between different countries are now so complex and so important that each country has lost its independence. It is impossible to take any major decision within one country without having an impact on and a response from other countries. The ideas of transnationalism and interdependence provide a basis on which we can understand the presence of pressure groups in global politics, whereas Realism does not. The chapter explores this debate between the two competing perspectives.

Chapters 2 to 7 outline the recent history of groups which have been involved in six major issues: racism in Southern Africa, Palestinian rights, individual human rights, development, conservation and women's liberation. With the exception of Palestinian rights, the chapters come from leading activists in pressure groups, that is from the Anti-Apartheid Movement, Amnesty International, Oxfam, Friends of the Earth and the women's movement. They are all describing and analysing the workings of pressure groups in light of their own personal experiences. These chapters stand on their own and can be read by those who do not wish to be concerned with the problems of theory which have been raised in Chapter 1. The case studies are independent of each other for those who are interested in just one of the issues. However, on all the six issues it is clear that the work of the groups does not fit in with a Realist approach and that transnational relations have been highly significant. It is interesting to compare the similarities and the differences between the six case studies.

The final three chapters make assessments of pressure groups in three quite different ways. Chapter 8 was written by a serving diplomat, who reports how one government, that of Sweden, takes account of pressure groups in its conduct of foreign relations. There must be a strong presumption that the Swedish Foreign Ministry sees the world in more complex terms than do most governments, because the author, Olle Dahlen, was the world's first Ambassador to Non-Governmental Organisations. Chapter 9 comes from a former member of the United Nations secretariat, who reports how pressure groups — always described at the UN by the neutral term, non-governmental organisations — have been of great importance in the UN's work for refugees. Lastly, a comparison is made of the groups from the six case studies, with respect to their formation, the targets of their pressure, the resources they can use and the way they choose the questions to be pursued.

The case studies in this book come from issues on which there is great public concern and cover groups which are household names, but this does not mean that their role in world politics is unusual. It would have been possible to have produced several more books filled with case studies from equally famous pressure groups, such as the International Planned Parenthood Federation or the Red Cross, the World Wildlife Fund or the World Veterans Federation, the International Commission of Jurists or the Inter-Parliamentary Union. While very many of the pressure groups have their origins in the Western world, this does not mean that we are considering a phenomenom which is only relevant to Western politics. Some groups are truly global in their membership, others have global support but are only organised in the West because it is Western governments which are blocking political change, yet other groups are strong in the West and seek to exercise influence throughout the world. It is hoped that the impact of this book will be three-fold. Whenever the reader is considering groups or issues which appear to be a matter of domestic politics, he or she should automatically ask what are the international connections. Secondly, whenever questions of traditional inter-state diplomacy are considered, there should automatically be an investigation of what non-governmental groups are involved. Thirdly, it should not be assumed that only sectional economic interest groups, such as companies and trade unions, are important: both general promotional groups, such as political parties and the churches, and highly specialised promotional pressure groups, such as the ones covered in this book, are major participants in global politics.

1   Pressure Groups as Transnational Actors

PETER WILLETTS

A variety of terms have been used to describe organized groups of people who seek to influence political decisions. Some like to call them pressure groups, while many others prefer to speak of interest groups and Professor Finer puts them all under the heading of 'the lobby'.[1] Diplomats nearly always talk of Non-Governmental Organizations and 'NGOs' has now become a standard piece of jargon in the world of diplomacy. It seems inappropriate to use the term 'interest groups' because it carries a strong bias towards considering sectional economic interests as being more important and more influential. Indeed some sectional interests may have never become involved in the wider politics of society. Most of them have interests to pursue *within* the group that take up far more of their time and resources. For the study of politics, it is preferable to refer to pressure groups, because this emphasizes our concern with the way such groups seek to exercise influence. They may try to bring about social change by the direct effect of their actions on other individuals, by their impact upon other groups or by affecting government policy. It is the act of applying pressure that brings them into politics. But this is not to say that all pressure groups are active in politics all the time.

Pressure groups have conventionally been considered relevant to the study of the domestic politics of each country. If international relations in the traditional view concerns the interactions between 'states', which seek to mobilize 'power' to promote their respective 'national interests', then pressure groups are not relevant to international relations. It used to be assumed by Realists that there were few non-governmental interactions between different countries; certainly they were not discussed. Now when faced with the large literature on transnationalism (that is, relations between different societies across country boundaries, which bypass governments),[2] the interactions may be dismissed as being of secondary importance, because they are not seen as affecting substantially the power relationships between different countries. Pressure groups cannot themselves be considered by Realists to utilize power. In addition, it is argued that governments have the authority to control transnational activities and tolerate them as long as they are compatible with the 'national interest', but stop them when the 'national interest' is threatened.[3] All of these theoretical assumptions will be challenged, but first of all it is worth considering the great diversity among the pressure groups.

Types of Pressure Groups

In the literature on British politics, a distinction has been made between sectional groups which 'seek to protect the interests of a particular section of society' and promotional groups which 'seek to promote causes arising from a given set of attitudes'.[4] It is argued that this distinction is related to the difference between aiming for a specialized small membership or a general mass movement; it affects a strategy of aiming to influence government directly or gaining support in public opinion; and it largely explains whether there will be success or failure in applying pressure.[5] For our purposes, it is worth making further sub-divisions among both sectional and promotional groups and it will be seen that the above relationships do not hold uniformly.

Sectional groups

The first of our eight categories of pressure groups covers *sectional economic groups*. These include companies, commerce, financial institutions, trade unions and agriculture. They are specialized groups, with restricted membership, are generally believed to have direct access to government and to be highly successful in achieving their goals, particularly on matters of economic policy. They are usually involved in a complex hierarchical structure of organization. For example, in Britain we have the companies, such as Imperial Tobacco Ltd, or Gallaher Ltd., both of which manufacture cigarettes, and the trade unions, such as the Tobacco Workers Union, the Transport and General Workers Union and the General and Municipal Workers Union, all of which represent tobacco workers. The individual companies co-operate in their employers' association and the Tobacco Advisory Council, while the unions have joint negotiating committees. Further up the hierarchy representing much more general economic interests, we have the Confederation of British Industry and the Trades Union Congress. However, the structure does not stop at the boundaries of Britain. Both the CBI and the TUC are members of world bodies, the International Organization of Employers and the International Confederation of Free Trade Unions, respectively. The CBI and the TUC each send delegates to the International Labour Organization, are members of European confederations, serve on OECD advisory committees and have been involved with the UN. The IOE and the ICFTU also have a formal consultative status themselves with the ILO and several other intergovernmental organizations, including the UN. The complexity of these arrangements shows that country boundaries do not necessarily provide major discontinuities for pressure groups

Professional associations form a second category. Doctors, nurses, lawyers, teachers, social workers, the various scientific and technical disciplines, journalists and so on, all have their own professional bodies. In some respects these act like trade unions in defending the sectional economic interests of their members, but in many cases they restrict membership to those who have attained certain qualifications and exercise some of the employers' functions in monitoring work standards. Their really distinctive feature is the promotion of a strong moral code, which can place loyalty to the profession and to the clients above loyalty to employers or to the government. If the organizational links for one of the professions was outlined in the same way as it was for the companies and the unions, the result would be very similar, with there being extensive links to regional and global professional associations and to intergovernmental bodies, particularly the UN specialized agencies such as the World Health Organization or UNESCO. But in addition, the professions are fundamentally transnational in two further ways. Generally speaking, the professional ethics of each profession are very similar in each country of the world, even though the political cultures may differ substantially. All doctors feel bound to observe the Hippocratic oath, wherever they practise medicine. Secondly, much of the work of the professional depends upon the free flow of information and the accumulation of knowledge within a single, global, professional community.

Recreational clubs are a third category of sectional groups. Even though recreation is a highly personal form of activity, these clubs also have transnational links and, with the great increase in the volume of tourism which has occurred since the Second World War, they promote exchanges between different countries and offer reciprocal facilities to their members. Some of these also form full-blown International Non-Governmental Organizations, (INGOs). There is a Boy Scouts World Bureau and a World Association of Girl Guides, both of which have a recognized status with several intergovernmental organizations. Among the most widespread and popular forms of recreation are the various sports. These too, in the competitive element to find the best performer, are intrinsically transnational. Here the groups are involved in a very special relationship with world politics. The individual sportspeople and their clubs usually have a strong commitment to sport for its own sake and the desire 'to keep politics out of sport', while governments try energetically to associate themselves with the prestige of staging and winning sporting competitions. Anyone who is tempted to think that sport is irrelevant to international politics should reflect upon the history of the Olympic Games.

Promotional groups

Next, we may turn to the five categories of promotional groups, starting with the *welfare agencies*, which run operational programmes and/or raise funds to provide education, health or social services or to relieve poverty. Very many of the charities, trusts and foundations are very specialized in their concerns and highly parochial in their area of work. Even with some of the larger agencies one would not presume that they would ever be involved in direct contacts outside their home country. However, among the top twenty British charities in terms of their annual income, two, Oxfam and Christian Aid, collect money almost entirely to benefit people overseas, another two have large overseas programmes, four more are members of INGOs and sixteen of the twenty are members of the National Council for Voluntary Organizations, which has an International Committee and 'attempts to represent the views of UK voluntary organizations internationally to bodies such as the UN agencies, Commonwealth Secretariat and the EEC',[6] and is itself a member of an INGO, the International Council on Social Welfare. Under British law, charities are not allowed to be active in politics, but such a concept is only tenable with a very narrow, 'common sense' definition of politics as covering the relationships between the political parties. If politics is taken to cover all the activities of governments, whether or not they are contentious, then there can be few charities of any size which do not at some point in every year co-operate with central or local government. Under the broadest definition of politics as the process by which society assigns the moral values which are to be supported and decides the distribution of resources to accord with those assignments, all the charities are fundamentally political. Thus, charities which choose to transfer resources or engage in other activities across international boundaries are taking part in world politics.

Religious organizations are concerned with the general promotion of values. In some countries there is a frequently held belief that religion should not be involved in politics, while in other countries few would find such a belief to be comprehensible. Even within the same country, religious organizations vary substantially in the amount they affect the political process: from helping to set a climate of opinion to being a major challenge to government, when issues central to their religious concerns are raised. What the religions have in common is that none of the organizations which have a significant number of adherents within one country is confined solely to that country. Most of them have a formal transnational structure, such as the Anglican Communion or the Baptist World Alliance, with the Protestant churches being further grouped in the World Council of Churches. The Catholics and Islam each have arrangements, which result in unique hybrids in a world where NGOs and governments are seen as being separate. The Vatican as the headquarters of a major INGO is for historical reasons treated as a state by the governments of the world and the rise in Islamic consciousness has contributed to the formation of the Islamic Conference, an intergovernmental organization. Nevertheless, despite its co-option by governments, Islam also remains a potent transnational political influence.

Communal groups arise when distinct segments of society, such as people of common ethnic origin or resident within a particular area, come together in order to promote their group identity and group status. They can have highly specialized concerns, such as the Welsh Language Society nominally concentrating on promotion of the use of Welsh, but frequently they beome active on a wide range of political questions: the Welsh Language Society has been involved in seeking to change policy on court procedures, road signs, education, television broadcasting and home ownership in rural areas. In many colonial societies, communal groups were the source from which nationalist political parties grew. Very few communal groups have established formal links in INGOs, such as the Celtic League or the Inuit Circumpolar Conference, but many obtain support from governments which are hostile to the government in their own country or have strong informal bilateral transnational communications with their ethnic kin. All communal groups can, in theory at least, have access to the United Nations via the Commission on Human Rights, Sub-Commission on Prevention of Discrimination and Protection of Minorities. Some communal groups move beyond specific cultural concerns to make economic or political demands, including claiming the right to form their own government. A few groups which have done this have become important global actors. African liberation movements have been accorded observer status by many intergovernmental organizations and at times have been given full membership. Even more successful has been the PLO, with membership of the Arab League, the Group of 77 and the Non-Aligned Movement, the right to attend all UN organs and conferences and recognition from a majority of the world's governments. To some people it may seem inappropriate to regard liberation movements as a type of communal promotional group, but really all that occurs is an attempt to move from domestic politics to an involvement in world politics. It is the claim for international recognition of the 'national right to self-determination' which converts a domestic communal group into a liberation movement.

Women's groups are another distinct sub-category among the communal groups. They do not have a narrow numerical base, which can often be a disadvantage for minority groups, but they are dealing with the same issues of group identity and group status. In many societies there is a large number and a great diversity to the women's groups. They have often been established since the early years of the twentieth century or the late nineteenth century and a dozen of the corresponding transnational associations date back this far. The majority of formal organizations have restricted memberships such as the Medical Women's International Association, or specialized concerns, such as the International Contraception, Abortion and Sterilization Campaign, but a few are more broadly based aiming for a general membership and covering a wide range of women's questions. An anomalous feature of the contemporary scene is that modern feminist groups do not co-ordinate well either by linking different issues or by moving beyond the local community, particularly to the transnational level. This may be due to a strong ideological predisposition towards seeing 'organization' as a male concept for promoting structures of hierarchy and domination. It is not unreasonable to assume that this pattern will change, in response to the desire to achieve political results, and that new feminist INGOs will in increasing numbers join the forty-seven relatively traditional women's INGOs already active in world politics by 1970.[7] The formation of ICASC in 1978 is evidence that the change is already starting to take place.

Political parties are normally considered to be analytically distinct from pressure groups, on the basis that they seek to take over office rather than to influence a limited range of policy outcomes. In practice this distinction does not accurately reflect how groups behave. Pressure groups, when they have widespread support, always have the option of converting themselves into political parties. Both agrarian parties and ecology parties have occurred in a variety of European countries. Anti-Common Market and unofficial Campaign for Nuclear Disarmament candidates have been markedly unsuccessful in Britain, but the Progress Party in Denmark achieved a spectacular growth mainly on the single issue of abolishing income tax. On the other hand, groups which have always claimed to be broadly based political parties, such as the National Front in Britain or refugee parties in West Germany, may appear to the government and to the electorate to represent minorities concerned with a very limited range of questions and only able to influence politics through their indirect impact on the other parties.[8] Even major parties, when they are in opposition and no election is in the offing, may have few strategies for applying political pressure on the government, which are not equally available to pressure groups. (In fact, in most countries the potential for taking office lies not so much with opposition parties as with particular economic–professional groups: the military and/or the police.) When they are in government, a certain distance still remains between government as an operational institution and party as a repository of ideology, so that the party is akin to a pressure group with privileged access to government. From the point of view of world politics, the distinction between party and pressure group is not at all appropriate. Legal doctrines assert that governments are the representatives of states and that relationships with *any* other body constitute interference in its domestic jurisdiction. From the Realist, theoretical perspective parties are like pressure groups in being unable to mobilize international 'power'.

In a manner similar to professional associations, political parties in the modern world are intrinsically drawn into a transnational exchange of ideas. Party ideologies provide a structure through which people may interpret the political world around them, but there is no logic by which our need for understanding is restricted to what is occurring within the boundaries of our own country. Baffling events in far-off places demand explanation; foreign people and institutions, which have a clear image, can be used as reference points for the advocacy of domestic policy; support from prestigious external sources is beneficial, while one's opponent may be discredited by being identified with hostile elements in the environment. From a perspective that sees political parties as being involved in global politics, it is not so surprising to find that major foreign policy failures can lead a party to topple its leader from office. There are some remarkable examples, from Lyndon Johnson in the United States, to Anthony Eden in Britain and Nikita Khrushchev in the Soviet Union.

However, not all political parties are formally organized on a transational basis. The socialists have the longest history, because international solidarity has been part of the ideology of most socialists. Two formal organizations were established successively in the nineteenth century. The Second International was seriously weakened by the failure of socialist parties to unite against the outbreak of war in 1914, but co-operation between social democrats did continue in the inter-war years. The current Socialist International, which is a successor to the Second International, was founded in 1951 and now has forty-eight member parties from forty-two countries. In 1919 the Third International of communist parties, Comintern, was formed, but it came under Stalin's domination and was disbanded in May 1943 as a gesture of goodwill towards the Western allies. A comparable organization, the Communist Information Bureau, Cominform, was established in September 1947, to assist in the strengthening of Soviet influence in Eastern Europe and the development of ideological uniformity. This was used as the instrument of Stalin's ideological war against Tito from 1948 onwards and was disbanded in April 1956 as part of Khrushchev's *rapprochement* with Tito. Since then no formal communist international has existed, but there has been an intermittent series of world conferences of communist parties. In addition, the party congresses of each of the ruling parties are usually attended by the First Secretaries or at least a Politburo member from the other ruling parties, with the result that they provide an informal basis for discussion and co-ordination.

In the Third World during the colonial period nationalist parties often had a close association with socialist or communist parties in Europe and met each other in lobbying at the UN and other international meetings. Since independence, the Afro-Asian Peoples' Solidarity Organization (AAPSO) founded in December 1957 and based in Cairo, along with the Organization of Afro-Asian, Latin American Peoples' Solidarity (OSPAAL) founded in January 1966 and based in Havana, have tended to attract only the minor and/or the more radical nationalist parties. In some regions where close party ties have at times developed, such as the 'Mulungushi Club' in East Africa around 1970, the party ties have been difficult to distinguish from intergovernmental relations.

Moving to other areas of the political map, we find that there has been a Liberal International since April 1947, but the right wing has been much slower to organize transnationally. A European Christian Democrat Union was founded in 1947, but it was not until 1961 that a Christian Democrat World Union appeared. In the Assembly of the European Community the Christian Democrats have remained separate from the European Democratic Group of conservatives, which only includes parties from the United Kingdom and Demark. Outside the Community, a totally different body, the European Democrat Union brings together twelve member parties (half from within the EC and half from the other European countries) with associate members from Australia, Canada, New Zealand and Japan. The EDU was formed as recently as April 1978. While it might eventually recruit world-wide, there is no sign yet of a global organization of conservative parties. Other types of parties, anarchist, agrarian, Islamic, fascist or ethnic parties, for example, and the Republicans and the Democrats in the USA, have not established substantial transnational links. Clearly, of all the groups which we have considered, political parties are the only ones to be completely absent from some countries and they are also among the least likely to have strong, institutionalized transnational links.

Lastly, in contrast to the three types of general promotional groups, there are *specific-issue, promotional groups*. These consist of groups of people who have come together solely for the purpose of promoting social change on a particular issue, usually by seeking change in government policy. They are the groups which most readily spring to mind when the term 'pressure group' is used. By the nature of their work, specific-issue groups are likely to be challenging orthodoxy. Often they are either raising new issues, which have not before appeared on the political agenda, or are trying to change the way existing issues are handled. Thus, they usually concentrate on influencing public opinion and the media and so they become household names. Frequently, new issues will not lead to specific-issue groups being formed because existing groups such as sectional economic groups or political parties can readily take them up. In many countries there has developed a consensus on questions of foreign policy which established groups become reluctant to challenge for fear of being regarded disloyal. As a result specific-issue groups do arise quite often on foreign policy. In Britain the development of nuclear weapons led to the Campaign for Nuclear Disarmament being formed; increasing public awareness of the contrast between decolonization in the Commonwealth and trends in the opposite direction within South Africa led to the Anti-Apartheid Movement; and the steady decline in the priority given to Official Development Assistance led to the World Development Movement. Each of the groups quoted is based in Britain and is known for its attempts to influence British foreign policy. However, it should occasion no surprise that such concerns frequently lead them into transnational activities in order to obtain information or to gain external allies. Furthermore, the events to which the groups were responding were also relevant in similar ways to those in other countries and so similar groups were formed elsewhere. In each case an INGO has resulted to provide a channel of communication between the groups in each country.[9]

New issues of the last two decades have also produced transnational activities through a totally different process. It has frequently been noted that problems arising from pollution and environmental issues cannot be solved by governments acting on their own. The technical need for co-operation is one of the factors producing interdependence. What is rarely, if ever, noted as well is that this has produced an international political process, in which pressure groups must engage in transnational lobbying in order to have any chance of affecting the outcomes. Friends of the Earth Ltd. in Britain is a member of Friends of the Earth International and is in frequent contact with the FOE groups in many other countries.

The Connections Between Different Pressure Groups

To some extent the eight categories of pressure groups given above are ideal types and very few groups belong unambiguously in just one category. The International Committee of Catholic Nurses is both professional and religious, while the International Council of Social Democratic Women involves both transnational links between parties and the group identity of women. Alternatively, some activities may have only one significant aspect to them for each of the participants, but belong in quite different categories according to which participants we are considering. The foreign tour of an orchestra may be an economic interest of the company, a professional opportunity for the players, recreation for the audience and a prestige promotion for the government which has subsidized the trip.

The first major point to note is the very great diversity among the pressure groups. The eight categories of groups are very different from each other in the motivation and goals which bring them together, yet there is both overlap between the categories and an enormous number and range of groups within each category. Secondly, although pressure groups are widely seen as a feature of Western democratic political systems, they do in fact exist in every country in the world, including both the least developed and the most totalitarian. There can be few, if any, countries which do not have groups from at least five of the eight categories. Thirdly, all types of groups can be significantly affected (from their own perspectives) by international politics and directly or indirectly engage in a wide variety of international and transnational interactions.

Any description of non-governmental groups being primarily concerned with promoting co-operation among their members and then moving from this base, with greater or lesser frequency depending upon the type of group, to seek influence in decision making by government, is too simple a picture. In most complex societies (and the term complex should not be equated with developed; India or even Uganda are considerably more complex than Iceland) several pressure groups arise within a single area of concern. Frequently these co-operate with each other by evolving distinctive specialization in membership, objectives or tactics; by exchanging information; and by co-ordinating activities, when they apply political pressure or engage in operational programmes. Sometimes by working together groups can obtain services and undertake activities which would be beyond the resources of any of the individual groups. The result can be not only a great deal of communication and co-operation but also a complex network of country-wide and transnational organizations.

If we take Oxfam as an example, it is part of an extensive network of research, fund-raising, educational and promotional groups concerned with development. The 'Development Guide', published by the Overseas Development Institute, lists 198 groups based in Britain.[10] In two major specialized areas of work Oxfam is in national bodies: the Standing Conference on Refugees includes Oxfam and thirty-one other agencies, to exchange information and make joint representations to government, and the Disasters Emergency Committee links Oxfam to four of the major relief agencies, primarily to enable joint fund-raising appeals to be made. To deal with its general concerns as a charity, Oxfam is a member along with 236 other non-governmental organizations of the National Council of Voluntary Organizations. For the purposes of sharing their experiences and skills in producing information, the Centre for World Development Education organizes a Public Information Group. In October 1980 this brought together forty-seven representatives from twenty-four agencies, four members of the UK government's Overseas Development Administration and forty-four press and broadcasting journalists, and the conference was funded in part by the EEC Development Commission and the UN NGO Liaison Office. Thus, in addition to its own activities, Oxfam has at least four other routes, SCOR, DEC, NCVO and CWDE, through which it can communicate with the public and with government at the national level.

The situation becomes more, not less, complex at the global level, as a pressure group can relate to the United Nations and the specialized agencies (1) directly, on its own initiative, (2) via national co-ordinating bodies, and (3) via transnational co-ordinating bodies (INGOs). Oxfam is a member of Euro Action ACORD (Agency for Co-operation and Research in Development), a consortium for the promotion of joint relief and development programmes. In Geneva, it works with the American based Catholic Relief Services and three INGOs, the League of Red Cross Societies, the Lutheran World Federation and the World Council of Churches, in a Steering Committee for Disasters. Oxfam is also a direct member of the International Council of Voluntary Agencies and an indirect member both via the national body, SCOR, and also via the INGO, Euro Action ACORD. For a while Oxfam's Director held the Chair of the International Council. Several other formal organizational connections of less direct concern to Oxfam exist, along with a whole multitude of *ad hoc* and non-formal links.

Not all groups work in as complex a network of domestic and transnational organizations as does Oxfam. Indeed, Amnesty International, as an explicit matter of policy, does not allow its National Sections to affiliate to any other organization, while for the Anti-Apartheid Movement it is not a matter of policy but there are few formal channels to other groups. On the other hand, both of them have extensive non-formal links. For example, Amnesty is strongly promoted by the churches and Anti-Apartheid maintains a close working relationship with the ANC and SWAPO offices in London.

It is not just co-operation between the bureaucracies which brings groups together. The structure of political beliefs also serves to integrate issues. Ordinary people do not necessarily relate environmental, development and disarmament issues to each other, but for political activists they are often seen as being inseparable. Thus, Oxfam run a Wastesaver Project to recycle aluminium and rags, partly in order to raise funds but also to reduce profligate consumption in a world of want. Oxfam's Youth Department runs work-camps in conjunction with Friends of the Earth, while Oxfam and the Conservation Society have a joint imprint on sticky labels for re-using envelopes. The Brandt Commission Report argued that expenditure on armaments represents 'a huge waste of resources which should be deployed for peaceful development',[11] a link which was also made in the Final Document of the UN Special Session on Disarmament.[12] In April 1980 the World Disarmament Campaign was launched in Britain with the objective being the implementation of the proposals in the UN Final Document. Three months later, 'Oxfam had donated £10,000 towards that part of [the Campaign's] work which emphasises the relationship of disarmament to development'.[13] Six months later, three local Friends of the Earth groups and four other ecology groups, along with some eighty United Nations Associations and more than 200 other varied groups were listed as 'Support Groups' of the World Disarmament Campaign.[14] These examples illustrate not just issue linkages but also how global political processes can have a major input to political interactions within a country.

Pressure Groups and the Intergovernmental Organizations

Reference has been made at several points to connections between pressure groups and the United Nations. This is not a new phenomenon and it dates back to the formation of the UN, yet it is not mentioned in standard works by as diverse a range of scholars as Alker and Russett, Bailey, Claude, Gregg and Barkun, Luard and Nicholas.[15] One thousand two hundred non-governmental organizations attended the San Francisco conference which finalized the UN Charter.[16] Although the original proposals drawn up at Dumbarton Oaks by the 'Big Four' made no mention of NGOs, they were successful in applying pressure, mainly via the United States delegation, so that NGOs were granted an official status.[17] The result was Article 71 of the Charter:

> The Economic and Social Council may make suitable arrangements for consultation with non-governmental organisations which are concerned with matters within its competence. Such arrangements may be made with international organisations and, where appropriate, with national organisations after consultation with the Member of the United Nations concerned.

The NGOs wanted to widen the UN's responsibilities as much as possible beyond security questions. They 'strove for the inclusion . . . of some provision for dealing with questions related to educational and cultural co-operation, human rights . . . and to the economic and social area in general'.[18] Some authors claim that the NGOs were directly responsible for the existence of the Charter's provisions on human rights.[19]

In implementing Article 71, ECOSOC has drawn up and regularly reviews a list of NGOs which have been granted 'consultative status'. The work is done through the Committee on NGOs, which has to apply several criteria before accepting any NGO on the list. The activities of the organization should fall within the Council's competence. It should have an established headquarters, an administration, authorized representatives and a policy-making body. Although one government urged that an organization should only be considered international if it had branches in ten or more countries, it has been accepted that two countries are sufficient.[20] It soon became plain that there was resistance to granting consultative status to 'national organizations'. But the possibility had to remain, because of the Charter provision, and in 1949 there were five national bodies along with eighty-five INGOs on the list.[21] When the arrangements were reviewed in 1968, provision was made for suspension or withdrawal from consultative status, if an organization was shown to be improperly under the influence of a government.[22]

The list of organizations originally was divided into Category A, those which have 'a basic interest in most of the activities of the Council, and are closely linked with the economic or social life of the areas which they represent;' Category B, those with a special competence but in limited fields; and Category C, those 'primarily concerned with the development of public opinion and with the dissemination of information.'[23] These categories might appear to match the ones we discussed earlier in this paper, with Category A covering the sectional economic groups, Category B the more specialized professional associations, recreational clubs and welfare agencies and leaving the other promotional groups in Category C. In practice by 1949, when the system had settled down, the major trade unions' and producers' INGOs were in Category A; the vast majority, seventy-seven out of ninety organizations, including ten religious and sixteen women's organizations, were in Category B; and the four in Category C did not have any obvious distinguishing feature to them. The two exceptions in Category A are not so surprising, when one remembers they were chosen by United Nations delegates rather than by impartial adjudicators. They were a professional association, the Inter-Parliamentary Union, a group with which diplomats must maintain good relations, and a specific-issue promotional group, the World Federation of United Nations Associations, a group promoting the organization in which they spend their working lives.

The classifications were modified in 1950 and again in 1968, when they became Category I, Category II and the Roster. The three categories are still supposed to correspond to differences in the breadth of the organization's activities and its relevance to ECOSOC's mandate, but 'in practice the Committee has tended to treat the consultative status categories as a hierarchy.'[24] Since 1968 the number of NGOs with Category I status has been increased from sixteen to thirty-one and in all except two cases the fifteen new groups have been promoted from Category II. Promotion from the Roster to Category II has also occurred regularly, but far more of the new groups admitted to Category II have not previously been on the Roster. When one scans the list it is clear that the Category I NGOs are the more broadly based, non-specialist groups, but it is impossible to see any operational criteria which distinguish those on Category II from those on the Roster. Thus, the three categories do appear as a status ranking.

Evolution of the system has produced other changes which are of general political significance. In an early report it was said: 'In order to avoid duplication, an organisation whose work is mainly or wholly within the field of activity of a specialised agency is generally not admitted to consultation under Article 71.'[25] Now, as part of the trend towards a decline in the independence of the agencies and the extension of the authority of the United Nations over their work, the situation has been totally reversed. Acquisition of consultative status with one of the specialized agencies, since 1968, has led automatically to listing in the Roster. Secondly, among the many small increases in the powers of the UN Secretary-General is the authority he was given in 1968 to place NGOs on the Roster on his own initiative. Thirdly, 'national organizations' which only operate in, or have personnel from, a single country have begun to gain consultative status in slightly larger numbers in the 1970s.

Apart from being a status ranking, the main significance of the different categories of consultative status has been in the differences in the procedural rights which are obtained. From the beginning Category A organizations had the same rights as governments to receive documents and to circulate their own written communications to all delegations as official ECOSOC documents. They could propose items for the agenda and be heard on the question of the inclusion of the item. If the item was accepted, they could open the debate and might be invited to reply to the discussion. Organizations in the other two categories could only have their written statements circulated, if it was requested by a government, and could only speak before the NGO Committee rather than the full Council. The Committee could also approve a request by a Category A organization to speak before the Council on any of the other items on the agenda. With the review of the arrangements, approved in new regulations in 1968, the procedures remain basically the same, except for a slight liberalization. Now Category II NGOs can also have their written statements circulated as an automatic right, but they are limited to 500 words whereas Category I are allowed 2000 words. Category II organizations have also gained the right, upon approval by the NGO Committee, to speak before the full Council when there is no relevant subsidiary body for the subject. The origin of the 1968 revision had been the disclosure that several non-governmental organizations had received funds, sometimes indirectly and without their knowledge, from the United States Central Intelligence Agency. The result was the addition of a requirement that the INGOs should in principle be funded by their 'national affiliates' and/or by individual members (i.e. individual people) and that any other sources of funds should be declared. This was backed up by a new requirement that those with consultative status should submit a report on their work every four years and a new provision that the NGO Committee could recommend suspension or expulsion from consultative status. Although several governments may be hostile to particular NGOs, notably those active on human rights questions, it seems unlikely that the provisions for suspension or exclusion will ever be utilized, except to delete groups which become moribund.[26]

In practice the system has not always worked smoothly from the NGOs' point of view. In 1974, as part of the general attempt to rationalize the Council's work, the NGO Committee was required after 1975, like many other subsidiary bodies, to meet every two years instead of annually. The result was that the ECOSOC session opened in early 1976 without there being any provision for participation by NGOs. Considerable pressure had to be exercised by the NGOs as a whole before those in Category I were allowed to speak. However, in 1977 the NGO Committee was authorized to meet outside the normal biennial cycle, so that the problem did not arise again in 1978 and thereafter.

ECOSOC started life as a relatively small group of eighteen members. With the Charter amendments which came into effect in 1965 and 1973, the Council increased to twenty-seven and then to fifty-four members. The volume of business has also increased substantially. In such a situation governments have tended to ignore rather than encourage the NGOs. When the contribution of a NGO has been unwelcome to particular governments, then the tendency has been to deny the legitimacy of the NGO and to deny its right to take part in the intergovernmental forums. As with most of the UN's activities, the legal authority provided by the Charter, by resolutions and by rules of procedure, is little guide to the regular political behaviour. Peacekeeping operations lie in an unspecified and ambiguous manner somewhere within the authority provided by Chapters VI and VII of the Charter. The independent role of the Secretary-General lies in Article 99. This legal authority has rarely been invoked, but the political legitimacy which it conveys has been used with great frequency. Similarly, Article 71 and the ECOSOC provisions have only been used by a small minority of the NGOs, but the legal authority they provide conveys political legitimacy to a variety of other links.

Firstly, consultative arrangements work much better in the Commissions and Committees of ECOSOC. The rules are applied more flexibly, giving NGOs more freedom to take part, and the Committee on NGOs does not have to be used as an intermediary. Here much depends on both the nature of the specific issue under consideration and which country is in the chair. In the case of the discussion of Chile during 1975–76 in the Commission on Human Rights, it would seem to be no exaggeration to say that the written report and oral statements of the NGOs dominated the debates and the decision-making.[27] On other occasions, Argentina and the Soviet Union have tried to stop Commissions from receiving any NGO communications and have used the control of the chair for this purpose.

Secondly, the existence of the consultative status with the Council has legitimized communication between the Secretariat and the NGOs. Without Article 71, it would have been possible to argue that, in dealing with anybody other than government representatives, the Secretariat was violating Article 2(7), which prohibits intervention 'in matters which are essentially within the domestic jurisdiction of any state'. Here the practice of giving overriding preference to INGOs has helped, as contact with the citizens of any country is not direct, but via the world headquarters of each organization. The Secretariat has found it useful, as it has been given more and more tasks, to tap the resources provided by NGOs. The General Assembly at its first session encouraged this contact in one specific way. The Office of Public Information within the Secretariat was asked to disseminate information about the United Nations through the NGOs. The OPI has established its own list of organizations with which it has contact in New York. Weekly briefings are given by top personnel, periodic conferences are held and documents on UN activities are supplied. Different United Nations organs and programmes now are developing their own constituencies, by using the OPI. Some go direct to the NGOs and the public, as with the monthly newspaper *Development Forum* or the journals, *United Nations Chronicle, Objective Justice*, concentrating on action against apartheid, and *Disarmament*. Others, such as the *Special Unit on Palestinian Rights Bulletin*, are aimed at the press.

It has now become standard practice, when specialized conferences are called, to set up a small unit to act as a secretariat for the conference and it is authorized to make contact with the NGOs. They are thus involved in the earliest stages of the preparations and provide an input before some governments have even begun to formulate policy. The intergovernmental preparatory committees for global conferences also work closely with NGOs. When the conferences actually take place, the diplomats become dominant and often do not allow formal NGO participation. At the 1980 UN Conference on Women, all the NGOs were given a total of 15 minutes between them to address the delegates. But the agenda for the conferences and the basic documentation have been prepared long before the delegates arrive and the NGOs have helped to set the frame of reference within which the debates take place. Since 1970 all the major global intergovernmental conferences have had 'unofficial' conferences take place alongside them, involving thousands of participants, from hundreds of INGOs and domestic NGOs, from all over the world.

The term 'unofficial' is rather inaccurately applied to these NGO Forums, as the basic administrative work to enable them to take place and the political briefing on the work of the intergovernmental conference is provided not by the NGOs themselves, but by the government of the host country and by the UN Secretariat. Among the more interesting features of the NGO work is the practice of a team of journalists working with the NGOs to produce a daily newspaper during the conference. This provides a communication channel between the official and unofficial conferences. In addition NGO delegates attend sessions of the intergovernmental conference, while diplomats do attend Forum events and direct contact occurs through lobbying. Increasingly the global media are reporting the activities of the Forums, as well as the official conferences, and commenting on the differences in the ways issues are handled in the two places (though there is sometimes amazingly little media coverage of either the official or the unofficial conferences). In the realm of the international law of diplomacy, we may have a world that has changed little since 1945, but in the realm of political behaviour the NGOs must be regarded as a significant component of the global conference diplomacy system.

Regional intergovernmental organizations also usually have some type of formal arrangements for relating to NGOs. The EEC provided in the Treaty of Rome, under Articles 193 to 198, for an Economic and Social Committee (ESC). This now consists of 144 members: twenty-four for the four largest countries, twelve each for Belgium and Holland, nine each for Denmark and Ireland, with six for Luxembourg. The members are non-governmental representatives, nominated by the governments and are divided into Group I, employers, Group II, workers, and Group III, other interests, such as agriculture, trade, small businesses, the professions and consumers. The Treaty of Rome obliges both the Commission and the Council of Ministers to refer to the ESC on a wide range of subjects, but it is noticeable that in the first three years there were very few referals and only after 1968 did the work begin to grow markedly. The Committee works through nine Sections, mainly demarcated by economic topics. The Economic and Social Committee as a whole, each country's delegation, the Sections and even their study groups are carefully divided out into employers, workers and other interests. The three Groups caucus separately and it is even provided in the Rules of Procedure for the chair of the Committee to rotate between Groups I, II and III.

The only authority the Committee has is to produce Opinions, studies and information reports and it is only since the Paris summit of October 1972 that the Opinions have been published in the Official Journal. However, members of the Commission frequently attend the Committee's plenary sessions, the Chairman and two Vice-Chairmen visit the appropriate national capital, when the Presidency of the Community is handed over, and they also have regular meetings with the Committee of Permanent Representatives (Coreper, a Committee of officials, which prepares the work of the Council of Ministers). On occasions, rapporteurs of the Committee have addressed committees of the European Assembly on their Opinions. Even now the legal position of the Economic and Social Committee within the Community looks extremely weak. Initially it was only supposed to deal with matters which were referred to it and hence it had no independent authority at all. In 1972, it was awarded the right to take up topics and to produce Opinions on its own initiative. This it used to go beyond its normal economic role, by contributing an Opinion to the debate on the Tindemans report.

As with the UN, the formal Treaty arrangements for non-governmental organizations are less important in frequency, breadth and impact than other contacts with officials. Lodge and Herman believe 'The ESC's role has been less restrictively interpreted than implied by the Rome Treaty, yet it is not the forum through which interest groups articulate their views, nor the forum on which public attention is focused,'[28] and they conclude 'that the ESC plays a negligible role in EEC decision-making'.[29] While there is strong evidence to support this position, it is perhaps overstated. A survey of twenty-two major European INGOs (of which all except one have representatives on the Committee) found that, when their leaders were asked to rank the extent of their contact with four European Community institutions, twenty-one of the twenty-two put the Commission first.[30] But the Economic and Social Committee came next, with an average rank of 2.6, followed by the Council of Ministers at 3.1 and the Assembly at 3.2.[31] One of the reasons that 'European interest groups' have more contact with the Commission is that there are forty-six Advisory Committees and other similar forums, which have been set up over the years outside the ESC framework.[32] In addition there are 'frequent encounters' through informal links with the Commission.[33]

The existence of a transnational political process centred on the Community is illustrated most plainly by the way that the formation of these twenty-two major European INGOs is based on the geographic area of the Community. Only one does not have an office in Brussels and seventeen have their headquarters there; eighteen were established after it was agreed to establish the EEC; and eighteen only have members from Community countries, without any from other European countries.[34]

Links between domestic NGOs or international NGOs and the United Nations, the ILO or the European Community are the most formalized and they effect the most extensive arrangements to enable pressure groups to influence intergovernmental organizations. Similar categories of consultative status also exist with UN specialized agencies, with UN subsidiary organs and programmes, with the Council of Europe, the Organization of American States and with other regional bodies. We must now consider what significance should be given in international relations theory to non-governmental transactions and lobbying in the world of diplomacy.

The Place of Pressure Groups in International Relations Theory

A distinction is commonly made between 'high' and 'low' politics, but like many concepts which are in popular usage it is hard to trace a formal definition of what the dimension is supposed to measure. If an issue is held to concern high politics because it engages the attention of those who are high in the government's hierarchy, the President or Prime Minister, the Foreign Minister or other ministers, then it may be merely a tautology to say that transnational interactions are not a part of high politics. But it is a tautology which still has a theoretical impact, because high/low carries a mental imagery of important/ unimportant. The more meaningful content to the distinction lies in the idea that all governments see the world according to similar priorities, producing a hierarchy of issues, in which 'the "high politics" of military security dominates the "low politics" of economic and social affairs'.[35] On this basis the state-centric, Realist theorist has no need to deny the existence of a vast range of transnational actors, engaging in many types of international economic trans-actions, nor is there even any problem in accepting that there may be a signifi-cant impact on economic outcomes. The analysis of international politics is not critically affected, because economics is held to be secondary to security questions and because governments are presumed to be able to establish control over the transnational actors whenever they so wish. It is probably the influence of such assumptions which leads Reynolds and McKinlay to say:

> As far as INGOs are concerned it is evident that the consequences of the activity of many of them are trivial . . . they may serve in some degree to alter the domestic environment of decision-makers, but with some exceptions their effect either on capabilities or on objectives is likely to be minimal, and in no way can they be seen themselves as significant actors.[36]

Such an approach begs as many questions as it answers. To whom are the con-sequences 'trivial' and what are the criteria of 'significance'? Any academic political scientist, who took this attitude to the purchase of books and journals published overseas, to dealings with visiting foreign academics and to the work of the International Studies Association, the European Consortium for Political Research and the International Political Science Association, would simply be regarded as incompetent!

It is ironic that the two established schools which challenge the Realists have a similar approach, inasmuch as they distinguish economic and social interactions quite sharply from security and diplomacy. The Marxists regard the economy as the basic structure of society and the institutions of the state as a superstructure which reflects the underlying class relationships. The main significance of the state arises from its ability to mobilize coercion in the interest of the dominant class. Similarly, the basis of international relations is the com-petition of the major capitalist institutions to secure markets and the co-operation between them to prevent challenges to the capitalist system. Military power is used to serve the interests of the multi-national companies and to maintain the structure of imperialism. At a high level of abstraction the Marxist and the Realist models are virtually identical, with the one major difference that they have opposite views as to which is the dominant and which the subordinate sub-system. With respect to international relations, Marxism is Realism turned upside down.

The Functionalists also see the state as being of secondary importance but differ from the Marxists in having a benevolent view of economic and social interactions. Mitrany saw the twentieth century as producing 'a new phase in political outlook and evolution', in which there is evident 'the very sign of our time — the sign not of power but of service':[37]

> the philosophy of the welfare state has grown fortuitously into that of a welfare world . . . Between the two, therefore, is not a political division based on 'sovereign' distinction, but a sociological continuity and affinity . . . with inevitably similar ways of working towards the service purpose of our time.[38]

Burton does not engage in the mystical reification of social systems nor does he have Mitrany's strongly teleological approach to explanation, but his 'cobweb model' is nevertheless a more analytical version of Functionalism, based on the same axiom that 'Communications, and not power, are the main organizing influence in world society.'[39] The high/low politics distinction occurs with an imagery of 'the ground floor level' which is 'narrowly concerned with inter-state relations, essentially power relations', contrasted to 'the basement level', which is 'concerned with world society as a whole, making no arbitrary boundaries between that which is national and that which is international.'[40] 'There is more cohesion in the world society of states, institutions and transactions than there is within most states.'[41] Again we have Realism turned upside down. In modern industrial societies, such as Britain, 'in form, authority is traditional state authority; in practice, it is a functionalist process.'[42]

The agreement between Realists, Marxists and Functionalists, that it is useful to distinguish high from low politics, does appear superficially to have some sound empirical base. Among our eight categories of pressure groups, if we ignore the smallest clubs and voluntary welfare agencies (say, by deleting all autonomous groups containing and/or interacting with less than 100 people), then sectional economic groups and professional associations must in virtually all countries of the world be more numerous than the other six categories of groups put together. Frequently, the economic and professional groups will also have the largest membership, but in some societies the religious organizations would be the biggest. In addition, among the 2,000 or more INGOs, the economic and professional INGOs are overwhelmingly the most numerous.[43] Furthermore, where the constitutions of intergovernmental organizations make provision for consultation with pressure groups, it is not designed for all types of groups on all sorts of topics. The links are specifically with the 'economic and social' organs of the institution.

In the 1970s, a body of academic writing has grown up, which is making such a different contribution that it may be identified as a fourth theoretical school. The literature on the domestic sources of foreign policy, bureaucratic politics, transnationalism and interdependence has been referred to as the 'pluralist perspective'[44] or more simply 'the international relations paradigm'.[45] Because the current author would wish to include greater emphasis on the way in which global communications are producing linkages between issues and the development of intergovernmental organizations, as separate loci of decision-making, the term 'Global Politics' school is preferred. The main writers in this school have been Rosenau, Keohane and Nye, and Mansbach.[46] They all accept that both governments and non-governmental actors are important and that both security issues and economic and technical issues are important. The argument about whether the state is dominant or subordinate is not resolved by simple assertion of an axiom, as it is with the Realists, the Marxists and the Functionalists, but is a matter for empirical investigation and dependent upon the particular issue process under consideration.

Keohane and Nye's book, *Transnational Relations and World Politics*, is the most relevant work for the study of pressure groups. Their approach was ambitious and they said 'the conclusion to this volume attempts . . . to introduce our alternative "world politics paradigm" as a substitute for the state-centric analytical framework'.[47]

> The difference . . . can be clarified most easily by focusing on the nature of the actors. The world politics paradigm attempts to transcend the 'level of analysis problem' both by broadening the conception of actors to include transnational actors and by conceptually breaking down the 'hard shell' of nation-state.[48]

The empirical material covered by Keohane and Nye is predominantly economic. The six chapters on 'issue areas' are all on economic and technological questions. Only in 'Part II. Transnational Organisations', where there are chapters on the Roman Catholic Church and on revolutionary organizations, does the emphasis change. This is not due to problems they had as editors in search of contributors. It is quite explicitly built into their theoretical perspective.

> In the modernized Western world and its ancillary areas the acceptability of multiple loyalties is taken for granted. Yet, this toleration seems to be extended more readily when the transnational actor is explicitly economic in purpose than when it is explicitly political. Thus, it seems less incompatible to be loyal to both IBM and France . . . than . . . for Americans to identify with Israel. In the West, therefore, nationalism probably hinders overt political organization across boundaries more than it hinders transnational economic activity.[49]

At three places they go further and speak of 'the decline of transnational political organizations', but no evidence is offered that such a trend exists.[50] In a more recent book, *Power and Interdependence*, Keohane and Nye backtrack in their attack. They offer 'complex interdependence' as an ideal type, an explanatory model in which transnational actors are important and the distinction between high and low politics is irrelevant. However, they also say 'sometimes, realist assumptions will be accurate, or largely accurate, but frequently complex interdependence will provide a better portrait of reality.'[51] They are not far from saying that there are two distinct types of systems of interaction: security relationships and economic relationships.

The overwhelming impact of all the academic literature is that transnationalism operates in a distinct realm and that the actors come mainly from our first two categories of pressure groups: sectional economic interests and professional associations. The Global Politics paradigm ought to make a sharper break with Realism, Marxism and Functionalism, because in each of the six other categories there are major transnational actors and significant transnational processes. In the area of recreation and culture, there is the International Olympic Committee, foreign broadcasting and cultural exchange. In the field of welfare, there is a myriad of development and relief agencies, such as Oxfam. The religions are high organized through the Vatican, the World Council of Churches, Jewish and Islamic bodies. Communal groups, such as the PLO, African liberation movements and women's groups, have an impact throughout the world. The Socialist International and communism bring political parties into international relations. Specific-issue promotional groups, such as Anti-Apartheid, Amnesty and Friends of the Earth, cannot be understood in terms of the politics of any one country, or even within the context of interactions between just two or three countries. From all the six categories, there comes a world of transnational politics which has its own impact upon both security and economic issues.

At this point it is necessary for us to clear up a confusion which occurs in the use of the word 'politics'. This has two components. Politics is the process by which groups take decisions, which will be regarded as binding upon the group. For the country as a whole, the government is considered to be the appropriate sub-group to take decisions which are binding on society, including all the pressure groups operating within it. A decision taken by the due process has legal authority. A second meaning to politics covers the process by which groups allocate moral values and hence derive preferences for different patterns of social relationships. Communication and debate produce each person's ideas of political legitimacy. Government generally is obeyed not just because it has authority but also because among a sufficient number of people it has legitimacy. The particular strength of government is that in most countries of the world nationalism and/or democracy (in whatever way it is defined and practised) promote the idea that government should be obeyed even when the individual disapproves of the decision that has been taken. The distinction between the two meanings of the word 'politics' is necessary because governments may have high authority and low legitimacy. Alternatively, pressure groups may have low authority and high legitimacy. Realists, Marxists and Functionalists tend to concentrate on the authority aspects of government, at the expense of its role for the mobilization of legitimacy.

The distinction between authority and legitimacy helps us to have a clearer conceptualization of the relationship between politics, economics and security. In the sense of politics being decision-making by governments, then it may well be true that some governments spend more time taking decisions about security and diplomacy relations with the rest of the world than they do about international economic relations. This is one aspect of maintaining their authority to continue making decisions. But there is nothing intrinsic in the nature of the exercise of authority to produce an automatic concern with security and diplomacy. William Wallace in writing about *The Foreign Policy Process in Britain* says 'High policy issues are those which are seen by policy-makers as affecting Britain's fundamental standing in the world: as involving national security or national prestige, as linked to values and symbols important to society as a whole.'[52] Where Wallace differs from other writers is in the assertion of the subjective nature of these questions: 'What is or is not a matter of high policy is above all a matter of perception, of definition.'[53] In other words, it is not the geographical situation of a country, its power in relation to its neighbours and questions of military strategy that determine security to be a matter of high politics. (On such a basis, the prevention of a military alliance between France and America would be the top item on Britain's political agenda.) The determination of 'high policy' is a matter of choice. As Wallace points out, the question of Britain's relations with the EEC was at first seen as mainly a matter of foreign trade policy and as such not 'high policy',

> to be redefined, rather painfully, as a matter of high policy when the Treasury, the Foreign Office, the Cabinet and the leaders of British industry realized that wider questions were involved and that a reassessment of the assumptions underlying British foreign policy might be necessary.[54]

For many governments of the Third World, such as Jamaica, Ghana or Sri Lanka, there may be no significant problems of 'national security' affecting their international relations. The security problems may be severe, but they arise from the domestic system. For them the high politics of international relations lies in trade and aid issues. The logic of Wallace's approach leads us to abandon the concept of high and low politics and replace it with the more precise and more widely applicable concept of *issue salience*. If priorities are a matter of choice, if they can change over time and can vary at the same time between one government and another, then to study any issue we need to know how much salience governments attach to the issue and how much they are attempting to exercise their authority on the issue.

The advantage of the concept is that we can generalize it to other actors, both intergovernmental organizations and non-governmental organizations. Pressure groups attempt to influence outcomes on issues which are salient to them. If certain outcomes, which they desire, require the exercise of its authority by a government, any government in any country, then pressure groups will seek to put their case to that government. They enter politics in the traditional sense of the word. The system of interest for the study of an issue consists of all those actors for whom the issue is salient. They are the ones that chose to engage in interactions to effect outcomes. The part of the global political system which we wish to study may or may not consist predominantly of governments. It may or may not contain large numbers of transnational political actors, from any of the eight categories of pressure groups. The situation will depend upon the issue under consideration and the time period under consideration.

The extent to which any actor will be the target of pressure will depend, significantly but not solely, upon the extent to which the actor has the ability to take and enforce decisions. Generally, this is perceived to coincide with the legal authority of the actor. As most governments have extremely wide authority, but never unlimited authority, they become major focal points for interactions. But it must be remembered that all other organizations possess some authority, either in a recognized legal sense or in some analogous rule-making capacity. Thus, virtually all organizations can determine eligibility and conditions of membership of their own organization. Usually they can freely dispose of their own resources. As a result any organization may become the target of pressure.

The issue of apartheid raises such a diversity of questions, which are of high salience to such a diverse range of actors and affects the exercise of their authority for so many of the actors, that virtually any organization with either wide global links or engaged in direct interactions with South Africa finds itself within the global political system on the issue of apartheid. In the UN, the process of delegitimizing the South African government is linked to most other issues with which it deals. Governments are under pressure, but specific-issue groups, notably Anti-Apartheid, and religious bodies also try directly to affect the employment policies of multi-national companies. The EEC is drawn in to harmonize the impact on companies. Recreational clubs are asked to break their contacts with South Africa; political parties are expected to take a stand; and professional associations have debated how to apply their professional ethics to work in a society practising apartheid.

When we move from politics as the exercise of authority to the second meaning of politics as the mobilization of legitimacy, once again governments, intergovernmental organizations and pressure groups are all involved. But governments are no longer the dominant actors. Legitimacy attaches to actors, in the way we perceive their status, and to ideas or policies, in the way we measure their moral value. The concept of power (as capability rather than as influence) is usually taken to cover the ability to utilize coercion, with the more recent emphasis in international relations on the ability to dispose of economic resources. The ability to mobilize legitimacy should also be seen as a power capability. In this domain, it is conceivable that Amnesty International, for example, has greater power than any single government. It derives global legitimacy both from its very high status, one recognition of which was the award of the Nobel Peace Prize in 1977, and from the high moral value that so many people attach to the policies it is pursuing.

One reason for the interaction between different actors can be the attempt of an actor to increase its legitimacy by association with another actor of high status. The United Nations may have little power, in the sense of a very limited ability to impose coercion or to dispose of economic resources, but it does have considerable power, by virtue of its high status and widespread support for the ideals it seeks to promote. This helps to explain the interaction between pressure groups and the United Nations and other intergovernmental organizations. On each side there is the potential for increasing legitimacy by participation in the relationship.

We can now produce a definition of global politics, which is fundamentally different from that of the three established schools. International relations is not concerned just with the exercise of power, predominantly in the form of military capabilities, in order to influence outcomes. Nor can interactions across the world be seen as predominantly concerned with the production and disposal of economic resources. Global politics covers the utilization of coercion *and* the disposal of economic resources *and* the mobilization of legitimacy, by governments and intergovernmental organizations and pressure groups. Governments are important as *loci* of authority and in the possession of military capabilities. Sectional interest groups are important as transnational economic actors. In addition we must regard the five types of promotional pressure groups, along with intergovernmental organizations, as important transnational political actors, mobilizing legitimacy. Indeed, all types of global actors may in principle engage in all three types of interactions. If we wish to explain political processes, we should not assume in advance that certain types of actors or certain types of interactions can be ignored. Our models of global politics, unfortunately, must become more complex.

References

1 Finer, S. *Anonymous Empire* (London, Pall Mall, 1958, second edn. 1966).
2 The most important early works on transnationalism were Rosenau, J. N. (ed.), *Linkages Politics: Essays on the Convergence of National and International Systems* (New York, Free Press, 1969) and Keohane, R. O. and Nye, J. S. (eds.), *Transnational Relations and World Politics* (Cambridge, USA and London, UK. Harvard University Press, 1971). Since then there have been many articles and books dealing with case studies, too many to be listed here. The more important general works are Mansbach, R. W., Ferguson, Y. H., and Lampert, D. E., *The Web of World Politics: Non-State Actors in the Global System* (Englewood Cliffs, N.J., Prentice Hall, 1976), Rosenau, J. N., *The Study of Global*

Interdependence: Essays on the Transnationalisation of World Affairs (London, Frances Pinter, 1980), and Mansbach, R. W. and Vasquez, J., *In Search of Theory. A New Paradigm for Global Politics* (New York, Columbia University Press, 1981).

3 For example, K. N. Waltz says that the 'study of transnational movements deals with important factual questions, which theories can help one to cope with. But the help will not be gained if it is thought that nonstate actors call the state-centric view of the world into question' — *Theory of International Politics* (Reading, Mass., USA and London, UK, Addison-Wesley Publishing, 1979), p. 95 — and in a section on 'Transnational Organisations', which predominantly discusses multinational corporations, H. Bull says 'It is sovereign states which command most of the armed forces of the world, which are the objects of the most powerful human loyalties, and whose conflict and co-operation determine the political structure of the world. The multinational corporation does not even remotely provide a challenge to the state in the exercise of these functions' — *The Anarchical Society. A Study of Order in World Politics* (London, Macmillan Press, 1977), pp. 272–3.

4 Kimber, R. and Richardson, J. J. (eds.), *Pressure Groups in Britain* (London, J. M. Dent, 1974), p. 3.

5 In making this summary, a paper by Grant, W. 'Insider Groups, Outsider Groups and Interest Group Strategies in Britain' (University of Warwick, Department of Politics Working Paper No. 19, May 1978), was most useful. More detailed references are given in his paper.

6 Quote from Lord Wolfenden, *The Future of Voluntary Organisations. Report of the Wolfenden Committee* (London, Croom Helm, 1978), p. 131. The list of the top twenty charities, in terms of their income, was derived from the Wolfenden Report, pp. 264–6. The data on income was from 1975. Membership of the National Council for Voluntary Organizations was taken from their *61st Annual Report 1979/80*, pp. 30–1.

7 The forty-seven women's INGOs are listed, with their dates of foundation and some other information, in Boulding, E., 'Female Alternatives to Hierarchical Systems, Past and Present — A Critique of Women's NGO's in the Light of History', *International Associations*, 1975, pp. 340–6. This article, as is indicated by the title, is an example of an ideological rejection of 'organization'. It is permeated with the sexist assumption that women have 'their traditional networking skills' as opposed to 'male organizational patterns' of dominance and hierarchy (p. 343).

8 The classic study of pressure groups in United States politics is Truman, D. B., *The Governmental Process. Political Interests and Public Opinion* (New York, A. A. Knopf, 1951, second edn., 1971). Truman also takes the view that political parties can be comparable to pressure groups in domestic politics. Minor ' "parties" essentially are weak political interest groups that adopt this form of activity [nominating candidates and electioneering] because they cannot command access to government through other means,' p. 282.

9 The Campaign for Nuclear Disarmament is a member of the International Confederation for Disarmament and Peace; the Anti-Apartheid Movement is on the committee of ICSA, the International Committee against Apartheid, Racism and Colonialism in Southern Africa; and the World Development Movement is a member of the International Coalition for Development Action. These three INGOs all have their headquarters in London.

10 *Development Guide. A Directory of non-commercial organisations in Britain actively concerned in overseas development and training* (London, George Allen and Unwin, for the Overseas Development Institute, 1978, Third Edn.). The overwhelming majority of the 198 organizations listed are technical or professional bodies involved in research and/or training. Perhaps about twenty groups have an overseas operational programme and another thirty or so are concerned with promoting interest in, knowledge of, and support for development.

11 *North–South: A programme for survival. Report of the Independent Commission on International Development Issues* (London and Sydney, Pan Books, and Cambridge, Mass., MIT Press, 1980), quote from p. 117 of the Pan edition.

12 *Final Document* of the Tenth Special Session of the United Nations General Assembly, Resolution S-10/2, adopted by consensus on 30 June 1978, paragraphs 16, 89, 94 and 95.

13 *World Disarmament Campaign Bulletin*, No. 2, November 1980, p. 1.

14 The source was a document, *W.D.C. Support Groups, November 1980*, supplied to the author by the General-Secretary, containing a list of names and addresses.

15 Alker, H. R. and Russett, B. M., *World Politics in the General Assembly* (New Haven and London, Yale University Press, 1965). Bailey, S. D. *The General Assembly of the United Nations. A Study of Procedure and Practice* (London, Stevens and Sons, and New York, F. A. Praeger, for the Carnegie Endowment for International Peace, 1960). Claude, I. L., *Swords into Ploughshares. The Problems and Progress of International Organisation* (New York, Random House, 1971, Fourth Edn.). Gregg, R. W. and Barkun, M. (eds.), *The United Nations System and its Functions — selected readings* (Princeton, London, Melbourne and Toronto, Van Nostrand, 1968). Luard, E., *The United Nations. How it Works and What it Does* (London, Macmillian Press, 1979). Nicholas, H. G., *The United Nations as a Political Institution* (London, Oxford University Press, 1971, Fourth Edn.).

16 Perkins, E. V., *Comparative Pressure Group Politics and Transnational Relations. The Case of Non-Governmental Organisations at the United Nations* (unpublished Ph.D. Dissertation, Texas Tech University, May 1977), p. 10.

17 Ibid. and p. 78. See also Eichelberger, C. M., *Organizing for Peace. A Personal History of the Founding of the United Nations* (New York and London, Harper and Row, 1977), ch. 17.

18 'Brief history of the consultative relationship of non-governmental organisations with the Economic and Social Council. Report of the Secretary-General', *United Nations Document E/C.2/661* of 7 May 1968, p. 1, quoted by Perkins, op. cit., p. 11.

19 Perkins, op. cit., p. 11, referring to Carey, J., *UN Protection of Civil and Political Rights* (Syracuse, Syracuse University Press, 1970), p. 131, and White, L. C., *et al.*, *International Non-Governmental Organisations; Their Purposes, Methods and Accomplishments* (New Brunswick, Rutgers University Press, 1951), p. 171. Eichelberger, op. cit., pp. 269–72, partially substantiates the point.

20 *Consultation between the United Nations and Non-Governmental Organisations. A Working Paper Transmitted by the Interim Committee to Consultative Non-Governmental Organisations* (Westport, Conn., Greenwood Press, 1978, reprint of 1949 ed., published for the Carnegie Endowment for International Peace), p. 23.

21 Ibid., the full list is given on pp. 69–71.

22 ECOSOC Resolution 1296(XLIV), adopted unanimously on 23 May 1968. This is a long and detailed resolution with forty-six paragraphs specifying the mechanisms for 'Arrangements for Consultation with Non-Governmental Organisations'.

23 Op. cit., in note 20, p. 24.

24 Perkins, op. cit., p. 83.

25 Op. cit., in note 20, p. 23.

26 For the original provisions see op. cit. in note 20, pp. 24–5, and for the current provisions see ECOSOC Resolution 1296(XLIV).

27 Perkins, op. cit., pp. 219–35.

28 Lodge, J. and Herman, V., 'The Economic and Social Committee in EEC decision making', International Organization, Vol. 34, No. 2, Spring 1980, pp. 265–84, quote from p. 269.

29 Ibid., p. 284.

30 Economic and Social Committee of the European Communities General Secretariat, *European Interest Groups and their Relationship with the Economic and Social Committee* (Saxon House, Farnborough, UK, 1980). A table on p. 15 gives the ranking of the amount of contact with Community institutions for each of the twenty-two groups.

31 Averages calculated by the author and not in the original source.

32 The forty-six committees are listed on pp. 45–8 of Economic and Social Committee of the European Communities General Secretariat, *Community Advisory Committees*

for the Representation of Socio-Economic Interests (Saxon House, Farnborough, UK, 1980).

33 *European Interest Groups*, p. 16.

34 All these figures were derived from counting up the entries in the table on pp. 5–6 of *European Interest Groups*. All three indicators of a Community orientation (being established after 1955, having a Brussels headquarters and being confined to members from Community countries), are satisfied by fifteen of the twenty-two groups. Seven of the eighteen which only have members from the Community area do have associates from other European countries.

35 Keohane, R. O. and Nye, J. S., *Power and Interdependence. World Politics in Transition* (Boston, Little Brown, 1977), p. 24.

36 Reynolds, P. A. and McKinlay, R. D. 'The Concept of Interdependence: Its Uses and Misuses', in Goldmann, K. and Sjöstedt, G., *Power, Capabilities and Interdependence Problems in the Study of International Influence* (London and Beverly Hills, Sage, 1979), p. 154.

37 Mitrany, D., 'A Political Theory for the New Society', in Groom, A. J. R. and Taylor, P. (eds.), *Functionalism. Theory and Practice in International Relations* (London, University of London Press, 1975), pp. 31–2.

38 Ibid., p. 32.

39 Burton, J. W., *World Society* (Cambridge, UK, Cambridge University Press, 1972), p. 45.

40 Burton, J. W., 'International Relations or World Society', in Burton, J. W. *et al.*, *The Study of World Society: A London Perspective* (International Studies Association, Occasional Paper No. 1, 1974), p. 5.

41 Ibid., p. 17.

42 Ibid., p. 16.

43 Table 5 on p. 79 of Skjelsbaek, K., 'The Growth of International Nongovernmental Organisation in the Twentieth Century', pp. 70–92 of Keohane and Nye, *Transnational Relations . . .*, see note 2.

44 When the Open University course team were preparing the new 'World Politics' course, which was first offered in 1981, they frequently spoke of 'the pluralist perspective'. The phrase does not appear in the course reader that has now been published. There is just a reference on p. 117 to 'a kind of pluralism at the international level'. The relevant section of readings is headed 'The Politics of Interdependence and Transnational Relations' in Smith, M., Little, R., and Shackleton, M. (eds.), *Perspectives on World Politics* (London, Croom Helm, 1981).

45 Banks, M., 'Ways of Analyzing the World Society', pp. 195–215 of Groom, A. J. R. and Mitchell, C. R. (eds.), *International Relations Theory, A Bibliography* (London, Frances Pinter, and New York, Nichols, 1978). Banks' labels for the four different paradigms are not the same as mine, but the distinctions made are the same, except that we disagree on how to categorize the work of Keohane and Nye.

46 See the references in note 2 and Section 2 of Smith, Little and Shackleton, *Perspectives on World Politics*.

47 Keohane and Nye, *Transnational Relations*, p. xxv.

48 Ibid., p. 380.

49 Ibid., p. 378.

50 Ibid., pp. 376, 377 and 378.

51 Keohane and Nye, *Power and Interdependence*, p. 24.

52 Wallace, W., *The Foreign Policy Process in Britain* (London, George Allen and Unwin, 1977), p. 11.

53 Ibid., p. 12.

54 Ibid., p. 13.

2 The Anti-Apartheid Movement and Racism in Southern Africa

ABDUL S. MINTY

This is a brief account of how the Anti-Apartheid Movement, a non-governmental organization based in Britain and specifically committed to working for an end to apartheid and colonialism in Southern Africa, works both nationally and internationally in order to secure support for its objectives. It is an example of how a pressure group can use the network of IGOs, INGOs and NGOs to further its purposes and of how other actors respond to such pressures.

To understand its present role and influence it is important to trace the history. It was established in June 1959 in response to the call of the late Chief Albert Luthuli, President of the African National Congress of South Africa (ANC), and other anti-apartheid leaders who appealed for an international boycott of South African goods and the total isolation of the apartheid regime. The Boycott Movement, as it was then known, was founded as an independent organization in Britain sponsored by public figures drawn from all walks of life, including the Labour and Liberal Parties, trade unions, churches and the arts. The campaign concentrated on winning support for a consumer boycott and rested on the proposition that international economic and other links with South Africa help to sustain the apartheid regime and should be ended.

Individuals who were opposed to apartheid could engage in personal action by refusing to buy South African products and thus demonstrate their support for the oppressed African, Indian and Coloured people of South Africa. The Boycott Movement did not suggest that a consumer boycott alone could bring the apartheid regime to its knees. For economic measures to make an impact of that kind it needed all Members of the United Nations to adopt a programme of economic sanctions which would need to be implemented strictly by South Africa's major trading partners.

As a result of the controversy surrounding the boycott campaign, the issue of apartheid was discussed and debated much more widely than ever before in Britain. The South African Foreign Minister was among the first to argue that the boycott would hurt the African people most and this was also claimed by business and other groups in Britain which had a vested interest in South Africa. However, the Boycott Movement found that its campaign developed rapidly and, in order to focus national action in a concentrated period, decided to organize a one-month intensive campaign during March 1960. On 28 February it was launched at a mass rally of over 20,000 people in Trafalgar Square which was addressed by leading public figures including the leader of the Labour Party, Hugh Gaitskell.

In virtually every town and city throughout Britain there existed a voluntary group to promote the Movement's campaign. The broad national support expressed for the campaign caused serious concern in Pretoria about the potential danger of a growing international boycott movement against apartheid. The fact that there existed so much opposition to South Africa in Britain, its biggest trading partner and largest overseas investor as well as long-standing ally, was particularly serious. Various pro-South African organizations were set up in Britain to counteract the Boycott Movement and existing business organizations in London also began to issue propaganda in defence of South Africa.

Once the British campaign got under way new groups were established in several Scandinavian and other Western countries to promote activities along the lines of the Boycott Movement. One important effect of the sharp controversy surrounding the issue of boycott was that a large number of journalists and television teams were sent to South Africa from various Western countries to report on conditions under apartheid — what was it exactly that caused so much international concern? Thus, on 21 March 1960 when the Pan Africanist Congress (a breakaway nationalist movement from the ANC) called for demonstrations against the Pass Laws and the police shot at unarmed crowds at Sharpeville and Langa, there were foreign reporters on the spot. Within hours the full horror of that massacre (in which 72 Africans were killed and over 180 wounded) was brought home to millions of people all over the world. It provoked deep international anger and spontaneous demonstrations took place outside several South African embassies. In Britain the demonstrations continued for three days and nights and the Embassy decided to keep its doors locked and the outer metal gates bolted.

The House of Commons expressed its sympathy with the bereaved in South Africa and similar motions were adopted in other parliaments as well as at the United Nations. Apartheid could no longer be considered as a matter 'essentially within the domestic jurisdiction' of South Africa by the major Western governments which had held that view until then.[1] It is important to recall that 1960 also marked the era of African decolonization and the Sharpeville shootings took place in the context of a wider African revolution.

The massacre and the subsequent reign of terror and brutality unleashed by the Pretoria regime against its opponents led to the Boycott Movement changing its name to the Anti-Apartheid Movement: it was essential to work more systematically and on a comprehensive scale with a long-term perspective because of the seriousness of the problem. Among the first issues to be taken up by AAM was the supply of British military equipment to South Africa. The Sharpeville photographs had clearly shown that British-made Saracen armoured cars had been used to attack the crowds. Special leaflets calling for an arms embargo against South Africa were printed. These were distributed at the Aldermaston march of the Campaign for Nuclear Disarmament in April 1960, as well as at other similar public events throughout the year. As the arms embargo campaign developed, the Conservative Government decided to ban the export of weapons designed for internal use. This was a minor victory but the campaign had to be intensified to secure a complete embargo on all weapons exports to South Africa.

The Arms Embargo

Britian was South Africa's major arms supplier and closest military ally. There was a defence pact between the two countries in the form of the 1955 Simonstown Naval Agreement which specifically provided for the supply of British naval equipment to the Pretoria regime. Any campaign which was aimed at reversing this policy and securing an arms embargo would have to overcome enormous pressures and problems. It was clear that nothing much could be achieved from within the Conservative Party which was in large measure sympathetic to South Africa. Support had to be secured from within the Labour movement in order to influence a future Labour Government, as well as winning much needed public support. The Liberal Party was sympathetic to the African cause as were several church leaders. Thus, the campaign was directed at winning broad public support expressed through resolutions, petitions, meetings and the like. After a long period of consistent campaigning the Liberal and Labour Parties committed themselves to the embargo in early 1963. At a mass AAM rally in Trafalgar Square on 17 March 1963, the newly elected leader of the Labour Party, Harold Wilson, committed a future Labour Government to the arms embargo but he urged that since the matter was urgent the Conservative Government should 'Act now and stop this bloody traffic in the weapons of oppression'.

AAM had already submitted detailed information to all Members of the United Nations about the need for an international arms embargo. At the same time the matter was taken up bilaterally with those governments which were selling weapons to South Africa.

An interesting and lengthy correspondence developed with the United States of America. AAM made representations via the Embassy in London and soon received a substantive response from the State Department in Washington which drew attention to South Africa's role in the last war and pointed out that it formed part of the Western world and was strongly anti-communist. These were some of the reasons why the USA considered it essential to sell military equipment to South Africa. AAM replied to each of the points in detail and concluded by asking whether Washington wished to have South Africa as an ally against communism despite the racist and fascist nature of the Pretoria regime — and if this was the case then the United States of America ought to say so clearly so that the world would know the position. Some weeks later, in the summer of 1963, the State Department informed AAM that it would operate an arms embargo against South Africa as from January 1964, but that all outstanding contracts would be honoured.

On 7 August 1963, the UN Security Council adopted a resolution which called upon all States to 'cease forthwith the sale and shipment of arms, ammunition of all types and military vehicles to South Africa.'[2] Britain and France abstained in the vote and explained that they would not supply South Africa with arms for internal suppression. The decision of the Security Council came about as a result of a number of factors. The most important was that it followed the summit conference in Addis Ababa, which had established the Organization of African Unity and had taken an uncompromisingly strong stand on apartheid. Secondly, the United Nations Special Committee Against Apartheid, which had been established by the General Assembly that year (following a proposal made by AAM to the United Nations) had just published a report on the rapid build-up of military and police forces in South Africa.[3]

AAM established close working relations with the UN Special Committee from its inception and was able to co-operate closely on all issues. From time to time AAM would make proposals to the Committee which related to suggestions regarding future United Nations policy on Southern Africa as well as proposals about the working of the Special Committee. For example, almost at the very beginning of the establishment of the Special Committee AAM urged that the Committee should take on an active role by making direct representations to those governments and organizations which were involved in collaborating with South Africa in one way or another. Today the Committee makes direct representations to governments and also to international and national organizations including sports bodies, trade unions, student groups, church organizations and the like. The Special Committee also organizes special seminars on South Africa to which representatives of AAM have been invited together with other similar organizations, and these opportunities are utilized to make specific proposals as well as to raise special issues of international importance such as the arms embargo and the question of investment and trade links with South Africa. Whenever AAM officials have visited New York they have been granted official hearings by the Special Committee and there are also further meetings held with specific sub-committees of the Special Committee. The Chairman of the Special Committee plays a vital role in the work of the Committee and regular contact is maintained with him or her. So far all the Chairmen have been African Ambassadors and their commitment to the anti-apartheid cause is a major factor in making the work of the Committee effective.

As a result of the close relations developed between AAM and various African States, both bilaterally and via the work of the Special Committee and other UN organs dealing with Southern Africa as well as contact made at Commonwealth and other conferences, it has been possible to channel relevant information with policy proposals both to the Organization of African Unity and the United Nations. It is difficult to assess the precise role and influence of AAM in securing certain decisions, but there is no doubt about the valuable contribution made by the information provided by AAM to international organizations and governments. By specializing on a particular question it is possible to secure changes in policy once the information collected is made available in the proper quarters. Such information provided by AAM was received with interest by those governments and organizations which supported the policy and work of the Movement. But governments which were unsympathetic could not altogether ignore AAM because of the wider influence it was able to generate both within Britain and internationally in Africa, Asia and the United Nations.

In Britain, the Labour Party was returned to office in October 1964. Prime Minister Wilson soon announced that a complete embargo would be implemented against South Africa although the Buccaneer aircraft already ordered and awaiting delivery would be supplied. But no new orders would be accepted. As a result France gradually became South Africa's main arms supplier and close military co-operation developed between the two countries. French public opinion was not as well informed about South Africa as British opinion. There were also fewer historical links between the two countries. Various organizations and individuals involved in public action over the Algerian war had stopped being active and it proved difficult to establish an effective anti-apartheid movement. France was also not subject to as much pressure as Britain from its ex-colonies in Africa. Meanwhile South Africa began to establish its own armaments industry with foreign assistance, mainly from its traditional trading partners.

The arms embargo soon became more difficult and complicated to monitor and enforce. The problem was serious because the decisions taken by the traditional arms suppliers did not come about as a result of any deep motivation: it was much more a response to national and international pressure. For example, spare parts for equipment already supplied were not prohibited by the United States of America or Britain; military patents for the production of equipment in South Africa were not banned; international armaments firms began to establish subsidiaries in South Africa without any discouragement or control by their governments. Thus multinationals which had been prevented from exporting arms to South Africa began to set up plants inside South Africa to make them locally. They were circumventing the international arms embargo and when the governments concerned were approached they refused to take action to interfere with this process on the grounds that they did not support a policy of interfering with normal economic relations with South Africa. South African military officials continued to visit high-level Western military institutions for research and training. It is difficult to organize mass national campaigns on technical questions particularly when the government is in fact operating a partial arms embargo.

All the loopholes in the international arms embargo were drawn to the attention of the United Nations regularly both through its committees and via Member States. AAM enjoyed close relations with various Commonwealth governments and the Commonwealth Conferences provided additional opportunities for raising the question of the arms embargo. At each Conference AAM submitted a memorandum to all governments and it usually drew attention to the operation of the arms embargo and made proposals for its strict implementation. Many governments in turn approached AAM for specific details about South Africa's defence policy and related matters which would then form the basis of their statements and proposals. This form of co-operation usually continued after the Conferences.

During 1963 and 1964 the Security Council adopted three resolutions on the arms embargo but the matter was not discussed in the Council again until 1970 following the return of a Conservative Government to power in Britain. The Labour Government had implemented a partial arms embargo during the period 1964–70. The Conservative Party, under the leadership of Edward Heath, put considerable importance on reversing this policy so that South Africa could purchase British equipment for external defence. In May 1970, a month before the British General Election was due, AAM had an opportunity to give evidence to the UN Special Committee on Apartheid in New York. Attention was drawn to Sir Alec Douglas-Home's visit to South Africa in 1968 when he discussed with South African leaders a plan to put the Cape sea route under the protective wing of NATO. AAM expressed its alarm at recent speeches and statements by Conservative leaders which 'not only cover the relaxation of the arms embargo but envisage the extension of the Simonstown Agreement and possible arrangements with NATO to help defend South Africa's so-called interest in the Indian and Atlantic Oceans.' The AAM went on to state that 'it is timely for the Security Council to once again consider the issue of South Africa and the arms embargo and to cover the following loopholes in the embargo.' Among the loopholes mentioned were: military patents, other military know-how and blue-prints, overseas investments in the South African domestic armaments industry, skilled technicians from Western countries taking up employment in the domestic armaments industry, the provision of military and police training for South African personnel in other countries, and finally, an end to nuclear co-operation between certain Western countries and South Africa.[4]

Following the return to power of a Conservative government in Britain the Security Council met and adopted Resolution 282 on 23 July 1970. The Security Council called upon all states to strengthen the arms embargo by withholding all vehicles and spare parts for South Africa's armed forces, by revoking licences and patents and by prohibiting training or investment for military purposes. Since the Resolution was comprehensive and clear it was not surprising that France, Britain and the United States abstained in the vote. But the interesting point is that the combination of pressure from the Commonwealth, the OAU and other governments internationally with the Anti-Apartheid Movement's work within Britain and globally meant that, despite the new British government's desire to reverse policy, a veto was not cast.

By this time the situation in Southern Africa had become much more critical for Portugal and South Africa since the armed struggle in the Portuguese colonies was making dramatic progress. Powerful forces in the major Western countries were now supporting South Africa's demand that the Western powers relax the arms embargo and develop even closer relations with South Africa in order to defend Western interests in the region. This tendency caused considerable alarm in Africa and the Organization of African Unity decided, in 1970, to send a special mission headed by its Chairman, President Kenneth Kaunda of Zambia, to several Western capitals. At an earlier meeting of the OAU Council of Ministers in February–March 1970 a resolution adopted on apartheid stated that 'any form of military and other co-operation with (the) minority regimes constitutes a hostile act against all African States and their peoples.'[5]

The OAU meeting with Prime Minister Heath in October 1970 was tense and it was followed by a visit to Washington which proved to be virtually abortive as a result of an apparent misunderstanding about the timing of a meeting with President Nixon — which in fact did not take place. The meetings in Bonn and Paris were apparently conducted in a much more pleasant atmosphere despite the seriousness of the issue.

The Commonwealth

British relations with African countries were seriously strained as a result of the determination of the Heath government to resume the sale of arms to South Africa. AAM intensified its national activities and a mass rally was called in Trafalgar Square on 25 October 1970. Special messages of support were received from all over the world, including one from the Indian Prime Minister, Mrs Gandhi. With the forthcoming Commonwealth Conference in Singapore due in January 1971, AAM issued a simple Declaration which stated: 'I am totally opposed to the sale of arms to apartheid South Africa.' This Declaration was issued at the end of November in the form of a petition to be presented to the Commonwealth Conference and within seven weeks over 100,000 British people had signed the statement and returned it to AAM. On 7 January they were taken to Singapore by a representative of the Movement to be handed over to the Chairman of the Commonwealth Conference, Premier Lee Kwan Yew.

It is not the normal practice of the Commonwealth to accept petitions and representations critical of member states. However, the Declaration did not mention any country by name and simply expressed opposition to all arms sales to South Africa. Since the arms embargo was a legitimate issue of international concern it was possible to engage in the campaign in this form and attempt to present the petitions. There was widespread opposition among the

Afro/Asian and Caribbean members of the Commonwealth to Britain's proposed arms sales. Before the Singapore Conference AAM had undertaken a series of visits to most Commonwealth diplomatic missions in London for consultations. It would have been politically difficult for the petitions not to be officially received and the Foreign Minister of Singapore accepted them on behalf of the Chairman of the Conference. This was the first case of its kind in the history of the Commonwealth.

The AAM Declaration was supported officially by the Labour and Liberal Parties, the British Council of Churches, the Trades Union Congress, the United Nations Association and a wide variety of other non-governmental organizations as well as 100 Anglican bishops. Earlier the Archbishop of Canterbury had himself written to Prime Minister Heath expressing his 'disquiet'.

Because of the uncompromising position taken by the Heath government, there was the real likelihood that the Commonwealth itself would not survive after the Singapore meeting. This danger led to even greater support for the arms Declaration and a special AAM public meeting held in London on 18 January, timed to coincide with the eve of the arms discussion at Singapore, sent a cable to Prime Minister Heath urging him to heed British and Commonwealth opinion and abandon arms sales to South Africa.

Several African and Asian countries had already stated that a British decision to reverse the embargo could lead to the end of the Commonwealth and Canadian Prime Minister Trudeau stated on the eve of the conference that a chain reaction could carry Canada with it. At the conference, when the item was reached, Heads of Delegations dispensed with their advisers and assistants and discussed the issue for two full days.

Finally, it was announced that an eight nation study group would be established to investigate the security of the maritime trade routes in the South Atlantic and the Indian Oceans. This was a compromise whereby Britain was expected to do nothing until the group had presented its report. However, within weeks the British government announced that it would supply South Africa with seven Wasp helicopters due to its legal obligations under the Simonstown Agreement. Nigeria immediately withdrew from the study group as did several other members and the group never met. However, no further supplies of major weapons were then made by the British government.

The fact that AAM was able to mobilize widespread support inside Britain for an end to arms sales made it possible for it to make representations to other governments on this subject with added credibility. Also, the level of domestic opposition in Britain to arms sales made it easier for certain Commonwealth leaders to take up the issue with increased vigour. The relationship between domestic pressure and international action has been very direct on the arms issue as with other campaigns of a similar nature. It is a two-way process in that the adverse reaction of Commonwealth leaders to the original intention of the Heath government to sell arms itself helped to strengthen the domestic campaign within Britain.

It can well be asked whether all this activity is useful since the Heath government in fact supplied seven Wasp helicopters despite domestic and international pressure — and the Commonwealth remained intact. There is no doubt that the campaigns on the subject of arms sales helped to focus attention on South Africa and demonstrated the considerable opposition to apartheid which existed in Britain and the Commonwealth. Secondly, it is likely that had there been no controversy surrounding the policy of the Conservative government in 1970 it would probably have sold even more arms to South Africa and developed closer military ties with the Pretoria regime. That was certainly its declared intention, announced by Premier Heath upon winning the general election in May 1970.

The role of the Commonwealth in relation to Southern Africa has often been underrated. There is also a widespread view that the Commonwealth is merely the last vestige of the British Empire and that it is not an effective intergovernmental organization. But judgement as to its usefulness depends almost entirely upon what expectations there are of such an informal organization. It is unique in that virtually all its Conferences are in fact attended by most heads of governments, so that it is in effect a special international summit meeting. The United Nations and the Organization of African Unity are both very important organizations in relation to Southern Africa but the Commonwealth provides a special opportunity to exert direct influence on Britain and other countries in relation to developments in Southern Africa.

It is instructive to examine the record of the Commonwealth in relation to Southern Africa. Soon after Sharpeville, in 1961, a Commonwealth Conference took place in London. Prior to that AAM lobbied all members over several months to seek support for the exclusion of South Africa from the Commonwealth. Within Britain support for this policy was obtained by AAM from the Labour and Liberal Parties as well as several major trade unions. When the Conference opened there was a seventy-two hour vigil (to mark the seventy-two killed at Sharpeville and Langa) organized by AAM and leading public figures joined the demonstration. It achieved considerable publicity and several heads of governments agreed to meet representatives of AAM. The South African Prime Minister, who attended the Conference, insisted that the Commonwealth should not discuss South Africa's domestic policies, but since the majority of Commonwealth members would not accept this position there was deadlock. Britain was not in favour of embarrassing South Africa and tried to suggest some compromise but the Afro-Asian governments would not retract their position. AAM wanted the apartheid issue discussed by the Commonwealth and also urged that South Africa be excluded from it. This created a very difficult situation for the Commonwealth which had never excluded a member before. On the eve of the conference, when all Commonwealth leaders had arrived in London, *The Observer* newspaper carried a long article by Dr Julius Nyerere of Tanganyika. In it he stated that if South Africa was still a member of the

Commonwealth when Tanganyika achieved independence at the end of 1961, then his country would not apply for membership of the Commonwealth.[6] This sealed the issue and it became highly probable that South Africa could no longer remain in the Commonwealth. Thus, when it declared itself a Republic in May 1961 the Pretoria regime did not bother to apply for membership. This was the first major blow to South Africa's external relations. Since then, the question of apartheid has been discussed at virtually every Commonwealth Conference either directly or indirectly over issues such as Rhodesia.

Following the seizure of independence by the Smith regime in Salisbury in November 1965, every Commonwealth Conference has given priority to that problem. The British government made several attempts to reach a settlement with Ian Smith and the fact that no sell-out was possible is in all probability largely due to Commonwealth pressures. The Commonwealth connection has been used very astutely by African, Asian and Caribbean heads of governments to impress upon Britain the danger of handing over power to a minority regime without taking adequate account of the majority African population. AAM has been able to lobby all Commonwealth Conferences since 1960 since most of them in the early years took place in London. More recently they have been held in a variety of Commonwealth capitals — Singapore, Ottawa, Kingston, Lusaka and Melbourne — and it has been possible to send a representative on each occasion. The Kingston Conference in April 1975 took the unprecedented step of inviting representatives of the African people of Rhodesia to take part in its proceedings when discussing that subject. These developments signify the fundamental transformation of the British Commonwealth into the Commonwealth where Britain and the older members no longer enjoy dominant influence.

The Arms Embargo during the 1970s

The Conservative government did not supply any other items of major combat equipment to South Africa besides the Wasp helicopters. However, the loopholes remained and nothing was done to strengthen the embargo. Meanwhile the Labour Party in opposition had adopted a much stronger policy on Southern Africa and the election manifesto contained a pledge to implement the arms embargo against South Africa. In February 1974 Labour was returned to office once again and it successfully increased its majority in the House of Commons in a further election in October. Within days of its victory the Royal Navy was participating in joint naval exercises with the South African navy. This was the second such exercise that year and both with a Labour Party in office. AAM organized a national protest campaign and obtained considerable support from within the Parliamentary Labour Party as well as the National Executive of the Labour Party. There was sharp domestic and international controversy and the Foreign Secretary, James Callaghan, responded to the protests by promising to review the Simonstown Agreement. By the end of 1974 it was announced that Britain had decided to terminate the Simonstown Agreement. This was a considerable victory for the anti-apartheid lobby, but whilst it ruled out future joint exercises between the two navies it did not mean that British warships would not call at South African ports. Upon returning to office in 1974 the Labour government also announced that it would implement the arms embargo strictly. This policy was warmly welcomed at the Kingston Commonwealth Conference in April 1975.

At the end of 1975 an employee of Marconi Ltd made public his decision not to work on a defence contract for South Africa which was for the supply of a tropospheric communications system. AAM investigations revealed that contracts of this type could be placed, since the relevant regulations in the Export of Goods (Control) Order 1970 permitted it. The Order provides that certain goods listed in Schedule 1 are prohibited for export but may be sent to any 'port or destination in the Commonwealth, the Republic of Ireland, the Republic of South Africa or the United States of America.' It is remarkable that South Africa is accorded a special status which is apparently denied to most Western European countries including members of NATO. It was difficult to organize a major campaign on this issue because of the claim by Marconi and the government that the equipment was in fact for civilian use even though ordered by the South African Armaments Board. If there had been a Commonwealth conference taking place shortly or some other major meeting with British and African leaders, it is likely that the Labour government would have banned the export of this equipment. As it is, the initial pressures of AAM led to the government later placing the tropospheric system under licensing control in April 1976. This meant that it could no longer be exported without government approval. In October that year it was granted a licence on the basis that it was not an item which fell within the British arms embargo. Since then AAM representations to the government about possible similar contracts in the future have produced the response that the government would not disclose such confidential information but that AAM should be assured that the arms embargo will be implemented. The problem arises not so much because the government opposes the embargo as a matter of policy but because of the way in which it interprets and implements that embargo. In 1976 it also became known that a firm in the Channel Islands had supplied South Africa with engines for its Centurion tanks. This was a clear breach of the embargo and Prime Minister Wilson condemned it. There was a prosecution and the firm concerned was fined by the court. These are only some examples of violations of the arms embargo.

Examples such as these have to be followed up and although campaigns result in considerable success it is not always possible to stop all the deals. What is crucial is that the matter should be kept under constant surveillance with prompt action. In matters of defence it is often difficult to obtain all the information, yet AAM had been able to reveal a large number of loopholes in the British embargo during the 1970s.

A Mandatory Embargo

Two unsuccessful attempts were made during the mid-1970s to get the Security Council to adopt a resolution making the arms embargo against South Africa mandatory under Chapter VII of the UN Charter. They were both tabled in debates about Namibia. The first was in June 1975 and the second in October 1976 — on both occasions the three permanent Western members, Britain, France and the United States of America, jointly used the veto. They held the view that the situation in Namibia and South Africa's illegal occupation of that territory did not amount to a threat to international peace within the meaning of Chapter VII of the Charter. It was difficult to accept that if Smith's UDI in 1965 was considered by Britain to amount to a threat to world peace, then the increasingly dangerous situation in Namibia in 1976 was less of a threat. Of course the problem could best be understood in the context of the 'no confrontation with South Africa' policy of the major western governments.

Intensified campaigning continued in a variety of forms. In August 1977, a joint UN/OAU Conference for Action against Apartheid was held in Lagos with high-level Western participation. The African liberation movements from Southern Rhodesia, Namibia and South Africa were well represented, as were national anti-apartheid organizations from many countries. At the time both the South African and the Rhodesian regimes were carrying out large-scale military attacks against neighbouring African countries, which supported the African liberation struggle. Thus there was widespread concern about the supply of arms and other military materials to the Pretoria and Salisbury regimes. Direct accusations were made in Lagos that the arms supplies were coming from specific Western and other countries, but in reply the named countries made blanket denials and claimed to be upholding the embargo. The anti-apartheid movements were able to provide detailed information which embarrassed several governments. On the eve of the Lagos conference it was learnt that Soviet and American satellites had spotted preparations by South Africa for a nuclear explosion in the Kalahari Desert. At the Lagos conference there was a general feeling among participants of the need to strengthen the arms embargo and end all nuclear collaboration with South Africa. Following informal consultations between African and other sympathetic governments and United Nations officials, the Chairman of the UN Special Committee against Apartheid met with the Honorary Secretary of the AAM and it was decided to explore the possibility of establishing a new organization to work specifically on ending all forms of military collaboration with South Africa.

The impact of the Lagos Conference, together with events in Southern Africa — particularly South Africa's intransigence over Namibia; the Soweto massacre of school-children in June 1976; its extended, turbulent aftermath; the death of Steve Biko while in custody in September 1977; and the subsequent government crackdown on sections of the press, the Black Consciousness organizations and sympathetic white individuals — created a political climate in which it was difficult for the Western members of the Security Council to persist in their protective role towards South Africa. In October 1977, Britain, France and the USA vetoed a series of African draft resolutions calling for sanctions, including once again a mandatory arms embargo. Under such pressure and in the context of the reaction to the killing of Steve Biko, the three Western permanent members felt compelled to present their own draft resolution, which was adopted on 4 November 1977. This resolution was a turning-point, not just for South Africa but also for the United Nations itself, as it was the first occasion on which Chapter VII of the Charter had been invoked to apply sanctions against a UN member. The Western countries still avoided accepting that apartheid amounts to a 'threat to the peace', by having the resolution determine instead that 'the acquisition by South Africa of arms and related materials constitutes a threat to the maintenance of international peace and security.' The resolution was also weak in its provisions: it called for a 'review' of existing contractual and licensing arrangements rather than ordering their cancellation; and each country is supposed 'to refrain from any co-operation with South Africa in the manufacture and development of nuclear weapons' rather than abandon all nuclear collaboration.[7]

Just a month after the embargo was made mandatory, the African Group at the UN tried to ensure its effectiveness by getting the Security Council to set up a committee to monitor arms supplies to South Africa.[8] Three days later the Anti-Apartheid Movement presented a detailed statement to the Special Committee against Apartheid listing fourteen areas in which immediate and urgent action was required and pointing out that the November 1977 resolution only covered two of them. Nevertheless, the South Africans could be affected significantly 'if the present mandatory decision is applied strictly . . . [it] will make much of their existing weaponary inefficient and non-operational.'[9] The consultations which had started at the Lagos conference were continued until, with the arrangements finalized, it was possible for the British AAM to launch the 'World Campaign against Military and Nuclear Collaboration with South Africa' on 28 March 1979. The 'Founding Patrons' were five heads of state, from Nigeria and four of the Front Line States, while four Western public figures were brought in as 'Founding Sponsors'. Messages of support came from the chairmen of the three relevant UN specialist organs, the Presidents of ANC and SWAPO, the Commonwealth Secretary-General and the Prime Ministers of Norway and Sweden.[10] Such a launch gave the Campaign an immediate ability to be accepted at high levels in international diplomacy. Indeed, the effect of having such Patrons is almost to give the Campaign a quasi-governmental status. Within a week of the launch the Director was giving evidence to the Security Council committee on the arms embargo.[11]

In June 1980 the Security Council called on the committee to recommend measures to 'close all loop-holes in the arms embargo'.[12] The Director of the

World Campaign again gave evidence, this time in closed session. The report which followed in September 1980 made sixteen recommendations — with the United Kingdom stating a general reservation on all sixteen recommendations, France expressing reservations on six and opposition to two, whilst the United States had reservations on five. The report was largely based upon the analysis which the AAM and the World Campaign had been putting forward since December 1977. It is also important to note from this report that, with one exception, complaints about violations of the embargo were not made by governments even when they had the necessary information available to them.[13]

At the end of 1980 further consideration of the issue by the Security Council was postponed on the grounds that South Africa should not be antagonized at a point when it looked as if progress might be made on the decolonization of Namibia. After the Geneva conference in January 1981, when implementation of the transition arrangements for the independence of Namibia broke down, with the responsibility clearly lying with South Africa, a flurry of diplomatic activity ensued. The General Assembly resumed its 35th Session in March 1981, solely to conclude its work on Namibia, and the Non-Aligned held a special Ministerial Meeting on Namibia in Algiers in April 1981. The UN Special Committee held a series of seminars in Western capitals; one of these was in London in April and was jointly sponsored by the World Campaign on 'the Implementation and Reinforcement of the Arms Embargo'. Although twenty-one governments sent observers, the seminar was essentially a dialogue between the UN Secretariat, officers of UN committees, individual experts and non-governmental organizations, of which twenty-three were present with representatives. Seventeen papers were presented, all except one coming from NGOs or individual researchers. Eight of the papers were specially commissioned reviews of enforcement of the mandatory embargo in eight Western countries, mainly prepared by the respective anti-apartheid groups.[14] Despite all the pressures, the Security Council debate on Namibia at the end of April again ended with the 'triple veto' being cast on four draft resolutions, by Britain, France and the USA. When this was being written the prospects for an early strengthening of the arms embargo were not favourable, particularly since the new Reagan administration had already begun to relax certain provisions of the USA's own arms embargo.

The Role of the Anti-Apartheid Movement in World Politics

In conclusion, it needs to be pointed out that the AAM is essentially a British organization and none of its six full-time staff concentrates on international work alone. AAM is financed by its members and donations from supporters including grants made sometimes by organizations such as the World Council of Churches. The Movement relies heavily on volunteer assistance and it is therefore remarkable that it has been able to work consistently on Southern

African issues since its inception in 1959. AAM is a membership organization based in Britain. It has a National Committee composed of one representative each from over fifty local AAM committees and of members elected by the Annual General Meeting: thirty from among the individual members of the Movement, twenty-five from among the 350 or so national and regional affiliated organizations, including the London offices of the African liberation movements, British trade unions, churches, student groups and the local branches of political parties. The National Committee is the policy-making body of AAM, working 'within the framework of the resolutions adopted by the AGM',[15] and it elects the officers and an Executive Committee, which meets monthly and is responsible for the day-to-day work of the Movement. The National Committee meets five times a year.

In contrast, the World Campaign against Military and Nuclear Collaboration with South Africa, although created by the British AAM, is a transnational organization without its own roots in any particular country. It is based in Oslo, sustained by support from the liberation movements and from anti-apartheid movements throughout the Western world and in Nigeria and Ghana, co-operates with the major transnational church groups and has a regular working relationship with African governments. It makes representations to individual Western governments, but the focus of its activities so far has been the committee work of the United Nations and public exposure of violations. However, it has also encouraged specialist research on particular aspects of the embargo and published a study, *South Africa's Nuclear Capability*, which has been translated into several languages.[16]

Although this account concentrates almost exclusively on the arms campaign, AAM also works on a large number of other issues. For example, for two years prior to the Olympic Conference in Baden-Baden, Germany in 1963, AAM made representations to all Olympic bodies throughout the world and sent a representative to Germany to work for South Africa's exclusion from the Olympics. South Africa was suspended in 1963. This was the first major victory in the field of sport. Later similar action was taken by the international football organization, FIFA. Once the process was started it was taken up in virtually all fields of sport. In cases such as cricket and rugby where the international organizations were much more sympathetic to South Africa, national demonstrations involving thousands of people in Britain, Australia, New Zealand and Ireland led to their eventual exclusion or put a stop to their overseas tours. However, the South African regime, as well as the various sporting bodies which practise apartheid, tried to deceive international opinion by instituting some 'reforms' which meant that token 'non-whites' were included in their teams. This attempt to overcome international isolation was partially successful, but at the same time resulted in even more intensified campaigns against apartheid in sport. The political process has been very much like that on the arms embargo. The Commonwealth has been important, particularly with the 1977 summit meeting adopting the 'Gleneagles Agreement', in committing each government to taking vigorous action to prevent sporting contact with racially chosen teams. Action in the United Nations, with SANROC, the South African Non-Racial Olympic Committee, being the NGO taking the lead, has resulted in the production of a list of sportspeople who have collaborated with apartheid sport and who themselves should be subject to boycott. As with the arms embargo, there have been some flagrant violations of the sports boycott of South Africa, the most notable being the Springbok Rugby tour of New Zealand in 1981. In this case opposition came from the New Zealand group, HART:AAM, Halt All Racial Tours: Anti-Apartheid Movement, and New Zealand experienced its most bitter political conflicts and civil disturbances in modern times.

The AAM has also worked closely with non-governmental organizations such as Amnesty International. In this case it tries to ensure that they have all the relevant information about political prisoners in Southern Africa and also to consider and organize joint action wherever possible. The World Council of Churches is another organization with which close relations are maintained so that its Programme to Combat Racism is more effective. AAM officials take part in some WCC conferences and send information regularly to its office in Geneva.

From time to time when appropriate, contact is also made with the UN specialized agencies such as the WHO, ILO, UNESCO, or FAO on specific issues relating to Southern Africa. Letters containing proposals are sent to the respective Director-Generals or suggestions are channelled through the UN Special Committee Against Apartheid.

If international work is done on a comprehensive scale to cover all organizations which may be relevant to Southern Africa, it could take up enormous resources and time. It is impossible to do that for a small voluntary non-governmental organization. The approach is much more to work on specific *issues* which are considered to be important and then to follow them up both nationally and internationally at various levels.

If important questions relating to South Africa are to be raised, it is important to be able to provide precise and reliable information. That basically is the main resource which the AAM and the World Campaign have at their disposal. Everything which is going to be used has to be most carefully checked. If we were to make just one or two mistakes our reputation would be seriously undermined and our credibility on future occasions would be open to doubt. It is a measure of the emphasis on getting correct information that respect and trust has been won. Governments from Non-Aligned countries now will respond without asking first whether the relevant information has been carefully checked. Often governments do not manage to obtain information which is available to specialist non-governmental organizations. Interpretation and presentation of information in a meaningful way is also important, so that government leaders, who are always hard-pressed for time, are not required to read through unnecessary detailed materials.

The AAM and the World Campaign have reached a unique position in the world of the NGOs. In the UN Special Committee against Apartheid and in the Security Council's arms embargo committee, they are often at the centre of the debate and the decision-making. This is due to a variety of factors. On the one hand, the UN has a commitment to self-determination and human rights and a consensus that change in South Africa is necessary, while on the other hand the issue remains one of high importance and high conflict for most of the governments involved. The Western governments are militarily and economically strong, while they are politically weak and risk damaging their legitimacy by siding with apartheid. A belief in democracy, combined with pressure at home from anti-apartheid organizations, makes it impossible to maintain unconditional support for South Africa in international diplomacy.

The AAM is not simply a lobby organization which makes representations to governments and organizations. It is basically a public campaigning organization committed to supporting the African freedom struggle in Southern Africa and aims to win the widest possible solidarity with that struggle. By working for international disengagement from South Africa and furthering the boycott movement, it acts in support of the oppressed majority in Southern Africa — it is by no means an easy task to accomplish in those Western countries which have long historical, economic, cultural and political ties with the white population of South Africa. The international economic stake in the apartheid system is substantial and it tends automatically to act in defence of the status quo in South Africa. Ultimately, freedom in Southern Africa will only be achieved by the oppressed people themselves, but international action in support of that struggle can make it a little less difficult.

References

1 Article 2(7) of the United Nations Charter reads 'Nothing contained in the present Charter shall authorise the United Nations to intervene in matters which are essentially within the domestic jurisdiction of any state' and was held to be an outright prohibition upon the discussion of the apartheid system. People who use this argument tend to forget that Article 2(7) continues, 'this principle shall not prejudice the application of enforcement measures under Chapter VII', which applies when the Security Council has determined under Article 39 'the existence of any threat to the peace, breach of the peace, or act of aggression'.

2 UN Security Council Resolution 181(1963) of 7 August 1963, adopted by 9 votes to 0, with 2 abstentions (France and UK), former reference number S/5386.

3 United Nations document A/5453 of 17 July 1963, second interim report of the Special Committee on the Policies of Apartheid of the Government of South Africa. The Special Committee was established by General Assembly Resolution 1761(XVII) of 6 November 1962 by a vote of 67 in favour, 16 against, with 23 abstentions. It was some years later that its name was shortened to the Special Committee against Apartheid.

4 For the text, see United Nations Unit on Apartheid, *Notes and Documents*, No. 17/70, May 1970, pp. 1–8.

5 OAU Council of Ministers Resolution on Decolonisation and Apartheid, CM/Res.209 (XIV), adopted at the Fourteenth Ordinary Session in Addis Ababa, 27 February–6 March 1970.

6 *The Observer*, London, 12 March 1961.

7 UN Security Council Resolution 418(1977) of 4 November 1977.

8 UN Security Council Resolution 420(1977) of 9 December 1977.

9 United Nations document A/AC.115/L.485 of 22 December 1977, reporting the text of the statement made by Abdul Minty to the Special Committee against Apartheid on 12 December.

10 The Founding Patrons were President Nyerere of Tanzania, President Khama of Botswana, President Neto of Angola, President Kaunda of Zambia and Lt. Gen. Obasanjo of Nigeria. The Founding Sponsors were Olof Palme of Sweden, Coretta King of the USA and Joan Lestor and David Steel, two British Members of Parliament. The messages of support from the UN came from Ambassador Harriman, Chairman of the Special Committee against Apartheid, Ambassador Salim, Chairman of the Special Committee on Decolonization and Ambassador Lusaka, President of the Council for Namibia.

11 Abdul Minty has testified on behalf of the World Campaign against Military and Nuclear Collaboration with South Africa to the UN Security Council committee on the Arms embargo on 3 April 1979 (UN document S/AC.20/SR.9), 5 March 1980 (S/AC.20/SR.25) and on 10 July 1980 in closed session (no summary record being issued).

12 UN Security Council Resolution 473(1980) of 13 June 1980.

13 Report of the Security Council Committee established by Resolution 421(1977), UN document S/14179 of 19 September 1980.

14 For the report on the 'International Seminar on the Implementation and Reinforcement of the Arms Embargo against South Africa', held in London from 1 to 3 April 1981, see UN document A/AC.115/L.547 of 8 May 1981 and subsequent addendum.

15 Quote from the constitution of the Anti-Apartheid Movement.

16 Smith, Dan, *South Africa's Nuclear Capability*, published by the World Campaign Against Military and Nuclear Collaboration with South Africa, Oslo, in co-operation with the UN Centre Against Apartheid, New York, February 1980; English, French, Dutch and Finnish editions available.

3 The Creation and Evolution of the Palestine Liberation Organization

DAVID GILMOUR

The establishment of the Palestine Liberation Organization was a consequence of the Arab Summit Conference of January 1964 which declared its intention of approving 'practical resolutions . . . to organise the Palestinian people to enable them to carry out their role in liberating their homeland and determining their destiny.'[1] The impetus behind the creation of the PLO came, therefore, not from the Palestinians themselves, but from the countries of the Arab League. Since the organization was to be an official body of the Arab League and thus easily supervised by the member states, many Palestinians regarded it with suspicion and hostility.[2] It was not for some years, and only after it had been radically transformed, that the PLO would be able to claim the allegiance of a majority of the Palestinian people.

The Palestinian cause had long been regarded, by both the Palestinians and the other Arabs, as an Arab cause, as part of the pan-Arab struggle against the Western colonial powers which they had been fighting since the French and British Mandates had been set up after the First World War. The monarchies of Egypt, Jordan and Iraq and the republics of Syria and Lebanon had all fought against Israel in 1948 and, although their performances (except Transjordan's) had been ineffectual, it was assumed that they would do so again in the future. Ten years later, the Arab nationalists had overthrown the Kings of Egypt and Iraq while Syria had become a part of Gamal Abdel Nasser's United Arab Republic (UAR). Many Palestinians believed that these progressive new regimes would soon be able to combine in order to achieve the last important goal of the pan-Arab programme, the liberation of Palestine.

But within three years, Arab nationalism as a coherent force at the governmental level was on the decline. Syria withdrew from the UAR and Nasser quarrelled bitterly with the Iraqi leadership. By then many Palestinians had become disillusioned by the failure of the Arab governments to help them and some began to reconsider their ideas on the nature of the Palestine question. Instead of viewing it as merely a part of the pan-Arab struggle, they came to see it more as a dispute between the Israelis and themselves which could be resolved by the creation of a Palestinian resistance movement. They were naturally both encouraged and influenced by the success of the Algerian War of Independence.

The increasing frustration and militancy of the Palestinians were noticed by the Arab governments and it was in order to contain these that they decided to create a political organization for the Palestinians.[3] At the Arab Summit Conference in Cairo in January 1964, Ahmad Shuqairi, a Palestinian who had previously been head of the Saudi Arabian delegation at the United Nations, was asked to prepare the groundwork for the establishment of a Palestine National Council (PNC).[4] Shuqairi visited the countries of the Palestinian diaspora and set up various committees charged with the task of nominating candidates for the new council.[5] When the PNC held its first meeting in Jerusalem in May 1964, its 422 members, though not elected democratically, nevertheless represented most of the Palestinian communities in the Arab world. The most important act of the first Palestine National Council was the proclamation of the Palestine Liberation Organization, whose Executive Committee was entrusted with the administration of the PNC's policy. The Palestine National Fund (PNF) and the Palestine Liberation Army (PLA) were both set up under the control of the PLO and a National Charter was adopted.

When the Arab League was set up in 1945, Palestine was still under the British Mandate and it was hoped that there would soon be a Palestinian Arab state. The Arab League Pact contained an 'Annex Regarding Palestine', which provided 'until that country can effectively exercise its independence, the Council of the League should take charge of the selection of an Arab representative from Palestine to take part in its work.'[6] The Palestinian representative was given the right to take part in the Council's proceeding, but could only vote on matters concerning Palestine and was not regarded as having an equal status to the full members of the League. From its establishment in Gaza in 1948, the Government of All Palestine had been recognized to speak for the Palestinians in the Council. In 1964 the PLO took over and fulfilled this role.

From the beginning, the PLO claimed to be the true representative of the Palestinian people, a claim much disputed by the Jordanian government which pointed out that a majority of Palestinians had Jordanian passports and lived under Jordanian sovereignty on both banks of the River Jordan (King Abdullah had annexed the Palestinian West Bank in 1950 and renamed his Kingdom Jordan).[7] Nevertheless, there were a number of Palestinians who accepted neither Jordan nor the PLO as their representative. They saw that the purpose of the PLO, as envisaged by the Arab League, was to contain rather than express Palestinian nationalism, to act as an outlet for Palestinian frustration — not to be an effective military organization which might drag the Arab states into a war with Israel. Above all, it was clear that Shuqairi and the PLO leadership would have no real independence and would always be subjected to the pressures and demands of the Arab governments.[8]

Those Palestinians who mistrusted the intentions of the PLO were divided into a number of different groups, small both in influence and in membership before the 1967 war, but they were later to take over the leadership of the Palestinian movement. Two such groups were the radical Arab Nationalist Movement (ANM), founded by Dr George Habash in 1933, and the Palestine Liberation Front (PLF) of Ahmad Jibril. A more active organization was the Palestine National Liberation Movement, known by a reversal of its Arabic initials as Fatah (conquest), which emerged in the early sixties and carried out its first commando operation in 1965. Although it received weapons and training from the new nationalist government in Algeria, the other Arab states, which realized that it was likely to be more active and troublesome than the PLO, disapproved of it. Fatah members were arrested in Egypt, Lebanon and Syria, and the group's future leader, Yasser Arafat, spent several weeks in a Lebanese prison.[9]

In the eyes of the Palestinians, the sweeping Israeli victory in the 1967 war discredited the Arab states and, by extension, the PLO. The Palestinians finally realized that the Arab armies were incapable of defeating the Zionists by conventional methods and so they turned increasingly to guerrilla warfare. In the aftermath of the defeat, thousands of them joined Fatah and a new grouping, the Popular Front for the Liberation of Palestine (PFLP), which was formed by Habash after the merger of three small guerrilla movements. These carried out numerous commando operations in the Israeli-occupied territories of the West Bank and Gaza and, in March 1968, they fought a pitched battle with Israeli troops at the Jordanian village of Karama. The Israelis suffered heavy casualties and the guerrillas emerged from the encounter with enormous prestige, although their success was largely attributable to the support of the Jordanian army.[10] In the following month Fatah made it public for the first time that their leader was Yasser Arafat.[11]

The rise of the guerrilla movements inevitably resulted in a temporary decline of the PLO. Ahmad Shuqairi, whose leadership had been bombastic but ineffective, resigned in December 1967 and his successor, Yahya Hammouda, realized that, if the PLO wanted to retain any support among the Palestinians, it would have to bring the guerrilla movements into the organization. In March 1968 an agreement was reached between the PLO, Fatah and the PFLP, according the guerrillas representation on the Palestine National Council.[12] During the year the guerrillas, particularly Fatah, were able to extend their influence over the organization and at the next session of the PNC in February 1969 they established their domination by electing Arafat as chairman of the PLO's Executive Committee.

The take-over of the PLO by the guerrillas was reluctantly accepted by the Arab states who realized that Fatah reflected the aspirations of the Palestinians more accurately than the PLO had done. No Arab government bordering on Israel can have welcomed the presence of well-armed guerrilla forces on their territory but immediately after the 1967 war they could not have afforded to antagonize public opinion in their countries by opposing the guerrillas. In the summer of 1968 President Nasser accorded Yasser Arafat official recognition by including him in an Egyptian delegation to Moscow.

The organization over which Yasser Arafat now presided soon transformed itself into what was in effect a government-in-exile (though the PLO has always refused to describe itself as one) with an extensive administrative machinery. The principal body remained the PNC, which continues to meet once a year, nowadays in Damascus, where it lays down the principles of PLO policy, elects the Executive Committee and approves the budget. While it is obviously not strictly democratic — it would be difficult to organize elections for a community so widely dispersed as the Palestinians — the Palestinians themselves feel that the PNC is as representative as it can be in the circumstances. The delegates come from all over the world, in numbers roughly corresponding to the strength of the communities in different countries. Forty come from Jordan and eighteen from Kuwait, while the United States provides eight, Brazil two and the rest of Latin America four. Of the 303 delegates, a hundred of them are from the resistance groups (thirty-five are Fatah members) who are selected at the annual conferences of the respective organizations. Fifty-seven are members of various syndicates, such as the Labour Syndicate, the Student Movement, the Teacher's Syndicate and the Women's Organization, and a small number are chosen as representatives of the refugee camps.[13] The remainder are independents chosen for their ability to contribute in one way or another to the cause. A significant number of PNC members are writers and historians who have written about Palestine, and businessmen who have made large contributions to the Palestine National Fund.

Although it possesses less than 12 per cent of the seats, Fatah is the dominant force in the PNC — as it is in all the bodies of the PLO. The independents receive a sympathetic hearing but they have no power base of their own. Most of them are linked in some way to one or other of the guerrilla organizations and the majority choose Fatah. The syndicates are also behind Arafat: thirteen of the fifteen PNC members from the Labour Syndicate support Fatah and so do 90 per cent of the students.[14]

The Executive Committee of the PLO is the Palestinian 'cabinet'. It is elected by the PNC to carry out the Council's policies and it likewise reflects a pro-Fatah bias. Its members administer the various departments of the PLO: the Political Department, which corresponds to a foreign ministry and is responsible for about seventy PLO offices all over the world;[15] the Military Department, the Palestine National Fund, the Departments of Education, Health and Social Affairs, the Department of the Occupied Homeland, and the Departments of Information and Culture and Administrative Affairs. The PLO also controls a number of supporting bodies such as the Palestine Red Crescent Society, which operates thirty-five hospitals and more than a hundred clinics throughout the Arab world. In Beirut it maintains a research centre, a news agency and a radio station.

The PLO's finances are controlled by the Palestinian National Fund. There are two main sources of income. One is 'Liberation tax' which is levied on Palestinians working in the public sector in some Arab countries. The Iraqi Law No. 130 of 1965 declared that the Iraqi government would deduct 3 per cent of the monthly salaries of Palestinians working in government departments and in both public and private companies, and credit the sum to the account of the Palestine National Fund.[16] Similar laws, providing for deductions of between 3 and 6 per cent, exist in a number of other Arab countries including Syria, Kuwait, Libya, the United Arab Emirates and Qatar. Palestinians living in countries not covered by these laws are expected to make voluntary contributions of a similar size.

The fund's other source of income is the Arab countries. Until 1979 particular governments could choose the guerrilla organizations they wanted to back and finance them directly without going through the fund. At a time when there was considerable disagreement with the PLO over its aims and strategy, such a situation was regarded as highly unsatisfactory. The Iraqi government, for example, could finance Habash and the PFLP without backing Fatah, which it regarded as too moderate. But it also meant that Habash would have to follow Iraqi policy if he wanted to remain on the payroll. At the Baghdad Summit Meeting in November 1978, steps were taken to end this state of affairs and so reduce the guerrillas' dependence on individual governments. It was then decided to raise 250 million dollars for the PLO, which would be distributed not by the Arab governments but by the Palestine National Fund. Of that sum, 50 million dollars were to be spent on development in the Israeli-occupied territories and the rest to be shared between the guerrilla organizations and the various departments of the PLO. However, largely as a result of the deep divisions of the Arab world since that date, it is extremely unlikely that the bulk of that sum was ever received by the PNF.

It is often said, by politicians and Israeli supporters in the United States and Europe, that the PLO does not properly represent the Palestinian people. This is obviously difficult to *prove* one way or the other, but it is certain that the people who make the charge have never substantiated it. There are a number of Palestinians in the West Bank, particularly among the landowners and the mukhtars, who identified themselves closely with the Jordanian regime before 1969: no doubt they would prefer to be ruled once more by the Jordanians rather than by the PLO. The same can be said about a number of people in the socially conservative Gaza Strip. But it is clear to anyone who travels through these areas, or indeed through any places where the refugees now live, that the vast majority of Palestinians support the PLO and regard it as their version of a government-in-exile. Nor is this particularly surprising since the PLO is a vast umbrella organization in which most political opinion, certainly anything between liberalism and Marxist–Leninism, can find a place. Although it is often diverted from its goal, its only real objective is the liberation of the homeland, and few Palestinians will disagree with that.

The pragmatism and lack of dogmatism of the PLO is a consequence of the ascendancy of Fatah within the organization. From the beginning, Fatah's message was a simple one: Palestine would only be liberated by Palestinians fighting a popular war. All effort should be concentrated on a nationalist uprising with a solitary goal: the liberation of the homeland. Everything else was secondary. Ideological debate and social revolution have therefore had little place in Fatah's activities. They are to be discussed later, after the liberation. Before that, only the question of recovering Palestine can be admitted. Fatah has thus appealed to all Palestinians, irrespective of class or profession, who support the resistance movement. Naturally it is not an entirely homogeneous group and it has its Marxist and other wings, but these have usually managed to avoid ideological disputes and to concentrate on a strictly nationalist approach. Fatah has thus been able to gain the support of both conservative and revolutionary regimes in the Arab world. This has given it an enormous advantage over the smaller, left-wing groups such as the PFLP, and has enabled it to dominate the resistance. But it has also meant that Fatah is always open to pressure from the Arab governments and depends for its survival on the skilful diplomacy of Arafat.

George Habash of the PFLP saw the struggle in different terms from Arafat and the Fatah leadership. He believed that Palestine could only be liberated by the joint efforts of all the Arab people and not by guerrilla warfare conducted by the Palestinians. When the Arab regimes revealed their feebleness in 1967, Habash reacted very differently from Arafat. While Fatah insisted that the regimes should now be ignored, Habash argued that they should be overthrown. If the Arab world as it stood was too impotent to regain Palestine, then it would have to be changed. But Habash, who had once led the Arab Nationalist Movement, now concluded that the slogans of Arab nationalism and the cry of 'unity' were no longer sufficient to bring the Arabs together to defeat Israel. A revolutionary creed was also needed and this explains Habash's late conversion to Marxism.[17]

Habash and his supporters believed that the Palestinians would never defeat Israel if they had to fight on their own or with pro-Western regimes such as those in Jordan or Lebanon. Their enemies, he argued, were not only the Zionists but also 'imperialism', by which he meant the United States and any other country which gave military or financial support to Israel, and the Arab 'puppet regimes' which, he claimed, were only kept in power by the West. He thus proposed the overthrow of the Arab regimes and their replacement by Marxist governments. If that were achieved, the PFLP argued, 'not only will Palestine be free from Zionism, but Lebanon and Jordan will be free from reaction, and Syria and Iraq from the *petite bourgeoisie*. They will be transformed in a truly socialist sense and united. Palestine will be part of a Marxist-Leninist Arabia.'[18]

Within a year of its formation in 1967, the PFLP had begun to splinter. A number of different groups left Habash, both for ideological and strategic reasons. The most important faction was that led by Nayif Hawatmah, who took his men out of the Front early in 1969 and formed the Popular Democratic Front for the Liberation of Palestine (PDFLP). Hawatmah, who had belonged to the left-wing faction of the Arab Nationalist Movement, had been quarrelling with Habash for some years, his principal complaint being that the PFLP leader was not revolutionary enough. The issue that caused many of the arguments, first in the Arab Nationalist Movement and later in the committees of the Front, was the role the 'petit bourgeois' were to play in the Palestine revolution. Neither Habash nor Hawatmah liked the petit bourgeois but while Habash believed that they should co-operate with them in the early stages of the revolution, Hawatmah refused to have anything to do with them. It was the quarrel over this and other, similarly recondite subjects, such as the relationship between military struggle and social revolution, that caused the other major split in the PFLP. Ahmad Jibril, a former Palestinian officer in the Syrian army who had founded the Palestine Liberation Front, had brought his group into the PFLP in 1967. But he was so disgusted by the time-wasting ideological disputes in which the Front specialized that he took it out again less than a year later and renamed it the Popular Front for the Liberation of Palestine-General Command.

From 1969 the PLO has included Fatah and the PFLP splinter groups, although the PFLP itself has frequently withdrawn or been suspended from the Executive Committee. These are the only important independent organizations of the resistance. There are others, however, on the Executive Committee which owe their existence to particular Arab governments which finance and support them and expect them to follow government policy in return. Two examples are the Arab Liberation Front (ALF), which is supported by Iraq, and Saiqa, which is supported by Syria. Both groups accurately reflect the policies of their protectors but, while the ALF is little more than a propaganda instrument of the Iraqi government, Saiqa is a serious military force which provides more commandos for the PLO than any other organization except Fatah. Its ideology is that of the pro-Syrian faction of the Ba'ath Party (a complicated compound of socialism and Arab nationalism), but inside the PLO it has generally supported Fatah against the PFLP.

Such a disparate number of groups inside the PLO has naturally led to disagreements about the organization's policy, even on the basic question of its ultimate aim. In the early years of the resistance, when it was clear that the struggle would last for several decades, there was no need to specify the final objective. 'Liberation' was a vague enough term that satisfied everyone. In October 1968 one of Fatah's leaders, Salah Khalaf, defined what later became the official PLO objective: Palestine was to form a single, secular, democratic state for the Palestinian people. The state would automatically cease to be a Zionist one, but all Jews who were established there and who wished to remain would be able to do so. As the PDFLP explained to the Palestine National Council in the following year:'[In the secular, democratic state] both Arabs and Jews shall live without discrimination, and will be granted the right to develop and promote their respective national culture.' In addition, the new Palestine would 'include Arabs and Jews enjoying equal national rights and duties.'[19]

The attitudes of the PLO were forcibly changed by the war of October 1973 which, together with the oil embargo that followed, persuaded the international community that a solution to the Middle East conflict had to be found. As the participants prepared for the Geneva peace conference, the Palestinians had to define their position and formulate their demands. Fatah and the other organizations which had official contacts with the Arab world had to take into account the positions of the relevant Arab governments; the Front and its offshoots, which considered all the countries of the Middle East as their enemies, except Iraq, South Yemen and Algeria, could afford to be less diplomatic. It was clear, for example, that Egypt, Syria and Jordan were prepared to accept a settlement if Israel evacuated the areas occupied in 1967, but they were not going to demand the rest of Palestine conquered in 1948.[20] The Palestinians, therefore, had to decide whether to go along with the Arab consensus or to reject it. They had to decide whether or not they were prepared to abandon their vision of total liberation and accept a lesser but more tangible thing – Palestinian rule in those small areas of their homeland, the West Bank and Gaza, which stood a chance of being restored to them by diplomatic means.

The compromise solution was implicitly accepted by Fatah, Saiqa, most of the Palestinian diaspora and the Palestine National Council which, at its twelfth meeting in Cairo in June 1974, declared that its new policy was 'to liberate Palestinian soil and to set up on any part of it which is liberated the militant national authority of the people.' Three years later it was made clear that 'national authority' meant 'state'.[21] This resolution, ambiguously termed as it was, represented a major change in PLO policy, one that clearly indicated that the majority of the leadership was now prepared to accept, in place of the secular, democratic state in all of Palestine as it was in 1947, an independent country in one quarter of the whole area. Since 1974 the PLO has remained divided over this issue, the PFLP and other groups forming a Rejection Front, to oppose these limited aims. It is this pressure inside the Palestinian movement which has prevented Arafat from being more specific about his present aims. Nevertheless, he and other leaders have frequently indicated their willingness to accept Israel's existence in exchange for a Palestinian state in the West Bank and Gaza. In May 1978 Arafat told the *New York Times* that 'the only possible solution was the coexistence of Israel and a Palestinian state',[22] and at the Baghdad conference later in the year the PLO confirmed its acceptance of Israel's pre-1967 borders when it committed itself to a 'just peace based on the total Israeli withdrawal from Arab territories occupied in 1967'.[23]

Although the official policy of the PLO is still governed by the PNC resolution of 1974, a large number of militant Palestinians have never accepted it. The principal groups of the Rejection Front have been the PFLP, the PFLP-General Command, the Iraqi-backed ALF and a dissident pro-Iraqi faction of Fatah led by Abu Nidal. All of them have refused to consider a compromise and have done what they could to wreck any chance of a peace settlement. Abu Nidal's group even precipitated an internecine war among the Palestinians over the 'mini-state' controversy. Prominent members of Fatah, including the PLO representatives in London and Paris, were assassinated because they were outspoken advocates of a peace settlement involving compromise and acceptance of Israel as an established fact.[24] While Fatah has claimed that its men were killed by Israeli agents who had infiltrated this pro-Iraqi group, few people doubt that the ultimate responsibility for the murders lies with Abu Nidal and his Iraqi backers. (Since November 1978 Iraq has withheld its support from the Rejection Front and the group's backers now include Libya, Syria, Algeria and South Yemen.)

The division inside the PLO over the 'mini-state' question roughly reflects a fundamental disagreement among Palestinians about whether diplomacy or armed struggle is the best method of achieving their aims. The parallel is not wholly accurate because Fatah and its supporters in the PLO have never denied the importance of the armed struggle and they have also resorted to acts of terrorism. Nevertheless, they do realize that diplomatic support is vital and in recent years they have concentrated on gaining this. Diplomacy has never had any part in the activities of the Rejection Front and from its beginning the PFLP decided that the best means of promoting its cause was terrorism. Nearly all the most spectacular acts — the hijackings, the attacks at airports and Israeli airline offices, the seizure of embassies and so on — were committed by the PFLP and by a shadowy group of dissidents from Fatah, the Black September Organization. The rationale behind the terror was simple. While the Palestinians remained harmless refugees the world could afford to disregard them; when they began killing people they would force the international community to find a solution to the Middle East conflict. As George Habash himself pointed out: 'When we hijack a plane it has more effect than if we killed a hundred Israelis in battle. For decades world public opinion has been neither for nor against the Palestinians. It simply ignored us. At least the world is talking about us now.'[25]

Although diplomatic methods have been scorned by the Rejection Front, which points out that not one inch of Palestine has been liberated by these means, the PLO nevertheless achieved an astonishing diplomatic success during the 1970s. By the end of the decade the Palestinians' cause had been adopted by the Third World and by revolutionary and liberation movements throughout the world. To the countries of Asia and Africa theirs had become the first among liberation movements and even the countries of Western Europe were making tentative moves towards some sort of diplomatic recognition of the PLO.

Of course, the PLO had long been recognized by most of the Arab world as the official representative of the Palestinian people and its prestige with the Arab countries had increased after the guerrillas' take-over of the organization at the beginning of 1969. Nevertheless, it was faced by a number of intra-Arab problems, particularly in its relationship with King Hussein of Jordan, who refused to accept the PLO's claim that it represented the Palestinian people. Hussein had ruled over both the East Bank and the West Bank of the Jordan before 1967 and he still claimed sovereignty over the West Bank after it had been occupied by the Israelis. Two-thirds of his subjects (including those on the West Bank) were Palestinians and to have admitted that the guerrillas were their rightful leaders would have threatened the whole basis of his regime. By 1970 both the extremist groups inside the PLO and the most conservative elements in the Jordanian army were eager to provoke a confrontation on the issue and, in the civil war that followed, the guerrillas were expelled from Jordan.

Although it was defeated decisively in the field, the PLO was able to survive as an organization and even to increase its stature within the Arab world in the following years. In the spring of 1972, less than a year after his last decisive victory over the guerrillas, a renewed attempt by Hussein to press his claims to the West Bank was rejected by the Arab world. His plan for a United Arab Kingdom on a federal basis, with two regional capitals in Jerusalem and Amman, was almost universally condemned by the Arab states.[26] The PLO, despite the near annihilation of its forces, still retained the loyalty of the Arab countries and in 1974, at the Rabat Summit Conference, Hussein was forced to admit the Palestinians' political victory and acknowledge, along with the rest of the Arab League, the PLO's claim to be the 'sole, legitimate representative of the Palestinian people'.[27]

The PLO, however, was still regarded by the Arab League as an organization representing a people rather than a government representing a country. A major change in legal status occurred in September 1976 in Cairo, when the sixty-sixth session of the Arab League Council accepted Palestine, as represented by the PLO, as a full member of the Arab League with the same rights as any of the member states,[28] even though the original Pact only allowed for independent states to become members. There was a similar change in the PLO's status in various other inter-Arab organizations. In the same year that it became a full member of the Arab League, the PLO, representing Palestine, was admitted to full membership of the Arab Monetary Fund and the Arab Fund for Economic and Social Development.[29]

The period of the mid-seventies also saw changes in the PLO's position elsewhere in the world. In 1974 the United Nations General Assembly voted by 105 votes to 4 (with 20 abstentions) to invite the PLO to participate in the Palestine debate.[30] Yasser Arafat's speech to the General Assembly in November of that year was proof of the PLO's new prestige. It was the first time in the history of the United Nations that a representative of a liberation movement, or indeed anybody who was not a governmental delegate (with the exception of the Pope), had been invited to address the General Assembly in its plenary session. In December of the following year, the UN went even further when the Security Council invited the PLO to take part in a discussion on Israeli raids into Lebanon. Significantly, as Anis Kassim has pointed out, 'that invitation was extended to the PLO as if it were a member state in accordance with rule 37 and *not* on the basis of rule 39 of the Security Council's provisional rules of procedure. Rule 37 applies to any "member of the United Nations which is not a member of the Security Council . . ."; rule 39 applies to "persons".'[31]

The PLO, however, was not given full membership status at the UN. Later in the session at which Arafat spoke, it was given a permanent Observer status at the General Assembly, and since 1974 it has been an Observer at all international conferences organized by the Assembly.[32] Further successes included its admission to the Non-Aligned Group in August 1975[33] and in January 1976 – at a time when it was still not even a full member of the Arab League – the PLO was accepted as a member of the 'Group of 77' developing countries.[34] In July 1977 it was also promoted from 'permanent Observer status' to a 'full member' of the UN Economic Commission for West Asia.[35]

The PLO's first major ally outside the Arab world was China, which recognized the organization within a year of its establishment. Mao Tse-tung was fond of drawing parallels between Israel and Formosa which he considered to be 'bases of imperialism'[36] at the extremities of Asia and his government began supplying aid to the PLO long before the Russians. Although their own ideology at that time was closer to Habash than to Arafat, the Chinese opposed the PFLP's use of terrorism and concentrated on giving weapons to Fatah. Later Arafat was to claim that China was 'the biggest influence in supporting our revolution and strengthening its perseverance.'[37]

The position of the Soviet Union and its East European satellites was far more ambiguous. Throughout the fifties and early sixties the Russians treated the Palestinian issue as a refugee problem without a political dimension. A PLO delegation did not visit Moscow until 1970 and even then it was met not by government officials but by the Soviet Afro-Asian Solidarity Committee.[38] The Russians' hesitancy towards the PLO is easily explained. They were exasperated by its lack of unity, embarrassed by its use of terrorism, and in disagreement, until 1974, with its ultimate aim. For the Soviet Union, which had voted for the creation of Israel and was committed to its survival, to have given full support to the PLO, which until after the October War called for a reunified Palestine, would have been inconsistent. Hence the Soviet Union remained ambivalent, keeping its distance from the PLO, partly in case it collapsed and partly because it did not wish to be associated too closely with Palestinian tactics and objectives. This approach was copied by Hungary, Czechoslovakia and Poland. However, the Russians seem to have realized that such a negative attitude would do nothing for their image in the Third World and would merely enable China to establish itself as the principal supporter of the Arab revolutionary movements. Perhaps as a result of such doubts, Bulgaria and East Germany became increasingly friendly towards the PLO and in 1974 the East German leader, Erich Honecker, sent Arafat a telegram in which he declared that 'the Socialist Unity Party again stresses its limitless support for the PLO in its struggle to attain the legitimate rights of the Palestinian Arab people.'[39] It was as recently as October 1981 that the Soviet Union finally decided to accord full diplomatic recognition to the PLO.

In the Third World the PLO has drawn its support from Asia and more recently from Africa. In the 1960s many African countries had diplomatic relations with Israel and received technical assistance. As late as 1969 the Algerians opposed the convening of a third Non-Aligned summit, because they feared that the African countries would prevent the adoption of Arab-sponsored resolutions on the Middle East.[40] Continued Israeli unwillingness to negotiate a peace settlement, and in particular the poor reception they gave to an OAU mediation mission in November 1971, began to change the attitudes of black African governments.[41] Algeria actually became the host for the fourth Non-Aligned summit in 1973 and there a *Declaration on the Struggle for National Liberation* was produced, which linked the situation in Palestine to racism in Southern Africa, as part of 'a single imperialist strategy'.[42] Six African countries had already broken diplomatic relations with Israel in the previous twelve months; Cuba, Togo and Zaïre broke immediately after the Algiers summit; and nineteen more African countries did so in the month after the outbreak of the 1973 war.[43] The decline in Israel's position was matched by a rise in the status of the PLO among the Non-Aligned. At the 1970 summit along with the African liberation movements, the PLO was classified as a 'Guest'. In 1973 they all became 'Observers' and in August 1975 the PLO was promoted above the other movements to full membership status.[44]

The PLO found more difficulty in gaining acceptance in the Americas and Western Europe. Nevertheless, by the end of the 1970s, Arafat had been officially received by the prime ministers or heads of state of Spain, Portugal and Austria while the PLO foreign affairs spokesman, Farouk Qaddoumi, had met the foreign ministers of Italy and Belgium. The most important of these diplomatic events took place in Vienna in July 1979. There Arafat was welcomed by Herr Willy Brandt, the chairman of the Socialist International and a former West German chancellor, and by Chancellor Kreisky of Austria. After talks between them, both Brandt and Kreisky claimed that the PLO had no intention of destroying Israel.[45] It was after this meeting that the Palestinian diplomatic initiative in Europe began to gather momentum. On 25 September in the UN General Assembly, the Irish foreign minister, who was speaking on behalf of the European Community, for the first time mentioned the role of the PLO in Middle East peace negotiations[46] and the following February the Irish government recognized the PLO and called for a Palestinian state.[47] In March 1980 President Giscard d'Estaing of France declared his support for the principle of self-determination for the Palestinians and spoke of the need to include the PLO in negotiations. Shortly afterwards, the European Community adopted a common position and moved close to recognition of the PLO, when in the Venice Statement of June 1980 it declared that the organization would 'have to be associated with the negotiations' for a peace settlement.[48]

By 1980 the PLO could claim recognition from more than one hundred countries and had opened offices in about seventy capitals.[49] The status of these offices varies. In most of the Arab world and in some Asian countries, such as India and Pakistan, the representative enjoys diplomatic status. This is also the case in a number of African countries, including Tanzania, Uganda and Guinea Bissau. In most other countries of Africa and Asia, as in Western Europe and Latin America, the representative usually heads an information office or works from the local Arab League Office. In the Soviet Union the PLO office was until October 1981 accredited to the Afro-Asian Solidarity Committee although its representative had the same rights and privileges as an ambassador. In the Warsaw Pact countries of Eastern Europe, it is the local Communist Party rather than the foreign ministry which deals with the PLO.

The PLO's diplomatic achievement cannot, of course, be explained only by its effectiveness in putting its message across. The shift in world public opinion towards the Palestinians in the last decade has had a number of causes, not least the policies of successive Israeli governments. Nevertheless some credit must go to the PLO and to particular representatives who have done much to encourage this shift in the countries where they have been posted.

In many countries of the world — the Islamic countries, the other countries of Africa and the communist bloc — the PLO representative does not have a difficult task. In these countries the Palestinian case is accepted by the governments and in general the position of the PLO is supported — although, as we have seen, with reservations in Eastern Europe. At the sixth Non-Aligned summit in Havana in September 1979 there was no problem in obtaining a forthright condemnation of the Camp David agreements and the Egyptian–Israeli peace treaty,[50] but the same conference also showed the limits of PLO and Arab influence in the rest of the Third World. In March 1979 the Arab League had decided to suspend Egypt from membership and to work towards its suspension from other Third World regional organizations.[51] Egypt was suspended from the Islamic Conference; the matter could not be formally discussed at all in the Organization of African Unity; and at the Havana Non-Aligned summit a long debate ended in deadlock with a decision postponed until the next conference.[52] Nevertheless, it is in the countries of the West, where public opinion is important and is not yet solidly behind the Palestinian cause, that the PLO feel they have to concentrate their main efforts. They begin with a number of disadvantages, since in Western Europe they do not have diplomatic status and they have to contend with a pro-Israel lobby which has had the ear of the public for many years. However, they do have the support of the Arab diplomatic corps.

Virtually all the PLO diplomats are members of Fatah and are usually protégés of either Yasser Arafat or Farouk Qaddoumi. Their work is similar to that of ambassadors although until recently in Western Europe they have enjoyed no official contacts with their host governments. Their job is to convince public opinion of the justice of the Palestinian cause and they set about this by writing letters to the press, addressing public meetings and making contacts with journalists and politicians. The sensitive nature of this work has meant that the PLO's image in any country can be heavily affected by the behaviour of one man. PLO representatives who have been notably successful in the political and intellectual circles of their host countries have been Said Hammami (Britain), Ezzedine Khallak (France), Wael Zuaiter (Italy) and Mahmoud Hamchari (France). All four were assassinated at their posts, the last two, it is generally believed, by Israeli intelligence.

Any evaluation of the PLO's success as a pressure group must take into consideration the peculiar nature of its 'success'. Clearly it has been immensely successful in convincing the world that the Palestinians have a just case. It has acquired status, prestige and support that no other liberation movement has been able to achieve.[53] More governments recognize the PLO than they do Israel, which in the international community now competes with Chile and South Africa as the world's most unpopular nation.

And yet the PLO has been conspicuously unsuccessful as a liberation movement: it has not been able to liberate a single inch of Palestine. Indeed, it has directed more of its energies into inter-Arab struggles than it has to the war against Israel. The PLO had to fight three armies between 1970 and 1976 and all three of them were Arab (Jordanian, Lebanese and Syrian). In Jordan it was dragged into a conflict which neither Arafat nor King Hussein wanted but which the PFLP and its offshoots, as well as the Jordanian secret service, did their best to provoke. It tried to avoid repeating the experience in Lebanon five years later, though once again the Rejection Front showed no hesitation in enthusiastically taking part. Fatah itself remained on the sidelines for nearly a year until the blockades of the refugee camps near Beirut by Lebanese Maronite forces brought them into the war. The following year the PLO (excluding Saiqa and other pro-Syrian groups) found itself opposing the Syrian army as the Damascus regime sent troops into Lebanon to prevent a victory for the Leftist-Lebanese and Palestinian alliance. Although these Arab civil wars were by no means entirely the fault of the Palestinians, they are a measure of the PLO's failure to concentrate on achieving its stated aims.

Ultimately, as many within the PLO do recognize, the success of the organization depends on its ability to convince public opinion in Europe and, more importantly, the United States. Some Palestinians admit that they should have worked on this from the beginning. Palestine could never have become like Vietnam or Algeria because the United States is prepared to risk fighting a world war to ensure Israel's survival. For the Palestinians to achieve even their limited aim of a 'mini-state', they need the United States' agreement. By their adoption of terrorist methods in the late sixties, however, they brought upon themselves a long period of American hostility. There are signs that this period may soon come to an end but the PLO still has a lengthy struggle ahead to persuade the USA that the establishment of a Palestinian state alongside Israel is the most just and reasonable solution to the Arab–Israeli conflict.

References

1 Quoted in Sabri Jiryis, 'The Nature of the Palestine Liberation Movement', a paper delivered at a seminar organized by the Committee on the Exercise of the Inalienable Rights of the Palestinian People in Vienna, August 1980. UAR, Ministry of National Guidance, *Documents and Papers on the Palestine Question* (Cairo, 1969), Vol. II, p. 1373.

2 Initially few Palestinian revolutionaries or activists joined the PLO. On 24 May 1964, the Political Bureau of United Action of the Revolutionary Palestinian Forces (which included Fatah), 'expressed doubt that an official entity would succeed in isolation from the revolutionary organisations.' Quote from Hamid, R., 'What is the PLO?', *Journal of Palestine Studies*, Vol. IV, No. 4, Summer 1975, pp. 94–5. Habash's Arab Nationalist Movement was more firmly opposed to the new organization, *Al-Hurriya*, 15 June 1964. For previous attempts at 'organizing' the Palestinians, all of which fell through, see Jureidini, Paul A. and Hazen, William E., *The Palestinian Movement in Politics* (Lexington, D. C. Heath and Co., 1976), pp. 9–11.

3 A biographer of President Nasser wrote, 'it soon became clear that [the establishment of the PLO] was intended, at least by Nasser, as a brake to precipitate action against Israel rather than as an encouragement of it . . . Nasser saw the PLO as a means of canalising Palestinian national emotions and restraining any rash adventures into guer-rilla warfare or more large-scale military operations against Israel.' Stephens, R., *Nasser. A Political Biography* (Harmondsworth, UK, Penguin Books, 1973), pp. 450–1.

4 Shuqairi had been appointed representative for Palestine at the Arab League by its Council in September 1963.

5 *Al Ahram*, 18 January 1964.

6 Gomaa, A. M., *The Foundation of the League of Arab States. Wartime Diplomacy and Inter-Arab Politics 1941 to 1945* (London and New York, Longman Group, 1977), p. 301.

7 See Kassim, Anis F., 'The Palestine Liberation Organization's Claim to Status: A Juridical Analysis under International Law', in the *Denver Journal of International Law and Policy*, Vo. 9, No. I (Winter 1980), p. 18.

8 It was recognized in the early days that the Egyptian government exercised effective control over the PLO, since its activities, training and organization all took place in Egypt. The Beirut paper, *Al Nahar*, on 31 October 1967 referred to the PLO as 'the Palestinian branch of Nasserism'.

9 See Hirst, D., *The Gun and the Olive Branch. The Roots of Violence in the Middle East* (London, Faber and Faber, 1977), pp. 277–81.

10 *The Times*, London, 22 and 25 March 1968.

11 *The Times*, London, 16 April 1968.

12 The agreement was reached in Beirut and gave the guerrillas half the seats on the National Council. It was reported in *Al-Hurriya* on 8 April 1968. See Hamid, op. cit.

13 The figures on the composition of the Palestine National Council came from information given to the author by Mr Khaled Fahoum, Chairman of the PNC.

14 Ibid. Even if allowance is made for the fact that these figures come from a commited source, it is clear that Fatah has a large majority in these groups.

15 Kassim, op. cit. on p. 19, says that the 'PLO has been recognised by over one hundred nation states. It has opened offices similar or equivalent to governmental diplomatic missions in over sixty states.' In November 1979 the British Foreign Office had a list of seventy-six PLO offices in a Background Brief, but in some cases, Kampuchea for example, it is not clear that an office was operating.

16 Kassim, op. cit., p. 25.

17 As leader of the Arab Nationalist Movement in the 1950s, Habash was a supporter of President Nasser. Habash opposed guerrilla warfare until 1966, when he formed a group to counter-act Fatah. His politics changed radically after the 1967 war. See Hirst, op. cit., p. 280.

18 Quoted in Quandt, William B., Jabber, Fuad, Mosely Lesch, Ann, *The Politics of Palestinian Nationalism* (London, University of California Press, 1973), p. 108.

19 Ibid., p. 104.

20 By accepting UN Security Council Resolution 242, these three countries accepted Israel's right to exist within its pre-1967 borders.

21 See Sharabi, Hisham, 'The Development of PLO Peace Policy', *Middle East International*, London, No. 133, September 1980, p. 7.

22 *New York Times*, 1 May 1978.

23 Communiqué of the Baghdad summit conference, 2–5 November 1978, United Nations document A/33/400 of 29 November 1978.

24 Said Hammami was killed in London in January 1978 and Ezzedine Khallak in Paris in August 1978.

25 Quoted in Hirst, op. cit., p. 195.

26 King Hussein announced the plan in Amman on 15 March 1972 and it was rejected by Iraq, the PLO, Syria, Egypt and Kuwait within a week. See Nielsen, J. S., *International Documents on Palestine 1972* (Beirut, Institute for Palestine Studies, and University of Kuwait, 1975), pp. 289–300.

27 Resolution of the Conference of Arab Heads of State, Rabat, 28 October 1974, in *The Middle East and North Africa, 1980–81* (London, Europa Publications, 1980, 27th Edn.), p. 73.

28 Kassim, op. cit., p. 22.

29 Ibid., p. 21.

30 United Nations General Assembly Resolution 3210(XXIX) adopted on 14 October 1974.

31 Kassim, op. cit., p. 20.

32 United Nations General Assembly Resolution 3237(XXIX) adopted on 22 November 1974, with 95 votes in favour, 17 against and 19 abstentions. It is noteworthy that the description of the PLO as the 'sole legitimate representative of the Palestinian people', referred to above and adopted by several regional intergovernmental organizations, was not used by the General Assembly. Resolution 3210(XXIX) specified 'the Palestinian Liberation Organisation, the representative of the Palestinian people' and the same formula continued to be used each year, the latest being in Resolution 35/169 A, adopted on 15 December 1980 with 98 votes in favour, 16 against and 32 abstentions.

33 Jankowitsch, O. and Sauvant, K. P. (eds.), *The Third World Without Superpowers: The Collected Documents of the Non-Aligned Countries* (Dobbs Ferry, N.Y., Oceana Publications, 1978), Vol. III, p. 1213 and paragraph 59 on p. 1221. The occasion was a Ministerial Conference in Lima, 25–30 August 1975.

34 See the 'Message from President Houari Boumedienne . . .' to the Third Ministerial Meeting of the Group of 77, Manila, 26 January–7 February 1976, in United Nations document TD/195/Add.1. While the Non-Aligned did follow up the precedent of admitting the PLO, by admitting two other liberation movements, SWAPO in October 1978 and the Patriotic Front of Zimbabwe in September 1979, it is notable that the PLO has remained the only non-state member of the Group of 77.

35 ECOSOC Resolution 2089(LXIII) of 22 July 1977, adopted by 27 votes in favour, 11 against and 12 abstentions, upon the recommendation of the Economic Commission

for Western Asia in Resolution 36(IV) of 26 April 1977. The quotes are from the latter resolution.

36 'Mao Tse-tung Urges Arabs Boycott West', *Arab World*, Beirut, 6 April 1965.

37 Harris, L. C., 'China's Relations with the PLO', *Journal of Palestine Studies*, Vol. 7, No. 1, Autumn 1977, p. 123.

38 Yodfat, A. Y. and Arnon-Ohanna, Y., *PLO: Strategy and Tactics* (London, Croom Helm, 1981), pp. 87–8.

39 Quoted in Hazan, B., 'Involvement by Proxy – Eastern Europe and the PLO, 1971– 1975', in Ben-Dor, G. (ed.), *The Palestinians and the Middle East Conflict* (Ramat Gan, Turtledove, 1978), p. 331.

40 Willetts, P., *The Non-Aligned Movement. The Origins of a Third World Alliance* (London, Frances Pinter, and New York, Nichols, 1978), p. 33.

41 Willetts, P., *The Non-Aligned in Havana. Documents of the Sixth Summit Conference and an Analysis of their Significance for the Global Political System* (London, Frances Pinter, and New York, St Martin's Press, 1981), p. 22.

42 United Nations document, A/9330, p. 27.

43 Willetts, *The Non-Aligned in Havana*, p. 22.

44 Ibid., p. 23.

45 *Middle East International*, London, 20 July 1979.

46 United Nations *General Assembly Official Records*, A/34/PV.8, 25 September 1979.

47 See the Joint Communiqué, published by the Foreign Ministers of Ireland and Bahrein, in *Middle East International*, London, 29 February 1980.

48 'EEC Statement on the Middle East. Issued in Venice, 13th June 1980', in *The Middle East and North Africa 1980–81* (London, Europa Publications, 1980, 27th Edn.), pp. 81 and 89.

49 See note 15. The text deliberately does not refer to the PLO having obtained *diplomatic recognition* by more than one hundred countries. While it is true that in many countries the PLO representatives are included in the official Diplomatic List, in others the situation is ambiguous. For example, Italy accords the PLO 'political recognition'. In Britain the PLO has been allowed to have an office in London and its representatives have been received by officials at the Foreign and Commonwealth Office; the British Ambassador has attended receptions given by the PLO in Beirut but has carefully avoided being photographed in company with Arafat; Britain for a long time said it recognized states and therefore the question of recognizing the PLO could not arise, but now the policy is not to announce recognition and to leave it to be inferred from current practice.

50 Paragraphs 107 and 108 of the Political Declaration of the sixth summit, given in Willetts, *The Non-Aligned in Havana*, pp. 100–1.

51 Resolutions of the Arab League Council, Baghdad, 31 March 1979, United Nations document A/34/160-S/13216, p. 3.

52 Willetts, *The Non-Aligned in Havana*, pp. 23–6.

53 Even SWAPO, which was formed long before the PLO and which always had broadly-based international support, has not achieved as high a status as the PLO. SWAPO was not made a permanent Observer at the UN General Assembly until two years after the PLO (Resolution 31/152 adopted on 20 December 1976, by a vote of 113 in favour, 0 against and 13 abstentions). It was by the same resolution given the right like the PLO to attend all conferences sponsored by the Assembly. SWAPO only became a full member of the Non-Aligned three years after the PLO (Willetts, *The Non-Aligned in Havana*, p. 19) and it is not a member of either the Group of 77 or the OAU.

4 Amnesty International and Human Rights

MARTIN ENNALS

Introduction

Amnesty International was publicly launched in Britain by a full-page feature in the Sunday newspaper, *The Observer*, on 26 May 1961. The article, written by Peter Benenson, called for a one year campaign for the release of 'The Forgotten Prisoners' — persons who were in prison because of their political or religious beliefs and who had been forgotten by the public, by the media and even by those who had imprisoned them. The Appeal for Amnesty, 1961, was reproduced in newspapers throughout Europe and appeared also in India and the USA.[1]

The launching of Amnesty International was, however, not the real beginning. Peter Benenson, a British barrister, had for many months previously been making contacts and seeking hard information on prisoners who fitted the categories he then described. The article featured six prisoners, included photographs and ended with an appeal for a campaign for their release and for the release of all others like them throughout the world, regardless of their political or religious ideologies, their geographical location or the political affiliations of the governments concerned. The article represented the first attempt at impartial research into political imprisonment and it sowed the seeds of the idea which has developed into the organization known and recognized today as the London-based human rights organization Amnesty International.

Associated with Peter Benenson were others from religious and legal fields, largely in the United Kingdom, but also including Sean MacBride, SC, from Ireland, who became the first chairman of the committee and remained so for thirteen years. In Britain the founders included Eric Baker, a well-known Quaker, the Hon. David Astor, editor of *The Observer*, and Gerald Gardiner, later to become Lord Chancellor. A small family legacy helped Benenson in the funding of the early days of the 'campaign' which became an organization and is fast becoming an institution.

The response to the *Observer* appeal for an international amnesty for forgotten prisoners was immediate and international. In July 1961 (six weeks later), the first international meeting was held in Luxembourg and an international committee was chosen to establish 'a permanent, international movement in defence of freedom of opinion and religion'.[2] At that first meeting were representatives from Belgium, Britain, France, West Germany, Ireland, Switzerland and the USA.

Work began in London to compile a systematic 'register' of prisoners of conscience and to develop groups of enthusiasts who were willing to write letters to governments about individual prisoners. The Amnesty membership was grouped into 'threes' — local groups who were occupied in working for three prisoners of conscience, one each from communist, non-communist and Third World countries. This balanced approach to the problem of imprisonment became and remains central to the concept of Amnesty International. The information was gathered at the London chambers occupied by Benenson in Mitre Court just off Fleet Street and then at Crane Court across the road, where there were several rooms available. Subsequently the headquarters moved to a long, lean building with the charming address of Turnagain Lane — now redeveloped — thence to Bloomsbury and currently in Covent Garden. In twenty years, Amnesty International has never moved more than one mile from its place of origin. As an organization, however, its development has been more striking.

There were critics and sceptics in those early days. The 'cold war' was abating and there were those who feared that Amnesty International, with its East, West and Third World approach would in fact become a tool in the prolongation of the cold war. Others believed that the whole idea of having an impact by writing to governments as John or Jane Citizen, the 'person on the Clapham omnibus', was naïve and would neither maintain its initial impetus nor have any effect on the prisoners. Both sets of sceptics have been proved wrong. Benenson and his supporters went on to prove their impartiality. Amnesty missions were sent in quick succession to Ghana, Czechoslovakia, Rhodesia and East Germany. Reports were published simultaneously in 1964/5 on prisoner conditions in Portugal, South Africa and Romania and in 1966 on prisons in Paraguay, Rhodesia and East Germany. In 1967 the British were criticized for practising torture in Aden. Amnesty International presented evidence to the Human Rights Commission at the Council of Europe about the torture practised in Greece under the Colonels. Amnesty International was already the centre of controversies which showed at least that governments are sensitive to accurate criticism.

Since those early inventive days, Amnesty International has really changed very little in its main purposes and its methods. The central theses remain: prisoners of conscience, freedom of expression and beliefs, impartiality of research and concern, financial independence and independence from governmental influences.

Structure

The *Observer* article was summarized in the following campaign points:

To work impartially for the release of those imprisoned for their opinions;
to seek for them a fair and public trial;
to enlarge the right of asylum and help political refugees to find work;
to urge effective international machinery to guarantee freedom of opinion.[3]

The Statute in operation for Amnesty Internation (after its amendment in 1980) cites as the purposes of the organization:

CONSIDERING that every person has the right freely to hold and to express his convictions and the obligation to extend a like freedom to others, the objects of AMNESTY INTERNATIONAL shall be to secure throughout the world the observance of the provisions of the Universal Declaration of Human Rights, by:

(a) irrespective of political considerations working towards the release of and providing assistance to persons who in violation of the aforesaid provisions are imprisoned, detained, restricted or otherwise subjected to physical coercion or restriction by reason of their political, religious or other conscientiously held beliefs or by reason of their ethnic origin, sex, colour or language, provided that they have not used or advocated violence (hereinafter referred to as 'Prisoners of Conscience');

(b) opposing by all appropriate means the detention of any Prisoners of Conscience or any political prisoners without trial within a reasonable time or any trial procedures relating to such prisoners that do not conform to recognized norms to ensure a fair trial;

(c) opposing by all appropriate means the imposition and infliction of death penalties and torture or other cruel, inhuman or degrading treatment or punishment of prisoners or other detained or restricted persons whether or not they have used or advocated violence.[4]

The objectives have been refined and the methods have been developed. The organization, however, remains rooted in its membership for the overall control of its activities and its finance.

The core of Amnesty International is the 'group'. This is a collection of Amnesty International members who undertake to work for the release of prisoners of conscience. The group may be of any size and may be composed of neighbours, friends, work colleagures or any other group of persons who are willing not only to endorse and apply the Amnesty International principles but are also committed to working systematically for the objectives of the movement despite often prolonged periods of absolute frustration. Letters receive no response, prisoners are not released and remain out of touch. There may be few indications that the efforts are worthwhile. On the other hand, money is still needed for research and other central activities and has to be raised by the membership in addition to letter writing, campaigning and organizing. Despite, or perhaps because of, this structure, membership has grown so that the movement in 1980 had over 200,000 members, organized in 2,427 groups with national sections in thirty-nine countries and individual members in another ninety-five countries throughout the world.[5] The international headquarters budget was £1,842,000 and the international secretariat in London numbers 150 paid staff.[6]

The Statute of Amnesty International provides for effective membership control exercised through *National Sections*, each of which sends representatives to an annual *International Council Meeting* where an *International Executive Committee* is elected. The Committee, consisting of the Treasurer, a secretariat representative and seven elected individuals, is responsible for the policy of the organization in between meetings of the Council which is the supreme governing body. The Committee also directs the work of the *International Secretariat* and appoints the Secretary General who is responsible to the Committee for the day-to-day affairs of the Secretariat and the implementation of the Council decisions. The finances of the organization are contributed by the National Sections on the basis of assessments agreed at the Council where the treasurers of each section meet with the directly elected international treasurer to agree a budget and the distribution of income and expenditure. Final approval, however, remains with the full Council, not the treasurers.

Each National Section is autonomous in that it has its own statute and structure which are, however, subject to initial approval by the International Executive Committee. The Committee may also recommend withdrawal of membership from any National Section or can refuse to recognize a National Section if its statutes do not conform to the international requirements. This right to withdraw recognition or to suspend a National Section or individual member has never been exercised but has been discussed on more than one occasion and emphasizes the strongly centralized nature of the organization as a whole. While it is the National Sections which provide the funds, recruit and organize the active members working for prisoners and against torture and the death penalty, translate and sell international reports and publications, and elect the International Executive Committee, Amnesty International as a whole applies to all its membership a very strict discipline in terms of its common actions, common voice and the independence of its finances.

This internal discipline takes a variety of forms but is expressed in a series of rules and guidelines prepared by the Committee and the Secretariat and approved by the Council and therefore the National Sections. One of the strictest of these rules is that no member, group, or National Section, member of the Committee, or member of the Secretariat is directly or indirectly responsible for Amnesty International's work on prisoners in his/her/its own country. It is the International Secretariat and the International Executive Committee which have a central responsibility for the adoption of individual prisoners, the publication of Amnesty International reports, the sending of AI missions or the issuing of AI press statements. On all policy matters, therefore, the movement has one voice. National Sections are not responsible for, nor expected to provide information about, human rights conditions, or repression, or imprisonment in their own country. This is a necessary precaution both for the movement as a whole and for the membership. In countries where AI may make criticisms, AI supporters could otherwise be held responsible for the passing of information. This could, in turn, result in charges being brought or hostages being taken by the government of the country concerned.

The National Sections, therefore, are not expected to comment on Amnesty International pronouncements about their own countries. Nor are their members expected to take action with regard to violations of human rights in their own countries. This is one aspect of Amnesty's activities which may take non-members and many new members a long time to understand. Some tend to support AI in the first place because they have been impressed by reports and actions undertaken concerning their own countries and therefore identify AI with a particular point of view. For this reason AI is cautious in its contacts and association with other pressure groups such as exiles, solidarity committees or refugees. The international statute is clear both in its purposes and in the limitations which are imposed on the membership. AI is above all therefore an international movement with national foundations, but with international policies based on restricted objectives universally applied. The national and international structure provides for the implementation and observance of these limitations and restrictions.

Membership

In a movement so strictly controlled by its participating membership it is surprising that there are few generalizations to be made about the type of person who joins and devotes spare time and money to the organization. From the beginning, Amnesty appealed to a widely varying age group. Its first volunteers came from the young who saw a new possibility of achieving something practical, using their own initiative and not just raising money and passing resolutions. But equally those with experience of the 1930s were represented, those who had lived through Nazism, knew about concentration camps and human rights violations and knew also the importance of information and international support. Perhaps one thing that all groups of members had in common from the very beginning was a certain scepticism about ideologies and 'isms'. AI recognizes that there are victims in all societies and that the individual needs protection. In the 1980s AI membership is still in the 20 to 40 age range with many who are older, but there is also an active school and student membership which is encouraging for the future.

The annual meetings of the larger sections such as those in France or West Germany stimulate the visitor with their wide age and class range, the vigour of their arguments and their amazing good humour which bursts out in laughter regardless of the apparent tension of the argument or the implicit tragedy which clouds all AI debates. The British section in 1979 undertook a survey of its membership with the help of the National Opinion Polls Company. The results were summarized in the AI newsletter and showed that the British section has also taken the lead in seeking to extend its membership systematically into the trade union movement. It has recruited the corporate membership of forty-six trade unions affiliated through their national headquarters or through local trades councils or union branches. Other National Sections will probably be equally active in this direction in the future. The average active group member of AI is educated and literate and finds in Amnesty an outlet for initiative and individual action frequently discouraged in the more conventional political movements.

Another generalization which is possible about the AI members is that they are not wealthy. There are exceptions, but the strength of the movement is the grass roots nature of the activities which it encourages and requires. The member is expected not just to contribute funds but also to work consistently both individually and in a group. The membership is linked not only by its group activities but also by the monthly newsletters issued by the London headquarters and adapted or translated by the National Sections. Each member is urged to take part in supporting the prisoners whose cases are selected each month for special attention. This is an intensely personal action which is called for. It cannot be delegated to anyone else. In this context the wealthy tend not to find the time. And so the AI membership stays active and on the whole not so well off.

Finance

Finance is always a major problem for any international organization. Ironically, by imposing strict and mandatory limitations on the sources of its funds, Amnesty has managed to develop a strong financial base where other comparable bodies continue to experience considerable difficulties. The sources of income remain the membership and their collective efforts. From a budget of £50,000 in 1970, AI was operating on a budget of £1,840,000 in 1980. Inevitably, the larger and richer Sections pay the majority of the contributions, but the assessments are made on the basis of membership figures, the number of groups recognized within the section and the overall income declared to the international treasurer. Constant efforts are made to find a fair system of assessment. The long-term answer to this problem is in a new world economic order and is unlikely to be found within Amnesty International. The North–South differences exist in any international organization, at least in financial terms.

The restrictions placed on income for AI are very important as they are designed to protect the independence of the movement from anyone who would hope by financial means to acquire a favoured influence in the policies of the movement. It is important to protect Amnesty from such influences both in reality and in the imaginations of the maliciously inclined. Guidelines have been established and are regularly reviewed to ensure that no section or group becomes in any way dependent on any single source of funds. The international treasurer may not accept government donations to the budget of the movement, although government funds may be received for relief purposes which fall within the AI mandate.

On the other hand, there are procedures whereby at the National Section level additional help, which may have financial consequences, has been accepted. For example, conscientious objectors to military service who opt for work with a peace or human rights organization have been employed. In Belgium several short-term posts have been recruited through a government scheme to combat unemployment. The key to these schemes, however, is that the recruitment must be made by the National Section itself and no one can be imposed on the national secretariat. Equally, no strings may be attached to the services undertaken by the employee, either by selecting the field of work or by excluding an area of activity. Such schemes, however, strengthen the conviction within the movement as a whole that research on imprisonment must remain the central responsibility of the International Executive Committee and the International Secretariat.

In some countries also there are schemes whereby the National Section of AI, along with other national organizations, may benefit from special tax-free concessions. In the USA the Amnesty section is 'tax-exempt'. This is not possible in the UK because of the nature of the laws on charitable status and the nature of AI activities and programme. In West Germany, in addition to a tax-exempt status, the section also benefits from being accepted as a recipient of fines for motoring offences where the judge orders that fines should be paid to an appropriate recognized institution. In Sweden there are local arrangements for lotteries which can benefit appropriate and approved organizations, including Amnesty groups. These are, however, marginal benefits which are not singled out to assist AI but are applicable to any organization which falls within certain defined categories of activity. Amnesty does not rely on or indeed accept any direct offers from governments for financial support.

The reasons for such stringency are that AI must be, and be seen to be, independent of all sources of pressure. There has been a long and continuing argument as to whether AI should accept — at any level within the organization —funds from well-known public foundations such as Ford, Rockefeller, Volkswagen, etc. This is not because there is fear that such public foundations would seek to influence Amnesty, but because in other parts of the world their reputation as being government-linked would be prejudicial to the work of AI for

prisoners of conscience and would influence the attitude to AI of either governments or their victims. There was some doubt as to whether AI should have
accepted the Nobel Peace Prize in 1977 for this specific reason. To counter
this difficulty, AI, in accepting the Nobel prize, made clear that the money
would be put into a special account to assist new and growing AI sections to
establish themselves. This approach remains current policy.

It is perhaps appropriate, when dealing with finances, to stress that the
National Sections and the membership are themselves very jealous of the democratic control they have over the organization. The issue of outside funding
is not merely one of reputation and appearances. It is a grass-roots issue of
who runs Amnesty International. The answer is, and will remain, that it is the
members who finance and control the movement at all levels.

Decision-Making

The democratic control of the organization is central to the structure; it is
reflected in the financing, it is equally important for the decision-making processes. However, decision-making is a more difficult area in which to stimulate
or maintain effective consultation, let alone control.

The decisions which have to be made within Amnesty International relate
to priorities of research and action, long-term strategies, statute amendments,
and day-to-day programmes. The priorities are to some extent decided not by
any internal mechanism but rather by international and national events. A
regular attempt is made to prepare an action calendar for a six-month period
based on anticipated research progress, the expected outcome of a mission to
a certain country or the progress of a publication. This information is sent
to the National Sections as an indication — no more — of what they may expect
from the International Secretariat during that period. They may prepare their
translators, their groups and their members. But the decisions have to be made
internally at the headquarters, on the basis of information available, and are
therefore largely a secretariat area of responsibility under the supervision of
and in consultation with the elected International Executive Committee.

On the other hand, priorities may be established by the recruitment policy
for researchers in the Secretariat, or for campaign organizers, or persons specialized
in particular types of activity. The report on *Political Imprisonment in the
Peoples Republic of China*, published in 1978, was the direct result of a decision taken by the Committee in 1976 to devote most of the time of a specially recruited researcher to develop work on China with a view to publishing
a report.[7] Previously it had been the view at headquarters that China was not
suitable for individual casework as there were risks that appeals from outside
China would do harm to the prisoners with the authorities. Furthermore, the
political system was so different from other countries and the area so vast
that it would be futile to try and absorb the work on China (along with all

the other countries in Asia) into the work load of two researchers. That decision was, however, unprecedented and has not yet been repeated.

During the early days of AI's existence the research department was so small that concentration of effort was not possible. The decision-making process did not really exist except in the most general terms of deciding to increase the size of the International Secretariat staff, particularly in the research department. Subsequently, however, other decisions were taken. In 1972 for example the Council decided that there should be a special campaign against torture and that a report should be prepared and published. This decision was taken against the advice of the international treasurer of the day but reflected the strong feeling of National Section representatives that more work should be done against torture and in the area of campaigning. The effect of this decision was the publication of the first major report on a world-wide theme.[8] This occupied the research department for several months and, without extra staff to offset the time spent, inevitably affected other work such as the preparation of the case sheets on individual prisoners, which form the basis of the daily activity both of the groups and the Secretariat itself. Another outcome of that decision was the establishment of a new structure within the Secretariat to deal with the issue of torture. This unit has now been extended to handle all campaigns and is involved in work on the death penalty as well as torture. A report on the death penalty was the second overall report based on a particular theme.[9] This also resulted from a decision taken by the Council.

Long-term decisions of this thematic nature can be taken by the Council, with its representatives from all the National Sections. But it is more difficult to involve the membership in strategy regarding individual countries. Attempts are made to plan strategy by calling regional meetings but the tendency is for the influence in such consultative processes to rest with the International Secretariat because it is they who have the professional experience. Tension may also be created between the centre and some of those in the National Sections who are particularly concerned with certain countries and who try to persuade the Committee and the Secretariat at headquarters that priorities should be changed. There is a real risk that the derogation of decision-making away from the centre would lead to pressure groups being established within the membership. The danger then is that the fashionable themes would replace the 'unknown prisoner' concept.

Amendments to the statute which relate to the very purposes and scope of the organization must be the sole responsibility of the membership expressed in and by the Council. The International Secretariat and the Committee may take part in these debates as part of the movement but the decision itself rests with the membership. On the other hand the major day-to-day decisions must remain with the Secretariat which decides which prisoners of conscience are to be adopted and which cases require further investigation because no decision can be taken immediately on whether they fall within the terms of the statute.

It is the Secretary General who decides whether and when to issue press statements from the centre. Approaches to governments may be the subject of discussion within the Committee and are decided by the Secretary General and it is almost impossible to involve the membership other than through their elected members on the Committee.

There is one further aspect which always has to be taken into account. Amnesty is responsible for the protection of the sources of its information. Amnesty is also responsible for discussions with governments about the release of prisoners and other sensitive topics. It is not possible to inform or consult widely where confidential information and sources are involved. Therefore, apart from the major concerns with long-range direction and thematic action, statutory aims and objectives, fund raising and expenditure levels, decisions have to be left to the day-to-day discretion of the central Committee and Secretariat.

It is possible to extend the process of decision-making, however, by involving more persons and members in the consultations which precede decision. This is an area which can lead to considerable expense and requires substantial continuity of personnel and expertise. It is an area of experimentation within Amnesty International.

Methods of Work

Every action taken by AI since its inception is based on information: about prisoners, their existence, their conditions, their trial, their families; about governments, their members, their policies, their friends, their enemies, their weaknesses and strengths; about the membership of AI and the people most likely to be effective users of that information. It is natural therefore that the majority of the resources of the organization are devoted to the collection and presentation of information. The entire structure of the movement is designed to collect, distribute and use information.

Although widely referred to as a 'human rights' organization, Amnesty International benefits from the very narrow mandate outlined in the first article of its statute. The information gathering is therefore focused on a relatively narrow field and almost always relates to prisoners who fall within the confines of the mandate. If there is any single factor which has contributed to Amnesty International's growth during its short existence, it is the blinkers with which it approaches the controversial human rights track. Amnesty has not become involved in debates about what human rights should be supported in society at large.

The research department is the largest unit in the International Secretariat. It is sub-divided into the obvious geographical regions and its task is to isolate and understand information about individual prisoners of conscience, to identify groups of prisoners and the core reason for their detention, to explain this information to its potential users and to suggest ways in which the information can be used for the purposes of the organization. The research department, however, does not and cannot work alone.

The sources of information are many and varied. Newspapers and other public sources, if selectively and carefully monitored, provide much information. In addition to volunteers who send newspaper cuttings on matters of interest to AI from all over the world, the Secretariat itself has a regular intake of 600 dailies, periodicals and journals from eighty-five countries. Over a prolonged period contacts are established with, and confidence develops in, individuals who are able and willing to transmit information much of which is obviously sensitive, controversial and even dangerous for the individual concerned. Such persons include: doctors with contacts with prisons, hospitals, torture victims; priests with knowledge of the victims of arrests, disappearances or the families of such victims; politicians with an axe to grind or journalists whose information is too much or too little for their newspapers to handle; released prisoners who bring information about those whom they have left behind; organizations, refugees, professional associations and trade unions; and sometimes even embassies and official channels. Each piece of information has one feature in common with every other piece of information: alone, it cannot be believed. Everything has to be checked and counter-checked before it can be safely used by AI. Those who act as sources of information may have a variety of motives in providing it, apart from the simple one of wanting to help prisoners or support Amnesty International. Information and propaganda may look remarkably similar in certain formats. Testing information is an acquired skill, but it must be acquired if AI is to be an effective instrument. One certainty within AI at all levels is that the organization cannot afford to make mistakes in its factual reports and must be willing to acknowledge any mistakes that may be made. The strength, if any, of AI lies in the credibility of the organization and the information which it collects and uses. Where governments have changed and more information has become available which enables previous AI reports to be checked, it is a fact that AI has always been shown to have underestimated the situation whether it related to torture or imprisonment. This is a sad fact. It should not be used to encourage AI to be less careful. It should, however, affect governments who are the subject of AI criticism.

AI is essentially a case-work organization and information is prepared with this in mind. However, the individual adoption of prisoners of conscience — Peter Benenson's original idea — which is still central to the AI philosophy, is more difficult to adapt to a mass movement spreading across the world. The preparation of individual case histories is very labour-intensive and in some instances it may even be harmful to the prisoner to single him out from his associates for special international attention. On some occasions prisoners have objected to being singled out from other prisoners because in AI terms they were 'non-violent' or because more was known about them than their colleagues about whom AI has little information. Such factors complicate the problem of finding suitable individual cases of prisoners of conscience for adoption by any one or two of the 2,400 AI adoption groups in thirty-nine countries. The technique of adoption is based on AI local groups working for the three named prisoners of conscience allocated to them from the headquarters on the basis of political and geographical balance. The lack of information about individuals should not, however, prevent the use of available information about groups of prisoners or about other aspects of the restricted AI mandate such as torture cases, threatened death penalties, disappearances, or prolonged detention without trial. The group adoption method is therefore central but not exclusive. As a method it is one which has been followed by other organizations.

The purpose of AI is to influence governments to release prisoners and it is therefore logical that AI should have examined the best ways of using information in arenas which governments respect or at least acknowledge. Intergovernmental organizations to which governments belong include the United Nations and the specialized agencies such as UNESCO, FAO and the ILO. There are also regional governmental bodies such as the OAS, the Council of Europe, both of which have incorporated machinery for protection of human rights and the OAU which is considering an advanced draft of a similar instrument for human rights protection. In the UN itself the Commission on Human Rights receives information from bona fide organizations (such as Amnesty International, the World Council of Churches or the International Commission of Jurists) which are recognized as having special experience. AI submits carefully prepared reports of situations which seem to reveal 'a consistent pattern of gross violations of human rights'. Such reports are studied by the subcommission of the Human Rights Commission and additional information may be requested from organizations or governments. The procedure is confidential and slow. But it represents considerable progress toward the international exercise of responsibility for the protection of human rights, whether or not the governments concerned have ratified the International Covenant on Civil and Political Rights. It is also important to realize that the very existence of such a procedure in the UN and other agencies and organizations provides another justification (if one is needed) for international non-governmental organization involvement in the field of human rights protection. Not only are the NGOs fulfilling a function which has been accorded to them by the intergovernmental organizations and their member states, but also NGOs have a better opportunity of submitting information without it becoming identified as a political gesture of hostility. NGO information is therefore available for use by governments. It is important for NGOs such as AI to find ways and means of making the information available to the governments who can best use it in the interests of victims. This method may be through the established machinery within intergovernmental agencies or it may be by direct approaches to govern-ments themselves.

For example, in the case of Indonesia the government held tens of thousands of political prisoners without trial for more than a dozen years. Remarkably little public attention was paid to this fact which was not in principle denied by the Indonesian government. Each year there were meetings of a group known as the IGGI (Intergovernmental Group on Indonesia), whose task it was to examine the aid programmes for Indonesia and to co-ordinate international assistance. Human rights was never an item on the agenda but AI and presum-ably other bodies made a point of briefing aid donors to ensure that human rights question would be raised informally at a time when Indonesia was sensi-tive to governments' opinions. There was often very little feedback from those briefings, but informally at least it was known that many of those approached did use the information and did obtain a variety of positive responses despite the official negative interest. The vast majority of these prisoners had been released by the beginning of 1980.

In a similar way information can be and is supplied to diplomats, businessmen, trade unionists, politicians, sportsmen and other delegations on a bilateral or multilateral basis either through the International Secretariat or through the National Sections who may use just the information produced by headquarters or check and update it themselves for the occasion.

One question which is frequently put concerns relations with so-called 'friendly' governments where there are few violations of human rights. For Amnesty International the answer must be simple. There are no special rela-tions with governments, no 'insiders' who may be trusted more than others, no friends with whom the organization can afford to be identified. Such special relations would carry the same risks as the receipt of funds from government sources and would risk creating the image that AI was the offshoot of a particu-lar government policy or programme.

Apart from information used by AI groups and national sections and by intergovernmental or national governments, there are also other channels into which AI information may usefully be fed. There are many specialist organiza-tions such as medical or professional bodies, trade unions both national and international, and other non-governmental organizations of women, youth, churches, or other interest groups such as political parties, all of whom may be prepared to work in the direction of AI's mandate in certain circumstances. It is therefore appropriate that AI supplies information to such organizations wherever it is felt that it would be productive to do so for the prisoners or the programme. International NGOs work closely together wherever their interests are common. Thus there have been joint resolutions and declarations submitted to intergovernmental agencies on the abolition of torture and others on the death penalty. Doctors have intervened in cases relating to mental hospitals and their abuse and to torture, where medical personnel are almost always involved. Trade unions have taken up cases of their colleagues in prison, or otherwise victimized, about whom AI has supplied information. Special groups of doctors, lawyers or mathematicians and others, have been set up to gain support for prisoners from a wider group of persons than would normally be involved. This is an important and effective area where AI information at both the national and international level can be used by those who are not AI members or supporters but who are willing to work on a specific issue.

Amnesty International has always made clear that most of its information is not copyright-protected and no credits are needed if the information is best and most effectively used without reference to AI as the source.

Apart from AI groups working for individual prisoners and information passed along into other governmental channels, there are other ways of using AI information on behalf of the prisoners. More and more AI has become a campaigning organization first on particular themes such as torture (and currently the death penalty), but also on individual countries such as Uruguay, the USSR, South Africa, Guinea, Indonesia, etc. Such campaigns are run by groups with prisoners adopted in the country, or by National Sections as national campaign programmes with material prepared for the press, the public and other normal campaign channels. This direct appeal for publicity is usually linked either to a national event, an election, change of government, national holiday or international event such as the World Cup football matches or the Olympics; or it may be linked to an AI activity such as the publication of a mission report or a special book such as that on *Prisoners of Conscience in the USSR*.[10] Special efforts are also made to provide material for Human Rights Day (10 December) or Prisoner of Conscience Week (15 October approximately). Such campaigns are hard to evaluate but certainly help to maintain the momentum of National Section activity and to brief membership, press and the public both about Amnesty International and about the problems in a particular country. These campaigns are prepared and planned in advance with consultation between headquarters and the National Sections.

Many other methods are used by the groups and Sections who have considerable scope for initiative as they work for prisoners or on particular campaigns. AI has, however, been systematic in refusing to extend its methods of work into areas which might lead to political confusion, for example advocating boycotts or economic sanctions. This is not because AI opposes sanctions as such but because it feels that it is not the role of the organization to be involved in activity which would lead to allegations of bias against countries selected for sanctions and might have little impact other than providing publicity.

International Standards

A call for effective international machinery to guarantee freedom of opinion was part of the initial 1961 appeal by Peter Benenson. It remains an important aspect of the programme. AI is represented by a permanent staff member at the UN in New York and by volunteers who devote considerable time to the task in Geneva, Paris, Strasbourg and Brussels where other international organizations have their headquarters. AI observers attend relevant UN meetings, congresses and conferences and specialists attend expert meetings where the setting of standards is discussed and instruments and guidelines are being drafted. The preamble to the United Nations Charter 'reaffirms faith in fundamental human rights, in the dignity and work of the human person, in the equal rights of men and women and of nations large and small.' The Universal Declaration of Human Rights, which provides the basis for the principles which AI supports, was adopted in 1948 and spells out the nature of the rights of man in both civil, political and economic, social and cultural affairs.[11] In 1966 the two covenants on human rights were approved by the General Assembly, but it was only in 1976 that they were both ratified by sufficient countries for them to come into force.[12] While therefore it may be said that in 1948, when the declaration was adopted, the UN was an organization of predominantly 'Western' countries, the Universal Declaration itself has since been reaffirmed in principle by the General Assembly: in 1968 it celebrated Human Rights Year and on successive occasions Human Rights Awards have been given, seminars organized, and resolutions approved by all member states. By September 1981, the Covenant on Economic, Social and Cultural Rights had been ratified by sixty-nine states, the Covenant on Civil and Political Rights had been ratified by sixty-seven and the Optional Protocol to the Civil and Political Covenant which provides for the right of individual petition to the elected Human Rights Committee had been ratified by twenty-six.[13] Amnesty International, therefore, in working for the establishment of new standards and for the implementation of existing standards, is acting in accordance with the United Nations itself and is exercising a function accorded to it by the UN when it granted the organization consultative status.

The UN Declaration against 'Torture and Other Cruel, Inhuman or Degrading Treatment or Punishment' was drafted on the initiative of the Dutch Government and presented and recast at the Fifth UN Congress on the Prevention of Crime and Treatment of Offenders held in Geneva in 1975. It was hammered out during the Congress and an Amnesty representative took part in the informal working group of government representatives.[14] The Committee on Crime Prevention and Control has drafted a 'body of principles for the protection of all persons under any form of detention or imprisonment.'[15]

The Amnesty International representative has participated in most of these meetings in recent years and has taken part in the discussions and in drafting the actual wording of the text. AI makes submissions to the UN Commission on Human Rights and to the ILO and the UNESCO Committees which consider complaints about violations of human rights. Similarly, AI makes submissions to the relevant organs of the Inter-American Commission on Human Rights

and to the European Commission where appropriate. It is through such participation in grievance machinery and in the drafting of new texts that AI makes
its most substantial contribution to the raising and maintenance of international
standards of human rights protection machinery.

In addition, the role of the membership, through the National Sections and
the groups, is to relate their letters and public statements to the apparent violations of these international standards whenever the case of a prisoner is taken
up or a case of torture is publicized or raised in any way with the government
concerned. Governments are more likely to be reminded of their responsibilities
and international commitments to such standards by AI than by any other
source. National Sections themselves may also play an important part in per-
suading their own governments to sign, ratify, publicize and apply the international standards for the protection and maintenance of human rights. The
Standard Minimum Rules for the Treatment of Prisoners were approved by
a UN Congress in Geneva in 1955, yet despite UN recommendations to governments and to the Secretary General to publicize the rules, they were totally
out of print fifteen years later when they again came up for consideration at
another meeting of the UN Congress. AI published and circulated the rules
at the Congress and to governments beforehand.

This educational function of AI is important but has yet to be defined or
refined in terms of priorities and programmes at the international or national
levels. There are those who believe that education about standards and rights
could be the first line of defence for individuals who may be unaware of the
existence of the rights, let alone the standards. Others argue that, in a period
where there are considerable constraints on the resources of AI, education
should be encouraged as a programme for others, that AI's role itself should
be to catalyse action in other organizations expert in education but less experienced in the defence of human rights. It is in this context therefore that
AI has collaborated extensively with other international NGOs recognized by
UNESCO, and AI members have been included in the various expert committees
established by UNESCO to plan the programme in the field of education for
human rights and peace.

AI, Strategy and Governments

Amnesty International is founded on the very simple precept that governments
respond to public opinion. It is for this reason that AI devotes its time and
effort to acquiring the information with which governments may be influenced
and to which they may be persuaded to respond. Such information, whether
it relates to individual prisoners or to the practice of torture, may be used in
direct communication with governments or for publicity by the media. It may
be channelled through other governments or through intergovernmental organizations. In seeking to influence governments by the use of factual information,

AI is taking part in the process of international relations which shapes all our lives. The interdependence of nations for trade and aid, arms and alliances, art and sport, law and asylum, natural disasters and man-made catastrophes, ensures that the participants in any of these relationships are affected by public opinion. In other words, all governments in the world are affected directly or indirectly by public opinion in their own and other countries. Amnesty International is one element in this process.

In planning its role in any situation AI always has one consideration above all others: what will be most beneficial to the interests of the prisoners involved. It may be that persuasion by friends is more effective than publicity by those thought to be hostile. It may also be that publicity on a massive scale is the only possible way of gaining attention and rights. Each case is different and each time there may be new factors to be taken into account.

The only power which an organization such as AI can hope to exercise is that of publicity or the threat of publicity. This is a very grave limitation but just as no one denies that even without 'divisions of troops' the Pope has an undoubted influence on international relations, so too do the many organizations which group people together with common interests or common ideals. Power is not only in the hands of the economic bases of society such as multinational corporations or governments. Public opinion can be influenced as effectively through common interest groups such as the trade unions, and the churches. Any specialist organization such as Amnesty International has a talent to contribute: accurate and embarrassing information. That talent is at the disposal of those who wish to use it. It is the task of AI to ensure that it is used effectively by governments and those who can influence governments. AI also uses the slow and systematic methods of persistence, reasonableness, courtesy, challenges at the international level, or publication. Governments, even the most repressive, like to be liked at home and abroad. It is a human reaction common to all. Exploitation of this desire to be liked is a part of the approach of organizations which try to confront governments with their own double standards, their cynical voting for principles and policies at the intergovernmental level which at home they ignore or destroy.

As such, AI is hostile to no government. AI criticizes the effect of government policies in terms of imprisonment and freedom of expression in speech and belief. Only in the case of South Africa did AI ever express the view that the system would have to be changed if human rights were to be respected. If the Greek Colonels had had no prisoners of conscience and no torture, AI would not have published reports on Greece at that time. Amnesty does not automatically attack military governments, or any other type of government for that matter.

Relations with governments inevitably vary according to the level of criticism and repression. During the period of fact finding, or talking to governments through missions, embassies or other channels, Amnesty International is often on official and apparently good terms with a government. After it is known that a report is to be published, efforts may be made by governments to postpone or prevent the date of publication by suggesting more talks or more visits. After a report has been published relations may appear to cool or even be broken off. But in recent years AI has on balance been received by governments either informally or formally. Its representatives are usually received or visas granted. There are exceptions regularly but it is not always the same governments who reject contact or who welcome talks. It would be hard to identify a pattern of relations with governments and if one could do so it would probably not be useful to make such a pattern public.

There are, however, certain lessons which can be drawn from past experience. It is never useful to make comparisons between governments. It is rarely effective to try and tackle two governments at the same time as if to balance one with the other. It is better to be absolutely sure of facts than to provide one weak link in the information chain which can be disproved by the government. It is always helpful to quote government commitments to international law and standards. It is also useful to indicate the extent of AI activities in other fields of interest to the government in question. Governments have little sense of humour when it comes to criticism. Governments may hit back at AI and its representatives and care should always be taken to anticipate the type of criticisms which may be made or stories which may be invented or developed. Care should always be taken not to claim credit for changes which may appear to result from AI action. Similarly AI should never feel responsible for the defects of new governments which replace governments of whom AI has been critical.

These lessons are generally applicable to organizations concerned with influencing governments from a position without any apparent power other than the truth of its information.

The Reality of Influence

Evaluation is problematic. The question invariably put to AI spokespersons is whether there are positive results which justify the work, the money, the publicity and the pressure. There can be no single answer; there can be no single reason for a prisoner's release or a government's fall. In order even to attempt to answer the question it is necessary to ask why was the prisoner detained? Who would feel threatened by his liberty? Why did the government practise restraint in the first place? Who put the government in power and who is keeping the government in power?

The conscientious objector in prison in Switzerland is hardly a threat to the Federal Government by his refusal to go into the army once a year for military training. Yet year after year persons who have neither practised nor advocated violence are put into prison in Switzerland because of their political or religious beliefs. The influence of AI or other bodies such as War Resisters International cannot at the moment be great in effecting the liberation of the Swiss CO. But AI members in Switzerland and AI itself will continue to work toward the realization of international standards in Switzerland whereby conscientious objection is recognized by law and men are not imprisoned because of it.

The Helsinki monitoring group in the USSR is treated as if it were a threat to the Soviet system. Charges are brought against the individual members, charges of anti-Soviet agitation and propaganda or perhaps of hooliganism. The information published in the West and pursued through a wide range of pressure points may not result in release but it is in itself a protection against worse things happening. It is certainly important for those who are the prisoners to know that they are not forgotten. This is true in almost all cases that AI takes up and is a theme which enters almost every conversation with ex-prisoners of conscience who have had their cases taken up by AI.

No government admits to acting under pressure or yielding to outside persuasion. Usually some prisoners remain after others are released. For AI to claim credit for the release of prisoners is therefore not only boastful but is probably only partially true. To make such claims is also counter-productive in terms of other prisoners of conscience who may have their release delayed if it is believed that it will be seen as a further sign of government weakness.

Prisoners are released for a variety of reasons including outside pressure. Internal confidence, internal politics, external relations, personal relationships, revolutions, elections, all contribute to a situation which sometimes results in surprise liberations. Amnesty International, however, helps by providing the information which is essential for any outside, or even on occasions inside, pressures to operate. It does appear that a person is more likely to be released if his/her plight and circumstances are known to the outside world.

Amnesty has sometimes been linked with the overthrow of a government or the downfall of a dictator. This could never be true. Governments exist for a variety of reasons explained daily by political scientists and writers. Governments are kept in power by other governments whether or not they have widespread popular support. The reasons may be economic or political but usually both. An AI report may be used as an excuse for questioning or even withdrawing such support. The AI report is, however, never the reason for the change of government. If AI reports changed governments, AI as it is today would cease to exist.

The publicity attracted by the AI statement on the assassination of children under the regime of Mr Bokassa in the Central African Empire did not lead to the fall of Bokassa.[16] The time was ripe for change and the AI report was one element in the change. It was the other African governments and the French government which ensured the change and Bokassa's downfall. If reports led to dictators being toppled, then the ICJ report to the UN Human Rights Commission on Uganda would have achieved the fall of Amin.[17] In fact Amin was removed by armed force from outside, with the connivance of other governments and world opinion. Equally, neither Amnesty nor the ICJ can be held responsible for the actions of governments which succeed those that have fallen.

It is not realistic, however, to avoid totally the issue of evaluation. The conclusion can only be personal opinion and impression not documented or provable fact. In my view therefore the Amnesty function of isolating information and using it to persuade governments to release prisoners, stop torture and respect international standards, is both worthwhile in general terms and is effective in specific cases. In the period since it was created, Amnesty International has contributed substantially to an international awareness that solidarity is not a slogan applied only to one's political friends. Solidarity exists and is needed in human rights without frontiers and without discrimination as in every other form of human disaster relief. Individuals are helped, families are supported, torture victims are relieved, executions are stopped. Not all prisoners nor all victims will benefit. Not all will be known or can be reached. Shortage of time, contacts, money and members are all constraints. Governments are still hesitant to intervene but are doing so more and more. Business and other transnational interests are slowly being persuaded that human rights means everyone and not just some, and that responsibility may have to be as transnational as profits.

Within this world framework AI is a small body. It has grown amazingly. Its resources can never match its ambitions. But in a small way Amnesty International may have done more than any other single group to make people aware that the human rights buck never stops anywhere and may have found the means of making a positive contribution to human rights and to peace.

References

1 Benenson, P., 'The Forgotten Prisoners', *The Observer*, London, 28 May 1961. An article appeared on the same day in *Le Monde*, Paris, followed by *Journal de Genève*, Geneva, 1 June 1961, *Die Welt*, Bonn, 2 June 1961, *New York Herald Tribune*, 11 June 1961, and hundreds of newspapers throughout the world in succeeding weeks.

2 Statement from the international meeting in Luxembourg, 22–3 July 1961, quoted in *Amnesty International 1961–1976. A chronology* (London, Amnesty International, 1976).

3 The original article in *The Observer* put these four points in a box headed 'Appeal for Amnesty, 1961. The Aims'.

4 *Amnesty International Report 1980* (London, Amnesty International Publications, 1980), contains the Statute as it stood in September 1979. The 1980 amendment will be incorporated in the 1981 report.

5 Ibid., p. 408.

6 Ibid., p. 372, 'Statements of Income and Expenditure for the Years Ended 30 April 1980 and 1979.'

7 *Political Imprisonment in the People's Republic of China* (London, Amnesty International, 1978).

8 *Amnesty International Report on Torture* (London, Amnesty International, first edn. December 1973 and second edn. January 1975).

9 *The Death Penalty* (London, Amnesty International, 1979).

10 *Prisoners of Conscience in the USSR: Their Treatment and Conditions* (London, Amnesty International, first edn. November 1975 and second edn. April 1980).

11 The Universal Declaration on Human Rights was adopted by the UN General Assembly on 10 December 1948 by a vote of 48 in favour, 0 against and 8 abstentions.

12 The International Covenant on Economic, Social and Cultural Rights was adopted by the UN General Assembly as part of Resolution 2200A(XXI) on 16 December 1966 by a vote of 105 in favour, 0 against and 0 abstentions and came into force on 3 January 1976, three months after its ratification by thirty-five states. The International Covenant on Civil and Political Rights was adopted as part of the same resolution by a vote of 106 to 0 with 0 abstentions and came into force on 23 March 1976, three months after its ratification by thirty-five states. The Optional Protocol to the International Covenant on Civil and Political Rights was also adopted as part of the same resolution by a vote of 66 in favour, 2 against and 38 abstentions and came into force on 23 March 1976, three months after its ratification by ten states. Resolution 2200A(XXI) as a whole was approved by a vote of 105 to 0 with no abstentions.

13 United Nations document A/36/455 of 25 September 1981.

14 The *Declaration on the Protection of All Persons from Being Subject to Torture and Other Cruel, Inhuman or Degrading Treatment or Punishment* was adopted by the UN General Assembly on 9 December 1975 as Resolution 3452(XXX) without a vote.

15 At the General Assembly 35th Session an 'open-ended working group' made progress with, but did not complete, a draft *Body of Principles for the Protection of All Persons under any Form of Detention or Imprisonment*, see United Nations document A/C. 3/35/14. By Resolution 35/177 adopted on 15 December 1980 without a vote the subject was transferred for the 36th Session of the Assembly from the Third Committee to the Sixth Committee which indicates good prospects for its completion in 1981, if sufficient time is available. Other work on torture has included the production of a *Code of Conduct for Law Enforcement Officials* which was adopted by the UN General Assembly in Resolution 34/169 of 17 December 1979. Amnesty International organized a seminar on Torture and Human Rights in Strasbourg, France, from 3 to 5 October 1977, at which one of the working parties drew up recommendations for the protection of individuals from torture by the application of professional codes of conduct. In January 1978 the Executive Board of the World Health Organization invited two NGOs, the Council for International Organizations of Medical Sciences and the World Medical Association, to prepare a draft *Code of Medical Ethics*. The UN General Assembly Resolution 34/168 adopted on 17 December 1979 asked the Secretary-General to circulate the draft code to member states, agencies, other intergovernmental organizations and NGOs for comment. No action was taken of any substance at the 35th session in 1980, but the question was put on the agenda for the 36th session in 1981.

16 Amnesty International News Release of 14 May 1979. See also *Amnesty International Report 1980*, pp. 35-8 and 391.

17 International Commission of Jurists, Violations of human rights and the rule of law in Uganda (Geneva, The Commission, 1974).

5   Oxfam and Development
ELIZABETH STAMP

Introduction

In the sphere of overseas aid, there are many and varied non-governmental organizations. Some of them specialize — working, for example, only with children, with the blind, or other needy groups. Some of them are operational, putting their own staff into the field and running their own programmes. But whether limited in objective or far-reaching, operational or only funding, almost all voluntary aid agencies are 'doers'. They work to grow more food, prevent blindness, help the victims of an earthquake, and have hundreds of other practical objectives.

Few of them aim to be primarily pressure groups. Many of them started in circumstances where 'the only way to get anything done is to do it yourself'. Some started as relief groups during or after a war coping with refugees. Many are church-related organizations following in the missionary tradition, helping establish and run medical services and schools in areas where none existed. Governments of the areas, whether indigenous or colonial, provided few or no funds. Private enterprise was still expected to fill the gaps and look after the poor.

Our perceptions of our responsibilities have developed dramatically in the last hundred years, particularly since the war. We expect the state to organize and provide medical, educational and other social services for all its citizens, levying taxes for the purpose. In recent years this concept is being internationalized — we all have a responsibility for our fellow human beings everywhere. But just as our social services were initially provided sketchily and individually, for centuries by charitable groups and the church, so it is similar groups who now aid the poor in the developing countries. Some of them campaign actively to work themselves out of a job pressing host governments and donor governments to take over responsibility. But many more 'get on with the job'. By influencing public opinion at home among donors and taxpayers, and in helping the poor in the receiving countries, they may ultimately be more effective. This has to be assessed by making a judgement between the effects of preaching and of practice.

Oxfam — the Early Days

When a group of people in wartime Britain from church, university and city backgrounds met at the Friends Meeting House[1] in Oxford in September 1942 to discuss reports of starvation among the civilian population in enemy-occupied Europe, they were concerned as to how they might help. At the subsequent meeting in the University Church, a famine relief committee was formed, and at ensuing meetings the thoughts were of immediate aid: of the organization for raising funds and supplies, and the methods of getting the aid to those in need. These two factors have remained central to the organization, which has grown to become the multi-million pound aid agency, Oxfam. But in those early years there was no thought of establishing a permanent organization.

The Committee decided to respond to an appeal from the Greek Red Cross. An appeal was launched within Oxford University and extended to the city in the autumn of 1943. A deputation was sent to the Ministry of Economic Warfare, followed by a petition with 8,000 signatures. The plea was for the blockade to be lifted so that supplies could be shipped into Greece, but it was refused, so the modest aid efforts were continued through the Red Cross. With the end of the war the focus of activity switched to the main continent of Europe where refugees, displaced people and local citizens alike were suffering from cold and hunger. Appeals were made for clothing, food and medicines as well as money, and distribution was entrusted to the Friends' Relief Service.

At the end of 1946 the first paid member of staff was recruited — a part-time organizing secretary. During his eighteen months of service some modest national advertising was initiated, and the property of '17 Broad Street' was obtained to provide a gift shop (which it still is) with an office above. In the year ending September 1948, just over £6,000 in cash and £32,000 worth of clothing and supplies were handed over to the Quakers for distribution.

The Committee, however, were undecided over their future. Should they close down — as the needs in Europe were increasingly being met by other organizations and governments — or should they stay in being? Members were feeling the strain of the continuing voluntary effort required to sustain appeals. Could they afford paid staff and could they find them? Then a temporary administrator was found, and a new problem erupted — hundreds of thousands of Palestinian Arab refugees were displaced by the creation of the state of Israel. The Committee immediately agreed to try and help. The registered objects of the charity were widened to read 'the relief of suffering arising as a result of wars or other causes in any part of the world'. From then on, any idea of closing down faded into the background. Whether they realized it or not, the Committee had set the foundation for a widening overseas programme, and with it the need for expansion at home.

A permanent Gift Shop Manager was appointed at the end of 1949, and in 1950 the Committee obtained the services of a Quaker advertising man who was to guide publicity for many years and who pioneered national charity press advertising. That year Professor Gilbert Murray, one of the founder members, made the Week's Good Cause appeal on the BBC radio which raised over £9,500 — a further step to make the Committee's work known more widely. But probably the most significant development was the appointment of Leslie Kirkley, a Leeds businessman and Quaker as General Secretary in 1951.[2] He was to provide leadership for Oxfam for twenty-three years, until his retirement in 1974.

From then on the appeals for help multiplied — a famine in Bihar, and the Korean war in 1951; a major influx of Chinese refugees into Hong Kong in 1952; an earthquake in the Ionian Islands in 1953. When the Algerian war sent refugees pouring into neighbouring countries in 1957, the Oxford Committee was the first relief agency to send help.

'It was all useful work,' wrote Mervyn Jones in his book about Oxfam, 'yet in significant respects the effort was still a limited one. Although horizons were widening, the bulk of the aid (52 per cent as late as 1957) went to Europe . . . the great majority of the aided were refugees or the victims of disaster, rather than people for whom poverty was the lifelong environment.'[3]

Participation in World Refugee Year (WRY) in 1959/60 when Oxfam contributed £750,000 in cash and supplies,[4] and the Congo famine in the following year[5] can, in retrospect, be seen as the end of one era and the beginning of another. Not only did Leslie Kirkley serve as chairman of the WRY Publicity Committee, thereby establishing himself and the Oxford Committee on the national scene, but nine regional organizers were appointed to raise funds around the country to build up and consolidate the formation of local groups which had been established over the years and the work of the one travelling appeals organizer who had been appointed in 1952. By the time the Congo horror pictures hit the newspaper front pages, the British public responded in their thousands to *that* famine relief committee in Oxford, bringing the cash income to over £1 million in 1960/1, £400,000 more than in the previous year.

Prosperity and signs of a new social conscience and internationalism showed themselves in the generosity of the British public in responding to these situations. With independence for some colonies on the horizon, and the launching of the Freedom from Hunger campaign by the Food and Agriculture Organization of the United Nations in 1960, Oxfam decided to turn towards 'development', and a deeper concern with the root causes of poverty among those people 'for whom poverty is the lifelong environment'.

The Structure for Longer-Term Work

Under the guidance of a grants sub-committee established in 1955 and an overseas aid officer appointed in 1958, the organization tackled the move into longer-term projects on three fronts. Firstly, it contacted FAO, requesting projects for funding under the Freedom from Hunger banner, suggesting a possible total of half a million pounds over three to five years.[6] Secondly, overseas organizations with whom the Committee had contacts were informed of the new policy and asked to submit requests for longer-term projects. Some vocational training and agricultural schemes had already received Oxfam funding during the latter part of the fifties, so this approach was more of an extension of recent developments. The third initiative was the most far-reaching — a decision to appoint a field representative with responsibility for a particular geographic area. The High Commission Territories of Basutoland (now Lesotho), Bechuanaland (now Botswana) and Swaziland were selected as three British protectorates where additional finance for new development programmes could make a real impact. After undertaking a survey of needs and possibilities for the Committee, Jimmy Betts was appointed to the field at the end of 1961. He was to oversee and help implement the initial £90,000 worth of projects he had recommended, and to take general responsibility for future work in Eastern and Southern Africa from his base in Maseru.

From then on the expansion of the overseas programme was rapid, and with it the further appointment of Field Directors. Relief and welfare projects had been assessed and monitored with occasional overseas visits by staff and committee members. But longer-term initiatives required more detailed background and on-the-spot discussion and investigation. The first Field Director for Asia was appointed in 1964 followed by one for India in 1965, with East and West Africa that same year. The first field office in Latin America was opened in 1968 in Lima, Peru, followed by a second in Recife in North East Brazil the next year. By 1970 there were eleven Field Directors, including three in India. Ten years later there were twenty-five in total — six in India, one each in Bangladesh and Indonesia, eleven in Africa, five in Latin America and one in the Middle East.

The Field Directors play a key role in Oxfam's overseas programme. Action can be taken quickly when the needs demand, but it is necessary to ensure that all applications are sound, so that money is used to the greatest effect. A standard application form is therefore provided. No project is supported unless a Field Director has visited 'the project' and dicussed the request with those responsible, only in rare circumstances of emergency is this rule broken. So when an organization or group requires help from Oxfam, they approach the Field Director for the area, or if they write directly to the headquarters in England, the application is sent out to the Field Director. He or she then seeks such local advice as may be needed before forwarding the application and a recommendation to Oxford. Here, background information is built up, the need is analysed, and the request is then considered for funding. Once approved the Field Director becomes responsible for visiting the project from time to time — to see that all is going well, to discuss any problems, and to give advice. At the same time, and to an increasing extent in recent years, the Field Directors take a more active role — seeking out possible projects for funding, encouraging local groups to formulate projects and programmes that Oxfam might help, and generally being 'the ears and eyes' of Oxfam in their part of the world. In this way the needs and priorities of different areas are fed back to Oxfam headquarters, where budgets, country priorities and guidelines for the most appropriate types of aid are worked out on a continuing review basis.

The old grants sub-committee, renamed the Overseas Aid Committee, gave way to four separate Field Committees for Asia, Africa, the Middle East and Latin America in 1964. They receive the project applications, which come in from the Field Directors, and, with powers delegated by Oxfam's Council of Management, they are responsible for making grants and for the development of overseas policy. But in turn, certain powers have been delegated to staff for approving smaller grants on a day-to-day basis; and special speedy procedures have been set up for dealing with emergencies. The Field Committees are composed of experts in different fields who give their time and advice to Oxfam. A voluntary medical advisory panel assists the committees, and a part-time medical adviser serves on the staff. More recently a rural development panel was set up in a similar capacity. In 1965 a further small change was made. The Oxford Committee for Famine Relief became Oxfam, the name being chosen because it had caught on, from various attempts at abbreviated postal names used in fund-raising appeals.[7]

At home

None of these developments would have been feasible or practical without expansion on the fund-raising side at home. By the time that Oxfam celebrated its twenty-first birthday in 1961/62, income was £1.6 million, with £1.1 million in donations, and sixteen paid regional organizers worked from their homes in different parts of the country. With income well over £2 million the following year and an overseas programme of £1.9 million, nearly half a million pounds was allocated to Freedom from Hunger projects. Four new gift shops were opened during the year administered centrally from Oxford, providing a new source of income; and in the mid-sixties a subsidiary trading company was set up to handle the sale of Christmas cards and to import handicrafts from overseas. Income rose steadily through the decade, and topped £3 million by 1967/68.

The seventies might be called the decade of the shop, as more and more Oxfam local groups started to run their own shops, initially taking premises temporarily, and gradually moving to more permanent locations. As early as 1967/68, shops emerged as the biggest single fund-raiser, with 136 groups (out of a total of 550) running shops for some or all of the year. By 1972, thirty-three regional organizers working from regional offices were servicing 649 local groups, with 430 running shops, which raised almost a fifth of the £4.6 million income. From then on the expansion of shop income was dramatic.

The secondhand clothing donated by supporters, which had been shipped overseas twenty years before, now became the major item of sales. It provided a useful social service to the poorer members of British society, and also met the fashion requirements of the young, who were busy searching the attics and market stalls for 'granny's garments'. So the last year of the decade, 1979/80, saw a net shop income of £4.5 million from the sale of donated goods and handicrafts imported from overseas, a sum nearly equalling the income of £4.8 million from direct cash donations, all contributing to a record of over £12 million. In addition, a further £6.7 million was raised by a special appeal for the Kampuchea consortium programme. The result was that during the course of the year, 583 shops actually handled some £10 million in all: their 'ordinary' income plus more that £5 million generated by the BBC 'bring and buy' appeal for Kampuchea.[8]

Other major sources of income included £1.1 million from the UK government and the EEC under their schemes for the joint funding of development projects (first started in 1974), over £800,000 profit from Oxfam's trading company — from the sale of imported handicrafts, Christmas cards and other UK produced goods, and over £300,000 from other agencies.[9]

The Overseas Programme

First steps in development

During the forties and fifties most of the agencies requesting help from the Committee were well known on the voluntary international scene — missionary societies, the Salvation Army, the Red Cross Societies, and various refugee organizations. The Committee plugged in to an existing relief and welfare network. With the decision to move into development work, Oxfam staff and Committees had to take on the responsibility for seeking out and even helping create new opportunities. Some of the long-standing church organizations were themselves beginning to think and plan along these lines, and modest agricultural and other types of projects were developed with funds from Oxfam, Christian Aid and other aid organizations. FAO and the Freedom From Hunger Campaign produced some larger programmes for funding. But in the final analysis it was the Field Directors who 'produced' most of the projects as Oxfam's growing income enabled expenditure overseas to increase. They were in a position to learn what governments and local authorities were doing, what voluntary agencies existed locally, who was doing what, and what might or could be done by these or other groupings.

Work with governments

Work direct with governments has been the exception rather than the rule. The scale of Oxfam funding is usually too small for government programmes, and they have usually attracted funds from other larger sources. But the overriding consideration has been the purpose and focus of any particular programme — is it realistically planned to help the poorer members of society in a particular area? Bechuanaland (Botswana from independence in 1966) was one of the exceptions, and part of Jimmy Betts' original programme in 1961 was worked out with local expatriate civil servants. A country the size of France but most of it Kalahari desert, it was poor and relied on Britain for aid just to sustain its annual budget. Cattle provided 80 per cent of the colony's exports and the bases of their livelihood for 80–90 per cent of the people. Then in the drought of 1961–65, one-third of the national herd perished.

Oxfam's aid to Botswana during the sixties totalled over £500,000, much of it going into Ministry of Agriculture projects linked with cattle raising. Seven cattle holding grounds were set up, one in each tribal area. They each carried a demonstration herd, provided a fattening service for local farmers' cattle, and generally served as a local focus for animal husbandry education. Two mobile animal husbandry units were also set up to provide veterinary and other services in remote rural areas with Oxfam funds; and a large dam-building unit jointly funded with Christian Aid helped with the provision of cattle watering points, crucial in this drought-prone country. To help with general agricultural education, one of the first projects was the establishment of a training centre at Mahalapye, built by the first intake of students. Here a new corps of local agricultural extension workers were trained; and later, with further funds, as a rural training centre it provided short courses for farmers, teachers and others, who learned about crops, vegetable growing, the raising of small animals, and the like.

While much of this Oxfam aid helped the better-off farmers — 40 per cent of the country's livestock were owned by only 5 per cent of the people in 1970 — it helped the small farmers too. As one civil servant remarked later, 'The whole of Gaberone (the new capital) was built with British money. But out in the country a farmer tilling his field knows about Oxfam.'[10] By 1977 minerals had overtaken cattle products as Botswana's major export earner, but cattle rearing still provides more income for the majority of people than the growing wealth of the mining industry. Botswana remains a net importer of food, with relatively little of her land area suitable for large-scale crop production. But sorghum and millet yields have risen by over 50 per cent in the last fifteen years, and maize production has gone up fifteenfold. Looking back, Oxfam can be modestly proud of the contributions it made to the basis for these improvements.

More recently, since Oxfam opened a field office in Tanzania in 1975, a number of initiatives have been taken at *regional* and *district* government level there, for the most part with small amounts of money for small projects. With rising transport costs making long journeys increasingly uneconomic, and as a result of the 'villagization' programme, there is a growing need for district services like chicken hatcheries, fish farms and tree nurseries. The structures for working such programmes are relatively new, and problems have been encountered with staff changes, the difficulty of realistic costing between estimates and execution, and the availability of building and other materials. But some progress has been made.

Most successful has been the development of tree growing in a number of schools and villages in Shinyanga region where deforestation threatens to denude the entire area by 1990. Oxfam has provided funds for water tanks, watering cans, wheelbarrows, hoes and similar homely items. But most important has been the financing of small 'seminars' where village leaders, teachers and others learn from forestry staff about fencing, planting, watering and manuring, ready to pass on their knowledge to pupils and fellow villagers. In 1980 Oxfam provided £106 for three forestry staff from neighbouring Tabora region to visit and see progress and problems, before they consider starting a similar programme. Oxfam encourages visits between projects even, on occasion, from one country to another as a most worthwhile learning process.

Helping the poorest

The main purpose of Oxfam's overseas work is to respond to the needs of men and women in the Third World, working with the poorest members of the human family. The traditional aims of a voluntary society are to relieve the suffering caused by poverty and to reduce the total number of the poorest. Oxfam is doing this, but it is also trying to do something more: namely, to encourage processes of change, and in such a way that the poorest can take charge of the improvement of their own living standards. In this way Oxfam seeks to reduce more permanently the bias against the poor in the development process . . .

Oxfam projects are aimed at two targets. They are designed:
(i) for the poorest to *have more*, particularly in terms of food and health, and control of a fair share of the earth's resources.
(ii) for the poorest to *be more* in terms of confidence and ability to manage their own future, and their status in society at large.

Oxfam Field Directors'
Handbook: Objectives, 1980.

A growing proportion of Oxfam's overseas work is concerned with seeking out ways of helping the poorest. This may take the form of encouraging small groups to work out what *they* want, with the resulting 'mixture' of many small grants. Or it may take the form of a general policy development of wide application which Oxfam promotes wherever practical.

Training health workers

Typical of this type of aid is the promotion of primary health care and the training of village health workers (VHWs). Projects of a variety of different types have been supported. It has been no part of Oxfam's policy to lay down a prescribed training or a particular method of working; rather more has it been a policy of supporting local initiatives and suggesting ways in which ordinary local people can help bring better health in their own communities. One contribution has been made from headquarters: Oxfam's Publications Unit has been helping with the translations of David Werner's book *Where There is No Doctor*, and a number of small grants have been made to provide the book to interested projects.[11]

One of the first schemes was at Savar in Bangladesh in 1972. After an initial attempt to train volunteers from local villages to work part-time was abandoned, because too much support and follow-up was required, it was decided to establish a group of paid full-time paramedical workers. Local recruits, both men and women, were given a year's training — half spent at the centre at Savar, and half out in the villages. They now undertake considerable curative work, immunization, family planning, and some preventive work. Local funds are raised by an insurance scheme and some clinic charges, and other funds are provided by outside donors including Oxfam. In 1975 a simple form of training was also devised for the village dais (traditional midwives) focusing on family planning and hygiene. Ventures such as this are often started by local doctors who want to bring health care to poor people in areas where medical services are few or non-existant.

By contrast, the health programme of the Kottar Social Service Society in Kanyakumari district in the tip of India works without a medical officer in charge. It started in the early seventies with mobile medical teams headed by nurses. But they did not like the rural work, felt little rapport with the villagers, and were soon leaving for better paid jobs in the cities or government service. The service that has evolved since then still relies on teams, but is made up of a complex variety of personnel — health guides, health educators, VHWs, a few nurses, all supported by several hundred voluntary village extension workers. They serve the 122 village health co-operatives, whose members in turn finance the programme's running costs. Oxfam and other voluntary agencies have paid for the training. An American social scientist who studied the programme in 1978 reported: 'Rates of popular participation average more than 90 per cent overall, a striking figure. Kottar's effectiveness is very much an outgrowth of the flexible approach and adaptability.' Further north in the Belgaum district of Karnataka, twenty-five VHWs, trained with assistance from Oxfam's Indian Nutrition Advisor, Sujatha de Magry, have taken over from twice-weekly, mobile medical clinics in eight villages. Here it was rising oil prices that cut back the forty-year-old health outreach programme of the Karnatak Health Institute, and thrust village women into positions of responsibility and leadership. By their own testimonies, they are bringing more than better health to their villages. They have unwittingly started a social revolution.

But the introduction of local health schemes is not all 'plain sailing'; existing medical services must be taken into account. In the Yemen Arab Republic, Oxfam is supporting a Catholic Institute for International Relations volunteer training team. The 'giddahs', or traditional midwives, are receiving one-week afternoon courses aimed at better hygiene and improved nutrition. In addition, there is a new phenomenon: the 'saheens', people who have picked up some experience working in hospitals often in Saudi Arabia or the Gulf, and who start dispensing drugs and injections in their home villages. They receive one week's training and further follow-up, which aims to broaden their knowledge of basic health care, and to include a preventive health approach. It is too early to assess this programme, but Oxfam's medical adviser comments: 'A case can be made for ignoring the Saheens and concentrating on training a new cadre (of health workers), but to do this is to ignore the situation as it stands. The Saheens are carrying the main burden of health care in rural areas; anything that can be done to raise the standard of their work will have immediate results.'

Local social structures can also cause problems. In one village in Indonesia a health programme supported by Oxfam has come unstuck because some people felt threatened by the new initiatives. Evaluating the causes of failure, Oxfam's Field Director summarized the constraints: '(1) an unwillingness on the part of the ruling élite to allow authority and responsibility to be exercised by a group outside the existing village government hierarchy. (2) An aversion on the part of men to allowing women to participate in decision-making processes. (3) A reluctance on the part of land-owning farmers to allowing participation of landless villagers in decision-making. (4) A certain distrust by sub-district and regency level health staff of village level initiatives that seem to threaten their positions of authority.' In the end, it was finance that proved the actual breaking-point of the scheme — disagreement over the organization of an income-generating agricultural project when the original health insurance foundered.

Creating employment opportunities

Encouraging employment through handicrafts production is another area of application in many countries. Oxfam imports handicrafts from a number of small producer groups, through the Bridge operation of its subsidiary trading company. Grants are also made to groups for staff salaries and working capital where markets are available locally. The production and sale of handicrafts can create employment and income where other work facilities are few or only seasonal. It can provide additional income especially for the women, thereby raising the standard of family living. Local raw materials are often available at relatively low cost, but the field is fraught with many problems: packaging and transport, marketing, pricing, product range, standardization, seasonal fluctuations in production and demand, and many more.

The women working at St Mary's Education Centre in Ahmedabad, Western

India, are too dependent on exports. Ten years ago Oxfam's Field Director encouraged the nuns, who did welfare work and taught embroidery, to start a small employment scheme. By the mid-seventies it had grown to employ more than 300 women, doing the traditional Gujarati mirrorwork embroidery, making bags and cushion covers: almost all for export to Bridge for sale in Oxfam shops. They tried to find other customers, but were offered derisory prices by middlemen. Oxfam's policy of paying a fair price to provide a fair wage had priced them out of their own local market. When Oxfam's sales in Britain slowed down gradually, a new skirt and waistcoat were proposed by a local designer, with approval from the Field Director. But the Indian women did not like the idea of doing something new. They downed tools for three weeks — the first ever Oxfam strike! After discussions all round, they started work again, and now cannot hope to satisfy the demand. Such are some of the hazards of trying to create employment opportunities — a microcosm of some of the larger world trading problems.

In Peru Oxfam is helping finance what one handicraft adviser says could be a resounding success or a spectacular failure — a handicraft marketing organization. Peru abounds with groups making a range of ethnic and other products which find a ready market in Lima, Cuzco and other tourist centres. The problem lies in the scattered nature of the groups, often in remote mountain communities. 'The average artesan is very much at the mercy of the middlemen who can afford to drive prices down by exploiting the vulnerability and lack of organisation of the artisans', writes Oxfam's Field Director. The initiative for this project came from several groups who approached Oxfam in 1979 asking for advice. They wanted help with marketing skills and wondered whether they could get together with other groups to share transport and other services. In September that year Oxfam hosted and financed a two-day seminar attended by sixteen handicraft groups. From this meeting came the idea for a marketing organization.

In January 1980 Oxfam approved a grant of £1,725 to get things going; and in July a grant of £21,000 was agreed to cover six staff salaries, rent, office running costs, transport, the production of a catalogue, and other small items. Initially the organization will work with three producer groups — one producing wooden items, silverware and some baskets, the second concentrating on basketry, and the third on pottery and cotton textiles. They will act as 'guinea pigs' for future expansion of the organization, in which each producer group will be a partner. The three groups represent more than 10,000 artisans who make handicrafts in their spare time.

It is estimated that 25 per cent of the Peruvian population, over four million people, produce handicrafts. When sold locally the handicrafts are marked up 100 per cent by the merchants. When exported, the mark up is 300 per cent or more. The new marketing organization aims to provide the artisans with a greater share of the final retail price and to foster traditional products and designs, at the same time encouraging high quality and standards.

The variety of local needs

Encouraging local initiatives covers a range of activities of amazing diversity. There are straightforward practical schemes where Oxfam is asked for funds for physical inputs. Examples of such projects include the provision of pipes and tanks to a group of communities in Rwanda for drinking water, or boats and nets for a group of poor fishermen in North East Brazil to improve their catch. Oxfam is not keen to put money into 'bricks and mortar' unless, for example, there are strong arguments for a community centre or somewhere to provide training. In one case a group of poor farmers in Bas Zaïre started building with borrowed funds, while their request for £2,000 was being submitted, and turned down. Reluctantly, Oxfam decided to rescue them, provided the money, and the simple mud block and thatch building was completed. Since 1977 it has become a focal point for local agricultural development, and a useful centre for short simple courses with sessions on soil conservation, nutrition and vegetable growing, fish farming, and other subjects.

'Change of Use' is a hazard with enthusiastic groups. Funds are allocated for one purpose, and the group decides to use them for something else. Even diligent Field Directors and a system of application and progress report forms cannot always prevent this happening. A recent example took place in Tierra y Libertad, a slum/squatter community on the outskirts of Monterrey, the steel town in northern Mexico. Here live 7,500 people who run their own community through a general assembly and a series of committees. They have set up their own school, a community clothing factory, a building block workshop, a communal laundry, a fuel depot, a taxi service and other enterprises. Oxfam's Field Director for Central America described it as 'The best community development project I have yet come across'. But it is a thorn in the flesh for the local authorities. Initially in 1973 the police came in and tried to evict the squatters, but were thrown out. Now they have plumbed themselves into the city water supply, and wired themselves into the electricity grid. But they pay no bills, as, they argue, the government has done nothing for them. In 1978 Oxfam agreed to provide finance to set up two revolving loan funds. One scheme to provide subsidized milk for the children, many of whom are malnourished, is progressing satisfactorily, linked in with a maternal and child health programme. But the second, an ironmongery project, was decided to be a non-starter, as the raw material prices were so high. Instead they are expanding the block-making venture, and the Oxfam funds are paying salaries of the administrator, the technical supervisor and two assistants.

Paying salaries or stipends for local experts or other staff is taking an increasing proportion of Oxfam's overseas expenditure. Those involved may be working in health, agriculture, technical training, or in more specialized fields where local demands require specific appointments. In the diocese of Juazeiro in North East Brazil vast irrigation and hydroelectric schemes are taking place along the Sao Francisco valley, part funded by the World Bank. Ironically, development schemes aiming to produce more power and increase agricultural output are displacing the small peasant farmer and labourer. As sharecroppers or squatters of long-standing, they are not 'owners' of their land, with the result that they receive compensation only for their houses, fencing and any fruit trees they have planted. The Bishop of Juzaeiro has taken up their cause and turned to Oxfam for help. Since 1977 Oxfam has provided between £3,000–£4,000 a year to pay the salary and travel costs of a lawyer.

A very different sort of educator is being paid for by Oxfam in Nairobi to promote breast-feeding among women's groups, in health clinics, hospitals and other appropriate places. The Breast-Feeding Information Group was set up in 1977 by a group of concerned people who were alarmed at the decline in breast feeding especially in urban areas in the face of the active promotion of manufactured baby foods. Initially helped by the Norwegian churches, they use materials prepared by the Kenya Government and UNICEF. The group members are all volunteers who are now finding that they cannot meet all the requests for talks and discussions; hence the request to Oxfam to pay a part-time promoter and provide funds for postage, etc., for distributing the materials more widely.

What the Kenyan promoter and Brazilian lawyer have in common, apart from Oxfam funding, is a 'fight' for the interests of the poor against the might of large and powerful interests. Working with small groups among the poorest members of society is one of the most difficult tasks. Relatively few groups are self-generating and self-sustaining. The pressures of poverty, lack of education and influence all mitigate against the establishing of permanent groups. But some groups are formed without outside leadership, and one such is a weavers' co-operative formed in 1977 in Adhalgaon, Maharashtra. Here fifty weaving families registered as a co-op in an effort to get themselves out of the clutches of the middlemen who provide their raw materials and the marketing outlets. They managed to subscribe share capital of just over £130, but not enough to purchase raw materials on the scale required. A doctor who worked in the area learned of their efforts, and arranged a meeting with Oxfam's Field Director. Oxfam agreed to provide £673 as working capital to help the fifteen poorest family members with raw materals.

More frequently one finds groups where the leadership comes from outside. In the sugar growing area of Satara district near Poona a young husband and wife, both graduate economists, decided to return home and recruit some old school friends to start a small organization to help poor labourers get better wages and fight injustice. By the time that Oxfam was introduced to them, they already had four animators working with labourers' groups in seven villages. Occasional paying jobs and money collected from friends just kept them going. Oxfam's assistant Field Director, musing on their first meeting, wrote, 'Faced with a group like this which has struggled for means to do what it wants and has been managing to do it, one wonders whether the money we give will kill it — slowly. It will enable them to work unhindered. But in giving this money are we damping the liberating fire that enthuses them to work for their cause?' Oxfam is currently paying stipends for twelve animators at the rate of £24 a month each, has provided a motorcycle and twelve bicycles, and is funding an imaginative programme of women's clubs, adult education classes, health education work, together with books and other materials.

An Oxfam committee member visited the project for three days in the spring of 1980. 'Great emphasis is placed on community involvement in all aspects of the work. The central team of animators works through local voluntary animators in each village. Care is taken to ensure that programmes respond to the needs of specific groups of landless labourers, marginal and small farmers.' The latest news from the group is that two of the animators have won prizes in a national competition for literature for neo-literates — one with a book about untouchability, and one with a book about collective action and the formation of a co-operative dairy society. The worry about Oxfam funding killing local initiative seems to have been unfounded here.

Emergency response to disasters

It is in the field of disasters and emergency operations that Oxfam has become best known in recent years both nationally and internationally, thanks mainly to the media which report disasters and seek up-to-date information from the NGOs on these occasions. In fact Oxfam's expenditure on disasters has not represented a major proportion of its overseas programme. It averaged 19 per cent per annum over the decade of the 1970s and only 10 per cent per annum over the last three years, if the special Kampuchea operation is excluded.

Oxfam sees its long-term development work as the major focus for its overseas expenditure from 'normal' income, relying on separate special disaster appeals to finance much of its emergency programmes. The main instrument for these appeals is the Disasters Emergency Committee set up in 1963 to provide a mechanism for the major British overseas charities to make combined appeals on television and radio. Meetings are also attended by Foreign Office representatives, including members of its specialist Disaster Unit from within the Overseas Development Administration, so that close liaison can be maintained with government and information on disasters can be shared. The committee is not operational in the field. Funds raised by the joint appeals are divided equally between member agencies to spend as they wish.

In recent years Oxfam has maintained a disasters register of 'volunteers' — medical and technical personnel who can go overseas at short notice on short-term disaster assignments. In the last two years or so a new and interesting development has taken place, largely with the United Nations High Commissioner for Refugees. Oxfam has been recruiting longer-term specialist staff to work overseas under UNHCR auspices, notably with the boat people refugees in

Malaysia, and with refugees in Somalia. Similarly with the World Food Programme in Uganda, Oxfam has provided logistics staff to help with the movement of supplies to drought-stricken Karamoja. In addition to these initiatives, doctors have been recruited to go out to Zimbabwe to help reopen mission hospitals after independence. So, to a limited extent, Oxfam has 'gone operational' with more than a hundred personnel working overseas – field staff and others – in 1980. This reflects the facts that Oxfam can recruit personnel for service overseas more cheaply and speedily than the UN system can.

In the Kampuchea famine relief operation of 1979–80, the speedy setting-up of a purchasing and shipping office in Singapore and the ensuing formation of a thirty-strong consortium of other NGO funding agencies with a joint team in Phnom Penh were operational initiatives, which would have been unthinkable a few years ago. As news of the horrors of the Pol Pot regime, food shortages and starvation trickled out of the country, Oxfam was willing to make an agreement with the new Heng Samrin government and was able to take quick action to procure supplies and shipping to start a relief programme. As the horrific publicity mounted and public opinion worldwide was moved to help, in spite of the political difficulties concerning recognition of the new regime, the consortium formation and the funding required came easily. Never before had public generosity in many countries been so spontaneous and massive.

Even in a disaster of these proportions, Oxfam was considering the longer term early on. Once the International Red Cross and UNICEF were established and were shipping in food on a larger scale than the voluntary agencies could contemplate, the Oxfam-led team were seeking out the most effective means of rehabilitation for Kampuchea. By early November 1979, within three months of the first plane load of relief supplies, barges were taking in hoe heads, diesel pumps, fishing nets, raw materials to get small factories going again; and several hundred lorries were brought in over the following months. The Kampuchea operation will without doubt attract other authors to write about it in detail. What it shows, in summary, is the speed and flexibility with which NGOs like Oxfam can respond to a disaster, that their operations are not necessarily small-scale and that they can work successfully in the most politically-sensitive situations.

The Influence of Oxfam

Oxfam's links with other oganizations

It would be quite impossible to list, let alone analyse, the other organizations with whom Oxfam has contact. Through the overseas programme itself, many hundreds receive funds every year. Oxfam field staff have on occasion initiated and normally support associations and groupings of voluntary agencies locally, finding that the exchange of information and the co-operation involved is useful to Oxfam and beneficial to all those involved. From time to time Oxfam has funded such initiatives, believing that the sharing of problems and achievements can in itself be a positive contribution to development.

In the last ten years Oxfam has built up a small technical unit to serve in an advisory capacity for Oxfam and agencies in the field. The unit has specialized in emergency housing, and water and sanitation. Through this work, contacts have been established with universities and research bodies around the world. Oxfam's new Publications Unit provides back-up material, focusing on simple technical manuals, leaflets and reports for use overseas, working in close co-operation with the London-based Intermediate Technology Development Group in some fields. Oxfam's committee members and advisers also provide regular contacts with universities, research bodies, banking and the retail trade, both in Britain and overseas.

Since the early sixties other Oxfams have been set up by groups of individuals with similar aims in Belgium, Canada, Quebec and the United States; and the Australian organization Community Aid Abroad has linked in with the Oxfam 'family'. This is the loosest of groupings — once every two years the six agencies meet together to discuss questions of mutual interest. Otherwise each organization is autonomous. They support their own programmes, occasionally linking in with the Field Director network. In emergencies information is shared and operations are sometimes jointly funded.

On a wider network, Oxfam is a member of the International Council of Voluntary Agencies, of the Liaison Committee of Development NGOs to the EEC, and a number of other agency groupings both within Britain and internationally. Some of these are permanent and formal, like the Standing Conference on Refugees. Others may be short-lived with a narrower focus — like the World Refugee Year Committee or the Freedom from Hunger Campaign Committee, wound up in the late sixties. To these must be added all the informal contacts between agency personnel, and other interested people — the sometimes unfairly maligned 'old-boy network' that can provide advice and assistance quickly when it is needed.

Oxfam and UN

Oxfam's first and most regular contact with UN agencies has been in the disaster field helping refugees through the UN Relief and Works Agency for Palestine Refugees (UNRWA), and with the Office of the High Commissioner for Refugees (UNHCR). Special contact was established at the time of the Congo famine when the Oxford Committee was the first agency to send in funds to the hastily-created ONUC (UN Operation in the Congo), before other moneys were made available. Here, too, as in the Cambodia crisis nearly twenty years later, donations poured in, many of them unsolicited.

Observers have been sent by Oxfam to various UN conferences as appropriate, and representatives have gone to several of the NGO forums organized alongside a number of these conferences in recent years. Oxfam's Overseas Director was invited to serve on the management committee of one of the earliest of the NGO forums, held at the 1974 World Population Conference in Bucharest. And Oxfam has provided both funds and journalists for some of the unofficial conference newspapers, such as PAN at the 1974 World Food Conference in Rome, that have become the daily news-sheets and sometimes caustic commentaries on the official proceedings. But conferences are attended only where a genuine contribution can be made.

Oxfam's most extensive contact with the UN has been at the grass-roots level. Projects have been funded with UNRWA, UNHCR, FAO, WHO and UNICEF. The Field Directors often establish a close working relationship with the UN Development Programme Resident Representatives and at times have gone on tour to inspect projects together. In emergency relief operations, where the UN now designates a 'lead agency' to provide field co-ordination for its many programmes and specialized agencies, co-operation may be particularly close and frequent. This was notably the case in the 1979–80 Kampuchean reconstruction operation. UNICEF, along with the International Committee of the Red Cross, co-ordinated most non-communist, governmental assistance, while Oxfam administered the international NGO consortium. UNICEF, ICRC and Oxfam made sure their work was complementary.

Consultative status in Category II with the UN was obtained in the mid-sixties, but only once has Oxfam used the formal channels to lobby at the UN in New York and that was to call for more aid for the Bengal refugees in India in 1971. Even Oxfam's lobbying tends to occur at the grass-roots. In 1980 when the UNDP representative in Uganda suspended the UN's convoys of relief lorries into Karamoja, it was pressure in Kampala from Save the Children and Oxfam, which helped to get supplies resumed. Normal contact between Oxfam and the UNDP would not involve public appeals of this type. Discussion, co-operation and exchange of information may result in influence of a less immediate or obvious kind. Finally, contact with the UN is more readily made through the International Council of Voluntary Agencies, which now is among the small number of NGOs with Category I consultative status. Joint statements with other NGOs are regularly made when development issues are debated in New York or Geneva and Oxfam's views will usually be in accord with the ICVA position, even if Oxfam has not been directly involved.

Oxfam at home

As part of its overall spending programme Oxfam allocates 5 per cent of income to educational work in Britain. An education department working in schools and training colleges was established in the late fifties. Teaching and discussion materials are produced in close and regular liaison with other NGOs working in development education. More recently a small Public Affairs Unit was set up to produce research and discussion publications on subjects relating to

Third World interests for debate mainly within this country. For a wider public on a regular basis, Oxfam and Christian Aid helped launch and finance the development magazine *The New Internationalist* for its first ten years, the only journal of its kind at the time. Helping take another initiative with over fifty other agencies in recent months, Oxfam has assisted in setting up an International Broadcasting Trust and small production unit to make films on development topics for the fourth television channel, which is due to begin broadcasting in November 1982.

Through its wider education work, much of it carried out with other agencies, Oxfam can take some credit for the wider interest in the Third World that has developed in Britain in the last twenty years — from the Freedom from Hunger Campaign in the early sixties, to the pressure for discussion of the Brandt Commission report in 1980/81. But not everyone is concerned. Oxfam has experienced more criticism and hostility probably than most other overseas aid agencies. Perhaps its very size, its early pioneering of press advertising, and the now omnipresent Oxfam shop have all contributed to an image which provides a ready target for the 'antis'. The 'anti-black' and the 'charity-begins-at-homers' naturally focus their attention on a prominent aid agency. Others suggest that tiny amounts of aid go overseas, that staff drive round in Rolls Royces and so on, unaware that the Charity Commissioners would close down any charity operating in so profligate a manner, a safeguard for the British public that many other countries do not enjoy.

Ranged on the other side are tens of thousands of supporters who give regularly to Oxfam, serve in Oxfam shops, run fund-raising events, knit blankets, sort stamps for sale, teach about the Third World, or help in many other ways. They will defend Oxfam to the last. And many more respond with astounding generosity when disaster appeals are launched. Most Oxfam supporters contribute and even defend 'the cause' in great faith. For in no way could they begin to know of all that Oxfam is involved with at any one time. Furthermore, the wider issues of trade and underdevelopment are infrequently discussed. Criticism can be levelled at Oxfam that in the constant search for funds and in getting on with the job overseas, educating and informing the supporters and wider public have taken a poor second place. But here lies the permanent dilemma. If time and money allowed, much more educational work could be undertaken at home. But recent government cuts have dried up that source of funding; and few donors large or small will contribute to development education. A further complication arises with the political limitations of British charitable law, making forceful campaigning on particular issues an uncharitable action.

Given all these limitations which affect all British overseas aid organizations, it is heartening that they have managed to develop a not inconsiderable body of support for helping some of the poorer members of this planet Earth.

The impact of Oxfam's development work

As a non-operational, non-specialist agency with Field Directors in so many parts of the world, Oxfam is in a singular position. Its flexible wide-ranging programmes provide contacts at all levels — from governments to some of the world's poorest small groups. It is not tied to any single political ideology, to any one specialist field, to any one 'type' of operating agency, nor to any rigid constitution. This has enabled Oxfam to be involved with an extremely wide range of initiatives in more than eighty countries, over nearly forty years.

Projects supported have, for the most part, been small. As more field staff have been employed, giving each one a smaller territory, so particular efforts have been made to seek out and encourage the small groups. The annual grants list now shows many more small grants for self-help than it did in the early seventies, with names unheard of outside the villages concerned. At the other end of the scale there have been larger grants than ever before — to UNHCR for staffing and running programmes for thousands of refugees in Somalia; to ministries and government agencies for literacy and agricultural programmes in post-Somoza Nicaragua; and to the Oxfam-headed consortium running the Kampuchea operation. Disaster relief and rehabilitation is costly.

Development does not necessarily require massive funds. Indeed money and the other forms of aid, outside materials and expertise, can be inappropriate or even swamp local initiative. The result may be to leave a group or an area no better off when the aid period is over than they were before it started; or, even worse, the better off are helped, leaving the poor even poorer. At best, aid should be sufficient to encourage self-help. Often the Field Director can give encouragement by just being there, representing an organization of ordinary caring people.

Much government and international aid has been devoted to large industrial projects and to infrastructure. Some of it has been useful, some not, but much of it has been relatively high cost for relatively few direct beneficiaries. Building a large dam, a highway, or an airport represents a tidy package to donor and recipient alike. It was hoped that some of the benefits of this 'easy aid' would trickle down to the poorer members of society. But too often the trickle never reached them, or else it washed them away.

The voluntary agencies never had the funds even to be tempted into this league, and few of them have worked with governments on any large and continuing scale. To appear to 'support' a particular government could prove unwise for the future should that government fall. And with much government initiative in the more sophisticated urban sector, too often benefiting only the richer members of society, the voluntary agencies including Oxfam have seen these areas as inappropriate for them.

For all the government planning that has become an accepted and common practice in most Third World countries, started by the Indian Five Year Plans, it is important to remember that government services rarely stretch satisfactorily outside the main cities. Schooling must be paid for, and secondary places are strictly limited. Health services are few or non-existent. Four out of five people in rural areas have no access to clean water. In other words, the government barely exists in large parts of the rural Third World, either because resources will not stretch that far, or because the government is not particularly concerned with welfare services, or a combination of both. (We should, perhaps, remember that government-provided medical and education services are relatively new in the developed societies, and were only made possible by a large and redistributive tax system to finance them.)

Some governments are concerned and willing to bring development to the rural poor. They are prepared to discuss with aid donors the provision of 'basic needs'. This aid concept, which was adopted during the late 1970s, implies rejection of large projects and the 'trickle down' approach. Even so, government ministries and departments are often ill-organized to meet the needs. Retention of Western governmental structures, such as the Whitehall model, which has survived coups and revolutions, perpetuates the divisions of Western-style administration, with its rigid demarcations and often competitive wrangling over resources. Women's development does not fit in to any particular ministry's purview, nor does the production and marketing of handicrafts — to mention just two aspects of the problem.

For these reasons, and many more, the voluntary agencies prefer to work at the 'grass roots'. Each situation, physical and human, will be different from what has been experienced before and the response can be made differently, an approach that is rarely possible in large government schemes. At the same time, groups can learn from one another's failures and successes. Oxfam has had the privilege of working with thousands of groups of people — on the principle of 'trickle up' rather than 'trickle down'. Its real contribution cannot be measured just in terms of the funds involved. It is often the advice, encouragement and support that are just as important; helping the poorest to *be more* as well as have more.

In the words of an 'Interpretation of Oxfam's Objectives': 'All people whether they be rich or poor, strong or weak, privileged or deprived, are interdependent and should share in the common task of seeking to achieve mankind's full potential.'

'Oxfam provides people in the United Kingdom and Ireland as well as overseas with the opportunity of playing a small part in a much larger struggle to eliminate poverty and to help mankind develop in a spirit of partnership and brotherhood.'

References

1 A Friends Meeting House is a building used by the members of the Society of Friends (Quakers) of a locality for religious and other meetings.
2 Leslie Kirkley remained with Oxfam as General Secretary from 1951 until 1961 and continued in the post of Director from 1961 to 1974. Since his retirement, Sir Leslie, as he became in 1977, has maintained close links with Oxfam and its work, being Vice-Chairman and then Chairman of the Disasters Emergency Committee, Chairman of the Standing Conference on Refugees and being on the Governing Board of the International Council of Voluntary Agencies.
3 Mervyn Jones, *Two Ears of Corn. Oxfam in Action* (London, Hodder and Stoughton, 1965), p. 35.
4 On 5 December 1958 by Resolution 1285(XIII), the United Nations General Assembly called for a World Refugee Year to be held from June 1959 to June 1960. The idea of such a year had originated with four young Conservatives, who wrote an article in the Bow Group journal *Crossbow*. The four, Christopher Chataway, Colin Jones, Trevor Philpott and Timothy Raison, had all been involved in voluntary organizations and felt the need for action of a dramatic kind to eliminate what appeared to be a permanent refugee problem in Europe. At that time not many 'international years' had been designated, but the four had been impressed by the impact achieved by the International Geophysical Year. The idea was supported by voluntary agencies and then adopted and sponsored at the United Nations by the British government. (Information from telephone conversation from Peter Willetts to Christopher Chataway, 24 October 1981.)
5 The Belgian Congo became independent on 30 June 1960. Within a few months chaos occurred as Belgians in administration, education and health withdrew from the country; the army mutinied, the richest province Katanga succeeded, and the two leading politicians, President Kasavubu and Prime Minister Lumumba, entered into a bitter dispute, refusing to recognize each other's authority.
6 The Food and Agriculture Organization of the United Nations launched the Freedom from Hunger Campaign in 1960. The idea had been proposed by the Director-General of the FAO and endorsed by the tenth session of the biennial Conference of FAO in Rome in November 1959.
7 Jones, op. cit., p. 30.
8 The BBC television children's programme, *Blue Peter*, took up Kampuchea for its Christmas appeal in 1979, hoping to raise £100,000 in seven weeks. However, this amount was raised in two days and £3 million was raised by Christmas.
9 These figures come from *Oxfam: accounts for the financial year May 1979–April 1980*, a leaflet produced by Oxfam.
10 Gill, P., *Drops in the Ocean. The Work of Oxfam 1960–1970* (London, Macdonald Unit 75, 1970), p. 106.
11 Werner, D., *Where There is No Doctor* (London, Macmillan, 1979 and Palo Alto, USA, Hesperian Foundation, 1977); translated from *Donde no hay doctor* (publishing details not available).

6 Friends of the Earth and the Conservation of Resources

TOM BURKE

Friends of the Earth was first formed in 1969 in the United States.[1] It was founded by David Brower, formerly Executive Director of the Sierra Club and then one of America's best known conservationists. The Sierra Club had been started toward the end of the nineteenth century by John Muir, a prominent naturalist: it was dedicated to the enjoyment of wilderness. From its earliest days the Sierra Club was involved in political battles to protect wilderness in the United States.

Under US law organizations which receive charitable (tax-deductible) donations may devote only a limited part of their time and resources to influencing public policy. In the early sixties Brower led the Sierra Club into a series of landmark conservation battles and strongly advocated the need to take the offensive in defending wilderness. He wished to challenge the underlying policies that generated specific projects which harmed the environment. The vigour of these campaigns provoked the Internal Revenue Service of the US Government into revoking the tax-deductible status of the Sierra Club. The consequent damage to the Club's fund raising ability led to a loss of confidence in Brower's leadership and his eventual resignation as Executive Director.

Shortly after leaving the Sierra Club, Brower was persuaded to establish a new organization. This body was to have as its specific purpose the task of waging political battles to protect the environment. From the outset it was intended not to seek tax-deductible status in order to be free to fight where, when and how the need arose. Thus it was that on 10 July 1969 FOE Inc. was formally established.

The internal pressures that led to its formation were classic. As threats to the environment grew in both number and intensity, it was inevitable that protecting the environment would cease to be an ancillary activity to enjoying it and would become an activity in its own right. It is a commonplace that institutions established with one purpose have difficulty in adjusting to new demands. Furthermore in any voluntary organization there are always stresses between young and old or new and long standing members; between those who are idealists and the pragmatists and between those who want immediate results and those prepared to wait longer. Changing external circumstances can accentuate these stresses. Impatience and inertia contend to determine the momentum of any institution. Often this results in a healthy tension which ensures that steps essential to the achievement of distant goals are not omitted any more than that the goals themselves are forgotten. When the containment cracks, as with the Sierra Club, the organization splits.

Splits need not always be destructive. Whether a split strengthens or weakens a movement depends, in part, on external factors. In this respect the Sierra Club could hardly have split at a better time. There was then a widely felt spirit of social activism in the United States. Civil rights and peace had both given rise to large popular movements drawing support from all sectors of society. The dominant style of the late sixties, especially among the young, gave prominence to natural things in rejection of the artificialities of the previous two decades. This fashionable critique of materialism was underscored by the begininnings of what became a sustained intellectual critique of the consequences of economic growth. Rachel Carson wrote 'Silent Spring'; Paul Erlich 'The Population Bomb'; Lake Erie was discovered to be dying. In April 1970 there was a massive popular and political outwelling of concern manifested during a day of environmental action in the US, Earthday. The environment joined peace and civil rights as one of a trilogy of issues that encompassed the fears and hopes of an emerging generation.

Friends of the Earth, committed not only to environmental issues but also to a forthright, even aggressive, approach to them was well placed to take advantage of this concern. Starting from scratch it was able to write its own agenda and to set its own style without the constraints of an institutional history. Having a nationally known figure as leader lent authority to its activities and encouraged financial support. It was able to respond flexibly and rapidly to the felt urgencies of the moment. Above all, however, it was fortuitous in its choice of name. Ideas are powerful instruments of change: good ideas are usually simple and infinitely transmutable to meet the needs of changing circumstances and personalities, whilst holding true to their intent. Ideas precede action, they impel change in attitude and behaviour and thus provide the basis for political change. The idea that the earth needs friends, in affirming the intimacy of mankind's destiny with that of the planet, touched a deep level of response throughout the world. 'Sahabat Alam', 'Jordens Vanner', 'Chikyu-no-Tomo', 'Prijatelyii Sveta', 'Les Amis de la Terre', are words in languages which have no common root, yet the actions they inspire share a common purpose.

FOE International

Friends of the Earth was conceived from the beginning as an international body. Originally David Brower simply appointed friends of his living outside the United States to be his personal representatives. This rather dirigiste approach to internationalization soon gave way to a more formal recruitment process, although certain of Brower's emissaries, and in particular Edwin

Matthews, then a Paris-based international lawyer, played an important catalytic role. Recruitment became a response to spontaneous initiatives in countries to which the idea spread by a process more akin to osmosis than conscious policy. It is difficult to see how any other name for the organization would have been sufficiently translatable in spirit as well as in letter to provoke such spontaneous reactions.[2] Friends of the Earth has subsequently developed into a genuinely international organization with national organizations now operating in twenty-five countries.[3] Collectively they comprise Friends of the Earth International.

It was in January 1971, less than eighteen months after the founding of FOE Inc., that substance was first given to the notion of FOE as an international organization. In that month delegates from six countries (France, Germany, Italy, Switzerland, the UK and the USA) met in the Forêt de Rambouillet just outside Paris. In June the same year, a second meeting took place at Roslagen in Sweden and a set of Governing Provisions was adopted by the participating delegates.[4] The aims of the organization were defined as 'to promote . . . the conservation, restoration and rational use of the natural resources and beauty of the Earth.' A Council of Friends of the Earth International was established as the supreme governing body of the organization with powers to admit and suspend members. The formal establishment of an international institution, nominally headquartered in San Francisco, enabled FOEI to obtain recognition by the Economic and Social Council of the United Nations (ECOSOC) as an international non-governmental organization. Subsequently FOEI has acquired consultative status at the Inter-governmental Maritime Consultative Organization (IMCO) and observer status at meetings of the International Whaling Commission (IWC).

The acquisition of formal identity was not, however, reflected in the internal organization of FOEI. Until 1980 the only structural components of FOEI were the meetings of the Council, usually annual, and the appearance of an occasional newsletter, FOE-Link. Although the idea of an international secretariat was discussed at a number of Council meetings, the dominant desire of the national organizations to assert their independence and autonomy led to successive decisions not to establish a secretariat. By 1980, however, the volume of international communication and the growing involvement of national organizations in international matters led to a decision to establish an international secretariat in Brussels. Even so, it consists of a single person whose main task is the production and circulation of FOE-Link and it is expected to find its own funding. The primacy of self-determination and consensus decision-making has been a defining characteristic of FOEI. It stems from a recognition, in part idealistic, in part pragmatic, of the need to accommodate diversity, both of opinion and approach. If this has, at times, resulted in a slowing down of the rate of development of FOE as an effective force internationally, it has also meant an absence of destructive divisions within the organization.

Few national FOE organizations have similar approaches or patterns of organization. Some have full-time staff, others do not; some are fairly centralized, others almost entirely decentralized; some work as pressure groups, some effectively as political parties, others as publishing houses. Each group tries to tailor its structure and approach appropriately to its own political circumstances. Continents require a different approach from islands. Authoritarian governments require a different style from liberal governments. Perhaps the hardest situation for many to grasp is the very real personal risks run by environmentalists in some countries. An adequate account of the work of each FOE group cannot be given in the available space. The following four groups illustrated are by no means typical, but the choice does show the diversity within FOE.

(a)   FOE in Spain has a structure not dissimilar to that of FOE in Canada. In the wake of Franco, regionalism is a strong political force. The introduction of democracy saw the birth of a number of regional environmental groups. These groups came together to form a national federation which operates under the name Los Amigos de la Tierra on national and international issues. Within the region each group operates under its own name. FOE in Spain has been particularly active in publishing environmental books as well as campaigning on energy, whaling, national parks and agricultural issues.

(b)   In New Zealand FOE employs a full-time staff of five people. It is organized in a similar way to FOE in the UK, with a national membership and local groups. As well as publishing a bi-monthly newspaper 'Earth', FOE New Zealand has active campaigns on transport, energy, pesticides, mining, industrial development and packaging. It is also the most active group in the FOEI network on Antarctica issues.

(c)   FOE in Mexico could not be more different. There is no attempt to influence national policy in the way that most European groups work. Instead FOE in Mexico, under the leadership of Arturo Aldema, is organized as a network of some 300 village-based groups. These groups work on an eco-nutrition project, seeking to educate the rural population in ways to improve their nutrition without destroying the environment.

(d)   Malaysia has one of the strongest Third World environment movements. FOE Malaysia — Sahabat Alam Malaysia — is an offshoot of the Consumer Association. The contents list of its monthly report for November 1980 tells its own story: nuclear power, river pollution, mining accidents, heavy lorries and water quality were all issues on which FOE Malaysia took action. They also wrote fourteen articles for national news media on these problems. At the time of writing they are in danger of becoming a proscribed organization if recently introduced legislation is enacted.

FOE UK

Friends of the Earth Limited is one of the two UK members of FOE International, the other being FOE Scotland.[5] FOE Ltd was formally incorporated in the UK on 5 May 1971 as the result of a chance meeting the previous August between Edwin Matthews and a Scots industrialist, Barclay Inglis. On 9 May FOE began its first significant campaign by dumping several thousand non-returnable bottles outside the London headquarters of Cadbury Schweppes Ltd. This action, together with the joint publication of a series of books on environmental issues, launched FOE Ltd as an organization.

Under UK law FOE Ltd, with its specific goal of achieving policy and legislative changes, cannot acquire charitable status. Thus the organization is structured as a company limited by guarantee having as subscribers the original founders. The subscribers appoint a Board of Directors to manage the company and the Directors in turn appoint the staff which currently numbers twenty. Strictly speaking, FOE Ltd is not a membership organization since no service is offered to supporters other than a thrice-yearly report on activities. The supporters play no direct role in forming the policy of the organization. FOE Ltd is associated via joint directors with two independent companies, Earth Resources Research and FOE Trust, both of which have charitable status. A network of local groups are FOE's contact with the community. By being seen to work in and for the local community, FOE groups are able to bring global problems into the backyard. In doing this they are the strongest source of political support for FOE. Not all FOE supporters work in their local groups and members of local groups are not required to support the national organization. Each of the 250 local groups is autonomous, choosing its own issues on which to campaign and its own policy to adopt on those issues.

Finance is a key preoccupation for every pressure group. In 1972 FOE spent exactly £11,000, mostly, then as now, on salaries. Six people were employed and most of the money not spent on salaries went into publications. By 1973 it had risen to £17,768, and this more than doubled over the next two years to £36,060 in 1975. In the next two years, as the economy went into recession, FOE's expenditure grew to £48,843 in 1976 and £123,782 in 1977. Current figures suggest that the cost of running FOE in 1980 was over £80,000 a quarter and, allowing for inflation, the budget for 1981 is approaching £300,000 a year. Throughout this expansion FOE has found its finances entirely from its own resources. Such an expansion could not have been achieved, however, were it not for the generosity of the Joseph Rowntree Social Services Trust in providing office space in central London free of charge and the forbearance of successive generations of FOE staff who have been willing to work long hours for low salaries. Although salaries are still the largest single item in FOE, accounting for over £120,000 in 1980, the salary of each staff member is only £4,500 a year, well below the national average.

Raising these substantial sums of money has largely been a matter of unremitting hard work leavened by moments of inspiration or pure fun and the occasional heart-stopping state of fear that an event would fail. Membership and trading between them account for some 65 per cent of FOE's income and it is here that the hardest and dullest work of generating income is done. The remaining 35 per cent of FOE's income comes from large donations, special events and campaign appeals. Inspiration is essential in deciding whether this is the year to invest £10,000 in an advertising appeal on whales; a wrong decision can wreck the budget.

Describing the finances of FOE Ltd, however, only tells half the story. The FOE local groups up and down the country also raise and spend a substantial amount of money on protecting the environment. Many FOE local groups are purely voluntary, raising a few hundred pounds a year to finance demonstrations, publications and meetings. Others are large operations in their own right, employing staff, maintaining premises and running projects. The activities of these groups are often financed by Government job creation programmes. FOE Birmingham for instance employs thirty people and has a budget of over £150,000 a year. As each FOE local group is an autonomous body, FOE Ltd does not consolidate their accounts into its own. Any figure for local group expenditure is an estimate. During 1980 we estimated local group expenditure at approximately £250,000, thus bringing the total amount of money spent by FOE on campaigning for the environment to over £500,000.

In 1970 the environment as an issue was the preserve of scientists, government specialists and private enthusiasts. By 1980 it was an issue high on the political agenda of most nations. FOE's early years coincided with a huge expansion in public and private discussion of environmental problems. 'Population' and 'pollution' were words on everyone's lips. The Club of Rome's famous book 'Limits to Growth' had defined, for the first time, the full scope of the problems. The publication by the Ecologist of 'Blueprint for Survival' had added colour to the sparse descriptions of the Club of Rome and, more importantly, had taken the first tentative step toward a strategy for solving the problems.

But the question to which everyone wanted an answer was 'What can I do?'. There was a sense of urgency and impending doom. Translating a broad general concern about the future of the planet into specific and effective actions is not a simple matter. All too often the impulse to do something collapses when confronted with the question of where to begin. It took FOE almost nine months of hard discussion to come up with three slight toeholds. By the autumn of 1971 these three campaigns were running: opposition to mining in Snowdonia, a beautiful mountain area, by RTZ, an attack on the fur trade's use of rare animal skins and the campaign against the non-returnable bottle.

Remote though these toeholds seemed from the great issues of resource depletion and ecological destruction, they were at least a start. As these campaigns developed and knowledge of the issues deepened, so the linkages between them became clearer. RTZ wanted to mine in Snowdonia because growing demand for copper was using up cheaper sources and making it economic to mine the low-grade deposit in the Snowdonia National Park. It was the availability of cheap energy that made it possible to mine low-grade ores economically, but that cheap energy was itself a non-renewable resource, oil. The economic growth fuelled by its wasteful use not only created the growing demand for copper but was creating a rapidly rising demand for luxury goods made from the skins and other parts of endangered animals.

For many people 'economic growth' was the enemy to be fought, for others it was over-population. To FOE what was most important was to challenge and to change the policies by which the people sharing the planet gave expression to their economic aspirations. Thus by the beginning of 1974 four areas of policy were emerging as those within which changes were most necessary in order to reduce human impact on the environment: wildlife, energy, resources and transport. FOE has subsequently developed campaigns on several fronts in each of these areas.

Over the years FOE's experience has been consolidated into a set of principles which define FOE's approach to running campaigns to protect the environment:

(a) *To remain politically non-partisan*: This principle arose, in part, from a feeling that none of the major political parties was really prepared to deal seriously with environmental issues, although there are many individual supporters in all the parties sympathetic to the environment, and, in part, from the pragmatic recognition that it would be necessary to influence whichever party was in power.

(b) *To seek the prevention rather than the cure of environmental problems*: Guided by this principle FOE's efforts have focused not just on a particular road, mine or factory, but on the whole policy that led to its development. This in turn has meant that learning to develop coherent alternative policies and thus to be able to say what FOE is for as well as what it is against.

(c) *To attack specific key issues*: Faced with the gross disparity of resources between FOE and its opponents, it was essential to avoid dissipating limited resources. No organization as small as FOE can attempt to do everything; thus it is vital to identify the heart of an issue and then to strike hard and accurately.

(d) *To build a strong full-time staff*: Organizations without a strong and professional staff have great difficulty influencing politicians, civil servants and industrialists. They are also very often unable to maintain the enthusiasm and commitment of voluntary workers through inadequate servicing. From its very first days, FOE has concentrated its resources on building its staff; salaries are the largest single item in the FOE budget.

(e) *To argue from information rather than ideals*: Not because there are no ideals, nor because moral arguments are less important, but because accurate information is the prerequisite for effective action. Few people disagree with the ethical importance of protecting the environment, but many are unsure of how to alter their daily lives or to change their decisions in order to help protect it. A small amount of accurate and concise information on how or what to do is often more helpful than reams of rhetoric.

(f) *To build a wide network of autonomous local groups*: In the final analysis it is the mood and opinions of the public at large that determines the limits within which decisions are taken. Creating a public climate in which solar power is essential and trade in endangered species unacceptable can only be done from the bottom up. The task of the local groups is to create the mass support without which the necessary shifts in national policy will not happen. But only the groups themselves can decide what issues to fight and when and how to fight them in their community.

No attempt to understand FOE Ltd would be complete without some account of the wider environment movement of which FOE is a part. The environment movement in Britain is by no means homogenous. It has developed in widely different forms, in response to varied pressures, over a considerable period of time. The bonds that hold it together are often loose, relying on temporary tactical or personal alliances more than shared analysis. It is really only in the face of the extraordinary growth in the scale of threat to the environment over the past twenty years that these very disparate groups have found any common identity at all. Nevertheless, for all the differences in both style and goals, there is now sufficient commonality of purpose for the idea of an 'environment movement' to have some meaning.

The roots of the environment movement in Britain can be traced to both the nineteenth-century naturalists and to the dissenting tradition that has been a feature of political life in Britain since the seventeenth century. From these roots have grown three interwoven, but discernibly different, strands that make up the environment movement at present: lifestyles, conservation, resources. FOE is unusual in having components of all three traditions.

The oldest strand in the environment movement is that which is least embodied in national institutions. The alternative lifestyle movement begins with the Levellers and Diggers, draws inspiration from Kropotkin and the nineteenth-century anarchists, as well as from Robert Owen and the co-operative movement in its diverse forms. Today it manifests itself in the rural and urban cooperatives, the radical health and personal development groups, the community arts organizations, the self-sufficiency movement and many other forms. A rejection of alienation and a refusal to pay the personal price of life in the industrial society are strongly characteristic of this part of the movement. But its strongest characteristic is a commitment to act rather than argue about change. Within FOE the very many people making conscious efforts to live their lives according to ecological principles constitute our strongest bridge to this part of the environment movement.

The next oldest part of the movement dates from the 1860s and 1870s. The founding of the Commons Preservation Society and the Society for the Protection of Ancient Monuments marked the beginning of the conservation movement in Britain. The primary focus of this part of the environment movement was, and remains, the preservation of something cherished for its aesthetic or amenity value. Within this group there are three distinct elements: the wildlife groups, the countryside groups and the built environment groups. Wildlife groups include the Royal Society for the Protection of Birds, the Fauna Preservation Society, the County Naturalists' Trusts, the World Wildlife Fund as well as organizations such as the Angler's Co-operative Association and the Wildfowler's Association and anti-cruelty groups such as the RSPCA and the Hunt Saboteurs. Countryside groups are those such as the Council for the Protection of Rural England, the Ramblers Association, the Youth Hostellers Association, the National Trust, the Conservation Corps and others which are primarily motivated by enjoyment of the countryside. Built environment groups would include such organizations as the Civic Trust, the Town and Country Planning Association and the Victorian and Georgian Societies. These bodies between them make up the respectable centre of gravity of the British environment movement. FOE's links to this strand of the environment movement operate both personally, in that many FOE members belong to one or more of the conservation groups, and institutionally, in that some of our campaigns, for instance on endangered species or motorways, have clear connections to the work of the conservation organizations.

The latest wave of environment bodies are those concerned with pollution and the rational use of resources. Although having some long-standing components, such as the National Society for Clean Air and the Noise Abatement Society, the main thrust of this part of the environment movement dates from the late sixties and early seventies. As well as FOE, it includes such groups as Greenpeace, the Conservation Society, Transport 2000, the Ecology Party and the Green Alliance. What is characteristic of these groups is their holistic approach and their sense of urgency. Inspired by the principles of ecology, most of the groups in this part of the environment movement are concerned with attacking the causes as well as the symptoms of environmental problems. This involves them in questioning basic values and institutional validity as well as specific policy questions. Furthermore, in the wake of publications like 'Limits to Growth' and 'the Blueprint for Survival', reinforced by later documents such as the World Conservation Strategy and the Global 2000 report[6] these organizations tend to give expression to the urgency of the problems by adopting a more aggressive and activist approach to influencing decisions.

FOE UK: International Work

Many environmental issues are intrinsically international in character — the carbon dioxide problem; the preservation of the Antarctic ecology or acid rain — demanding bilateral or multilateral agreements to produce effective action. Most environmental issues have an international dimension to them, either because they are common to many countries or because they involve trade. Problems like the environmental impact of the motor car or of building nuclear power stations occur in several countries and ideas; initiatives and policies from one country can be used elsewhere. The trade in endangered species or in resources such as tropical hardwoods or metals is a major source of environmental damage. Attempts to control this trade can involve bilateral or multilateral activities in both producer and consumer countries. FOE Ltd operates internationally at five levels; creating a national constituency for international issues, bilaterally with non-governmental (and rarely, governmental) organizations, through the Environment Liaison Centre in Nairobi on global environmental issues, through the European Environment Bureau on EEC issues and via the FOEI network. Since 1979 FOE Ltd has employed the author on a part-time basis to co-ordinate international work.

— One of the influences on the position adopted by a government in international arrangements is the visibility of the issue in question within the nation. By creating public awareness of an issue and by focusing this awareness on key decision-making points such as agenda deadlines, preparatory committees or plenary sessions, it is possible to broaden the scope of the interests reflected in national policy. The larger the domestic constituency taking an active interest in an international issue, the less easy it is for a government to deviate from a position in the interest of expediency or under pressure from commercial lobbies.

Thus, one of FOE Ltd's primary tasks has been to create a large and vocal constituency which both monitors the performance of British delegations and lobbies for the incorporation of its view into the official British position. This is important not only to achieve changes in official British policy, as for instance in obtaining British support for a ten-year moratorium on commercial whaling at the International Whaling Commission, but also for ensuring that international agreements are actually implemented. FOE pressure in the UK on the trade in endangered species led to British ratification of the Convention on the Trade in Endangered Species (CITES) earlier than would otherwise have been the case. Furthermore, by amending the legislation and monitoring its implementation, FOE has been able to ensure more vigorous application of the law by the appropriate authorities.

Pollution at sea, habitat protection, toxic substances, radioactive waste and Antarctica are other issues on which FOE has attempted to influence the British government's international behaviour by creating domestic pressure.

As well as direct lobbying of civil servants and the scientific community, FOE has used the media and its network of local groups to create popular concern. This has been notably successful in the case of whales. In recent years FOE has co-ordinated its activities closely with other environment and conservation organizations. As a result of these efforts, Britain has from time to time taken a more responsive stance to environmental matters internationally and has on occasion taken initiatives it would not otherwise have taken. It is clear that on issues where FOE and the other environmental bodies have failed to create a public visibility for the issue, most strikingly in the case of the Law of the Sea negotiations, the British position has been governed by a narrow definition of interest.

Information is the currency of politics and the ability to move accurate, up-to-date information rapidly around the globe has been one of the key factors in the growing strength of environmental groups. Whilst there are formal networks along which information is passed, the most valuable material is usually a product of bilateral links with organizations in other countries. This is especially important in the North Atlantic and OECD contexts where common problems and common responses has meant that information generated in one country, particularly scientific, technical and economic information, has been immediately relevant elsewhere. The operation of Freedom of Information Acts in countries such as Sweden and the USA has greatly increased the volume and importance of bilateral information exchange.

This aspect of the international operations of FOE has been most important in the field of energy policy and of nuclear energy policy in particular. The almost universal adoption of the pressurized water reactor throughout the non-communist world has led to a large flow of information on reactor design, safety, economics and a whole range of other related issues. Much of this information has originated in the United States where the openness of government, the large policy review community and the large number of academic institutions has generated a huge availability of data. FOE Ltd in Britain has often received information through unofficial channels close to, and even on occasions in advance of, the transmission of that information through official government channels. There have also been occasions when FOE Ltd was able to obtain, officially or unofficially, information to which we had been denied access by the government in the UK.

At the Windscale inquiry into a nuclear fuel reprocessing plant a considerable proportion of the evidence submitted by FOE Ltd was based on information originating in other countries and transmitted to FOE Ltd via environmental organizations. Uranium mining and radioactive waste disposal are other issues in which FOE has participated in extensive bilateral exchanges of information with organizations in Canada, Australia, France, Ireland, the United States, Sweden and elsewhere. Uranium mining as an issue has also generated exchanges of information with indigenous people's organizations in Australia and Namibia.

The potential for co-ordinated action on common issues between groups in different countries is still largely unexploited. Whaling is one issue in which demonstrations and other actions have been co-ordinated internationally, largely as a result of the focus provided by meetings of the IWC. In the energy field FOE has participated in Sun Day celebrations aimed at consciousness-raising on solar energy. There have also been a small number of specific initiatives such as the joint publication in Australia and the USA of leaked documents revealing the existence of a uranium cartel, or FOE Ltd's participation in a USA day of action on recycling by demonstrating outside the US embassy in London. On a small number of occasions FOE UK has participated with the Natural Resources Defense Council in the United States in taking legal action in American courts. Generally, however, bilateral action requires co-ordination of planning which is still too expensive for environmental groups to arrange.

One process that does bring groups from different countries together is joint participation at sessions of intergovernmental organizations, particularly the United Nations and the European Community. The UN Conference on the Human Environment held in Sweden in June 1972 was a turning point for global awareness of environmental questions (see the section in chapter 10 on how this conference was convened). In preparations for the conference many governments were confronted for the first time with the necessity of having an environmental policy. A large number of non-governmental groups focused their work on trying to influence the outcome of the conference and the Swedish government had to respond by organizing an unofficial Environment Forum alongside the official diplomatic conference. Here the discussion was more wide-ranging, with attitudes generally being highly critical of the government delegates, but on some subjects, notably whaling, delegates did attend Forum events and influence was exerted on the conference's decisions. Since 1972 this innovation has been copied and all major UN conferences have been held alongside a non-governmental forum.

A second innovation to the world of diplomacy was introduced at the Stockholm conference: the production by NGOs of an *ad hoc*, specialist newspaper to cover the proceedings of the conference and the Forum. The idea of a daily newspaper for this conference had originated six months previously in discussions between FOE representatives and the *Ecologist* magazine. A response in part to the confusion that surrounds all large international gatherings and in part to the heavy dominance in the conventional media of the official view, the newspaper was seen as allowing NGOs to comment on the Conference issues as they emerged. In particular it gave the NGOs a tool for co-ordinating lobbying and for introducing items omitted from the official agenda. The newspaper, called the 'Stockholm Conference ECO', was delivered before breakfast each morning to delegates' hotel rooms, embassies, press centres and other locations. It was widely read by delegates, NGO representatives and journalists, often succeeding in breaking news ahead of the main media. It thus had some influence on the way the Conference was reported to the rest of the world. One enthusiastic member of the USA delegation was reported as saying, 'The crew that put out ECO should attend all international conferences so we'll know what the hell is going on.' Subsequently FOE has played a part in publishing newspapers at several UN conferences, at meetings of the IWC and at other international gatherings.

The Environment Liaison Centre (ELC) was established in Nairobi, Kenya in 1974 by non-governmental organizations (NGOs) concerned about the environment and human settlements. It is a communication link with the United Nations Environment Programme (UNEP) and the UN Centre for Human Settlements (HABITAT), both headquartered in Nairobi. The ELC was also created to strengthen communication and co-operation among NGOs in the developing and developed world, working in the field of environment, development, natural resources and human settlements.

The idea of establishing such a centre in Nairobi was first considered by NGOs at the 1972 UN Stockholm Conference. In 1973 they formed the International Assembly of Non-Governmental Organizations Concerned with the Environment (INASEN). It consisted of major international NGOs, including the International Institute of Environment and Development (IIED), International Council of Voluntary Agencies, International Union of Architects, Friends of the Earth and the International Union of Local Authorities. INASEN, in turn, created the Environment Liaison Board, charging it with the responsibility of establishing the Centre. In 1977, with the Centre firmly established, INASEN and ELB were dissolved.

At present the ELC has almost 200 member organizations from all regions of the world and in February 1981 was recommended for Consultative Status with the UN Economic and Social Council (ECOSOC) by its NGO Committee. The ELC annual budget is US $300,000. The secretariat is composed of five professional and four administrative employees. Usually, five medium-term volunteers per year work at the ELC's office. The Centre is incorporated as a company under Kenyan Law. It holds an Annual General Meeting in Nairobi which elects the Members of the Board of Directors. The Board can have up to fourteen members, of which FOE International is currently one.

The ELC publishes a quarterly bulletin, ECOFORUM. The bulletin acts as a focal point where NGOs from around the world can share information, programmes and strategies. It also functions as a 'window' on UNEP and HABITAT, analysing programmes, reviewing areas of activity, describing past and future meetings, noting personnel changes, reporting on Governing Council decisions; and generally advising NGOs on positions being taken by the two UN programmes. ECOFORUM is published in English, French and Spanish; it is distributed to 4,000 NGOs, the majority in developing countries. In co-operation with UNEP, the ELC has promoted the marking of World Environment Day each year on 5 June. The ELC has published special NGO resource packs, distributed to over 7,000 organizations each year. Since 1978, the ELC has focused the packs on the theme 'Development Without Destruction', emphasizing the need for environmentally-sound development in the Third World and a 'conserver society' in the overdeveloped industrialized countries. FOE Ltd in Britain has not participated actively in the work of the ELC since its early involvement in founding it. Other FOE national groups, however, have played a more active part. FOE Inc. in the USA is currently working closely with the ELC in preparation for the United Nations Conference on New and Renewable Sources of Energy.

The European Environment Bureau is a coalition of sixty-three leading non-governmental organizations concerned with environmental matters within the European Community. It was founded in 1974 with FOE Ltd as one of the founding members and has a small Brussels-based secretariat. Its mission is to co-ordinate the input of the environmental NGOs into EEC policy-making. The main work of the Bureau consists of organizing seminars and conferences on a range of specific issues, including agriculture, energy, transport and toxic substances. Those meetings provide an opportunity for member organizations to establish personal relations with officials of the Commission, experts and their colleagues in other countries, to educate themselves about the European dimension of the issue in question and to develop common positions on key policy questions. The meetings often provide the basis for Bureau publications such as that on 'The Community's Financial Instruments and their Impact on the Environment' or 'Toxic Substances'. The Bureau also publishes a bi-monthly magazine, 'Eco-Forum', in three languages — English, French and German — which is circulated widely to the member organizations and elsewhere. Other important publications have included a manifesto, *One Europe One Environment*, summarizing the general approach and concerns of the Bureau's members, and recently a memorandum to Gaston Thorn outlining the Bureau's view of the priorities to be adopted by the newly appointed Commission.

The Bureau also alerts member organizations to initiatives by the Community institutions and co-ordinates environmental response to these initiatives. In recent years, to facilitate the responsiveness of the Bureau, and its members, a number of permanent working parties have been established. Currently these cover the Common Agricultural Policy, Energy, Transport and Toxic substances with an additional working party on Economics and the Environment in the process of formation.

FOE Ltd has played a very active role in EEB affairs both at the European level and within British politics. FOE provides an honorary press officer for the Bureau to advise on media relations and to assist in the presentation of Bureau policy. This has been an important institutional function enabling FOE to contribute its experience both politically and administratively to the development of the Bureau. It has also meant that FOE in Britain has been able to establish strong links with both other FOE and other organizations in Europe.

As one of the few environmental organizations with a relatively large and experienced professional staff, FOE has been able to provide information and policy advice to the Bureau. Thus, FOE has found itself playing an important role in Bureau policy on energy, toxic substances, whaling and beverage containers. As the EEC has taken an increasingly more vigorous role in many areas of policy, and on environmental policy in particular, FOE has been able not only to infuence directly the emergence of European policy but to open a new avenue of approach to influencing national policy. On the beverage container issue, for example, FOE was able, through the Bureau, both to exchange technical information with the Commission and to co-ordinate its actions with those of the Commission. Since much of the opposition to Commission proposals in this area stemmed from the British government, it was advantageous for the Commission to have a link to British NGOs. Careful timing allowed Commission initiatives to reinforce and be reinforced by FOE initiatives in Britain. Furthermore, the personal contact, mutual respect and confidence established by this co-operation provided a good basis for future joint actions. The existence of the Bureau has created another focus within Britain for co-ordination and co-operation between environmental organizations. There are thirteen British members of the Bureau who meet from time to time both to discuss Bureau internal matters and to co-ordinate efforts to influence British positions on European matters.

The FOE International network functions much more as an information exchange than as a policy or action co-ordinator. This primacy of information exchange is in part a result of the widely different priorities and perceptions of the member groups which would make policy co-ordination or joint action difficult to agree, and in part due to the cost and difficulty of co-ordination. Few of the FOE national groups have full-time staffs and fewer still enough resources to employ a specific person on international affairs. Even, as in the case of the USA and the UK, where full- or part-time staff are employed on international matters, there is little, if any, money for travel and communications. Thus, real attempts to co-ordinate policy or action are few and those tend to be arranged in an *ad hoc* manner as a result of coincidental meetings. What co-ordinated international presence exists is normally a result of one national group seeking a mandate from the Council to act as 'lead' group for FOE International on a specific issue or at a specific meeting. Thus FOE UK leads for FOE International at both the IWC and at IMCO since both those international agencies are based in Britain. FOE New Zealand leads on Antarctica issues and FOE US has normally taken a lead on energy issues and in the production of NGO newspapers at UN conferences.

The bulk of the routine work of FOE UK in relation to the FOE network is, however, information exchange. All the FOE sister groups receive copies of all newsletters and publications sent to our own local groups. Wherever possible we support this by more detailed information on request. A number of FOE UK publications have been translated and published by other groups, normally without any copyright charge. As part of the assistance that we supply to new or potential national groups, FOE UK usually sends a full set of publications and promotional materials. Recruitment of new national bodies is not the specific responsibility of any part of FOEI and it is a clear policy of the organization that initiatives must originate from the country in question. In practice, FOE UK and FOE US have played the largest part in developing initial inquiries through to the point of formal application. FOE UK has recently played an important part in helping groups of people in Cyprus, Sri Lanka and Papua New Guinea acquire the necessary confidence and expertise to found new organizations. Currently we are also encouraging initiatives in India and Taiwan.

The Campaign against Whaling

There is no typical way in which FOE approaches the international aspects of its work. On an issue like energy, the emphasis has been on an intellectual critique of conventional policy; on the trade in endangered species, the emphasis has been on harmonizing national and international initiatives. Although not typical, the FOE campaign on whales does illustrate most of the approaches used in campaigning on international issues. FOE is frequently asked how a particular campaign is chosen from all of the possibilities available. Why not elephants or turtles? Why animals rather than plants? Isn't the build-up of carbon dioxide in the atmosphere more important than anything else? It would be reassuring, but deceitful, to say that options are carefully considered, pros and cons finely weighed on deeply scientific and political grounds, arguments analysed and measured decisions finally arrived at. In fact enthusiasm, personal commitment, popular opinion, strong hunches and the availability of desk space and funding are just as important as purely intellectual factors.

The campaign to save whales did not so much begin as emerge. No one is quite sure exactly when FOE decided to take up the cause of the whales, but during the early part of 1971 the fate of the great whales was a recurring feature of discussion within FOE. The success of our transatlantic colleagues in influencing their governments' policy may have been the catalyst that turned discussion into action. Or it may simply have been the enthusiasm of Joan McIntyre of Project Jonah. Whatever it was, the late spring of 1971 found FOE's director, Graham Searle and its newly joined, and as yet unpaid, wildlife campaigner Angela King, engaged in conversation with Christine Stevens of the USA-based Animal Welfare Institute. Out of that conversation came a definitive decision to campaign on whales. By 21 June a directors' meeting was formally noting a decision to proceed with 'the whales project'.

But how could the issue be tackled? Stopping fleets of ships with arguments is a largely unpractised art and no one in FOE had any previous experience. So there then followed almost a year of solid research: going through the International Whaling Commission records to establish the history of the organization, writing to hundreds of companies seeking information on goods containing whale products, collecting and reading every book ever published on whales. Meanwhile the whale became a major issue at the 1972 Stockholm conference. An American group, the Hog Farm Commune of New Mexico, held a teach-in on the subject and, because the Secretary-General of the conference, Maurice Strong, agreed to take part, many of the delegates attended. The following day a demonstration was held in the centre of Stockholm, with a bus made up as a near life-size model of a whale. Among the conference decisions the delegates voted 53 to 0 for a ten-year moratorium on commercial whaling. Then just before the 1972 IWC meeting in London, BBC television showed a film called 'Whales, Dolphins and Man' by Simon Campbell-Jones. In the *Radio Times* it announced that anyone wanting further information should contact FOE. Within a few days 2,000 letters had arrived and the whale campaign was under way.

Politically, FOE's campaign has had two main prongs: to obtain a ten-year moratorium on commercial whaling and to challenge the record and legitimacy of the IWC. Since the Stockholm vote for a moratorium indicated the depth of global support for an end to whaling, FOE has concentrated its efforts on ensuring that this issue was raised at each IWC and that it was supported by the British government. On several occasions a majority of IWC members voted for a moratorium only to have the motion fail by a whisker to obtain the necessary three-quarters majority. Even if it had succeeded, there is no guarantee that the Japanese or Russians would have accepted the IWC's verdict. Under the Commission's '90-day' rule any member can object to a decision within 90 days and have it set aside. The Commission has been fatally flawed by its dual responsibility to protect both whales and whalers. In practice this has often meant that it ignored its own scientific advice, in order to protect the whalers rather than the whales. It was for these reasons that FOE in 1976 proposed that the role of the IWC be taken over by the United Nations Environment Programme.

Economically the issue has been simple. If there were no market for whale products, there would be no incentive to catch whales. How then can the market for whale products be eliminated? FOE's research found that there were substitutes for every single whale product from pet food to leather treatment oils. Thus we argued that there was no reason why the whale-using industries should not stop using whale products and why governments should not ban the import of whale products. On the basis of this evidence whale groups all over the world launched boycotts of goods containing whale products.

Ignorance has been the predominant characteristic of the science of whales.

Data collection has often been a hit and miss affair and much of the data that have been collected have not been properly processed or interpreted. Because most of our knowledge of whales is of dead whales, we are unable to construct reliable models of how whale populations grow or decline. This is a situation that cries out for error on the side of caution. As the arguments developed FOE and other groups fought for and won the right to be present at meetings of the scientific and technical committees and mounted a sustained attack on the scientific basis of IWC policy.

The sustained critique of policy by non-governmental observers is not normally a powerful influence on government delegations. However, FOE mounted a series of publicity events around each IWC meeting, some of which drew global attention. The positions and votes of the delegates came under increasing scrutiny by the media. These efforts in London were complemented by major publicity drives in other countries with the result that the public in each nation was constantly aware of its government's position on whaling. Thus we were able to establish the classic position for effective pressure of squeezing the officials between sustained and informed policy critique on the one hand and public opinion on the other.

There have been whale funerals, floating whales, all-night vigils, pickets and flying whales; concerts by David Bowie, Mike Oldfield and Georgie Fame; posters from thousands of children; once a model whale, complete with blood, was slaughtered on the pavement; on another occasion 15,000 people gathered in Trafalgar Square. But ensuring that the IWC met in the full glare of public opinion is only one of the tactics that FOE has used in its whale campaign. Other tactics have involved direct pressure on the Russian and Japanese Governments by demonstrations, boycott of goods, urging adults and children in the UK to write to the Prime Ministers of the two countries. There can be few documents that both Sir James Goldsmith, a right-wing industrialist, and Hugh Scanlon, a left-wing trade unionist, would find themselves able to sign, yet both signed a petition to the Prime Ministers of Japan and Russia asking them to stop whaling. On one occasion FOE organized a large advertisement in *The Times* urging the IWC to agree a ten year moratorium on whaling signed by a whole string of the very famous. At the last minute a phone call came from the Duke of Edinburgh's secretary. The Duke had heard of the advertisement and wanted to add his name to the list.

But the real successes of the whale campaign have not been won by the very famous, important though their help has been. It has been the unremitting efforts of thousands of committed individuals that has made the real difference: above all the hundreds of thousands of letters to government, to politicians, to industries. Although it is often an apparently unrewarding task, it is quite clear from the feedback received that it was the sheer volume of correspondence that persuaded 335 MPs to sign a parliamentary motion calling for an end to commercial whaling. It was the same pressure of correspondence that persuaded the sperm oil-using industries to find substitutes ahead of the EEC ban, and that also persuaded the main refiners of sperm oil to cease operations.

Whales have been a dominant campaigning issue in FOE for ten years. The first positive progress occurred in 1973 with the achievement of a ban on the import of Baleen Whale products into Britain. Between 1974 and 1979 intensive lobbying at each and every IWC led to major reductions in the numbers of whales taken and to a considerable strengthening of the whale management regime and more stringent standards for whale science. Although progress was slower in 1980, it is clear that the five years of intensive campaigning have substantially altered the posture of the IWC.

The campaign in Britain reached a peak during 1979 and this domestic success established a base for further international action. In this year a major shoe manufacturer, Clark's, ceased using whale products as a result of consumer pressure and the availability of alternatives. They were rapidly followed by other leather users and manufacturers and by the Ministry of Defence. The Conservative Party pledged to end the trade in whale products if elected and when it took office launched an initiative at EEC level to obtain a ban on the trade in whale products within the European Community. This initiative was strongly supported by both the European Commission and the European Parliament, both of which institutions were lobbied by FOE. In 1980 the Council of Ministers approved a directive prohibiting the import of whale products into the European Community. A further distinct step forward was a decision by the 1981 session of the IWC that there should be a complete moratorium on the killing of sperm whales and also that non-explosive harpoons should be banned on the grounds of cruelty. It remains to be seen whether countries such as Japan, Iceland and Norway will observe these restrictions.

Conclusion

It is beyond question that in the twelve years since FOE began the prospect for the human environment has darkened rapidly. This statement imples no criticism of FOE's efforts, nor of the great many other organizations that have worked on environmental problems. Neither is it a counsel of despair. But in viewing the future of any institution it is vital to distinguish effort from achievement, movement from progress and commitment from strength. A spate of recent major studies, including the Brandt report, the US government's 'Global 2000' report, OECD's 'Interfutures' study and the World Conservation Strategy, have all confirmed the main thrust of the fears that led to the founding of FOE. Emphasis has certainly shifted: renewable resource issues are now perceived to be much more pressing than non-renewable resource problems (with the exception of oil); institutional, political and social barriers to change are now a more urgent threat than physical limits. But the central critique, that the ecological basis of the economy is being undermined, is more valid than ever.

The Global 2000 report concluded that: 'If present trends continue, the world in 2000 will be more crowded, more polluted, less stable ecologically and more vulnerable to disruption than the world we live in now.' Its hope was that these trends could be changed. But to do so will require co-ordinated and far-sighted international effort on an unprecedented scale, precisely at a time when the conditions for such an effort are deteriorating. The rapidly changing pattern of financial surpluses has stressed the international monetary system that has sustained economic growth since the war. The uncertainties generated by the slow collapse of the Bretton Woods arrangements have led to a retreat into nationalistic policies, added momentum to arms expenditure and a decline in confidence in international mechanisms.

Joint actions require a shared perception of the problems, a common will to solve them and authoritative and fair institutions to implement that will. At a time when governments everywhere are confused into inertia by a coalescence of internal and external pressures, the role of the international NGOs becomes increasingly important. Single-issue groups such as FOE can act as bridges of co-operation independent of political belief, ideological commitment and cultural difference. It is vital for the future that FOE, together with the international NGOs working on peace, development, poverty, human rights and other issues, construct such bridges in order to provide a foundation of understanding on which to build the necessary international institutions.

References

1 A small nature protection organization, Los Amigos de la Tierra, has been in existence in El Salvador for more than thirty years. Shortly after Friends of the Earth was established, the existence of this organization became known and it was invited to join the Friends of the Earth International network.
2 Only in Holland, where the name Freunde der Erde has unpleasant associations with the Germany occupation, has this not been true. The Dutch group operate under the name Vereniging Milieudefensie and state their affiliation to Friends of the Earth International in English.
3

Australia	France	Italy	Portugal	Thailand
Austria	Germany	Japan	Scotland	UK
Belgium	Greece	Malaysia	Spain	USA
Canada	Holland	Mexico	Sweden	Yugoslavia
El Salvador	Ireland	New Zealand	Switzerland	

Four countries: Brazil, Cyprus, Papua New Guinea and Sri Lanka have applied for membership and will be formally admitted in October 1981.
4 The six founding countries were different from those which attended the Rambouillet meeting, consisting of France, Germany, Holland, Sweden, the UK and the USA.
5 Until 1977, FOE Ltd was the only UK member of FOEI. In anticipation of devolution and in response to environmental sympathy for regional movements, it was decided in 1977 to establish FOE Scotland as a separate legal entity which then applied to the FOE Council for membership in its own right. For a short period FOE Quebec was similarly separately represented from FOE Canada.
6 The most readily available source for the World Conservation Strategy is Robert Allen, *How to save the world. Strategy for world conservation* (London, Kogan Page, 1980). Barney, G. O., *The Global 2000 Report to the President of the US. Entering the 21st Century* (Oxford and New York, Pergamon, 1979).

7 The United Nations 'Women's Conference' and International Linkages in the Women's Movement

GEORGINA ASHWORTH

The contemporary women's movement is not one single international or national pressure group. As a phenomenom of the 1970s and 1980s, it has taken many forms and there have been many different stimuli to indigenous activity all over the world. It was described as 'the most global social movement' by Maria Lourdes de Pintassiglo (who was briefly Portugal's first female Prime Minister — a doughty revolutionary, chemical engineer and feminist, now in exile). The occasion for the remark was what many take to be the most visible expression there has been of a global women's movement, that is, the opening of the *United Nations Decade for Women Conference* in Copenhagen in July 1980. The conference was held at the mid-point of the UN Decade for Women (1975–85), and the principal object was to assess progress made since 1975 by governments in the implementation of the World Plan of Action for the Decade adopted at a previous conference in Mexico in 1975.[1] It was also to debate and adopt a Programme of Action for the remaining five years. Although this gathering became known as the 'Women's Conference', it was officially at all times an intergovernmental conference and not a conference of the women's movement.

While 145 governments sent delegations,[2] some 135 international non-governmental organizations in Consultative Status with the UN were present as Observers, with representatives from France to Fiji and Alaska to Australia.[3] With the exception of a few brief interventions (statements) in the First and Second Committees and a single fifteen minute joint statement in Plenary, presented after numerous delays by the President of the Geneva-based Conference of NGOs,[4] they were restricted to listening, lobbying and grumbling.

The diplomatic conference was held in the Bella Centre — a stark industrial exhibition hall with manœuvrable false walls that were not without symbolism. Two miles away was the non-governmental 'Forum'. This was an 'alternative conference' simultaneous with and symbiotic to the intergovernmental conference, as has become customary at all major United Nations conferences since the 1972 Conference on the Human Environment. Here, in the modern maze of the University of Copenhagen's Amager campus, was the 'global movement'. The Forum attracted some 8,000 participants from formally recognized NGOs, from national women's organizations and action groups to individuals with no formal association. In the space of ten days, these 8,000 daily organized or attended between fifty to seventy 'workshops' (discussion seminars) on every aspect of the human condition.

This chapter will trace the origins of the diplomatic conference and of the Forum, the relationships between them and the issues involved. The focus for the Decade for Women is on 'Equality, Development and Peace', with sub-themes of health, education and employment.[5] The currency of ideas available in Copenhagen in 1980 on these issues will be explored.

The Position of Women in Society

The women's movement is about participation, and the absence of participation, in different forms of power. The substance of political power and the power of capital, even state capital, is concentrated both physically and metaphysically in the hands of men. The power to re-create the species belongs to most women. They are not alternative forms of power, although they are often contraposed or perceived as such: they have different dimensions. It is the relationship between these dimensions that is fundamental to democratic participation in every sphere and form of decision-making in human society. That is, no social or political philosophy has yet developed an integrated and workable role for women within it.

The emanicipation or advancement of women is frequently envisaged as a progression from access to the vote to a gradual, modest and dispersed scaling of hierarchical ladders, when and where an expanding economy allows. The conical edifices of state, corporation, religion, armed, civil and social services are the means and end for the accession of women to the nation's political and economic life. Instruments of non-discrimination may be enacted to demonstrate equality of opportunity into these cones of privilege. This gradualist approach chooses to neglect the changes in and proliferation of international and transnational institutions, particularly since World War II, and the reproduction of heirarchical structures in the 'new' states all over the world. The immense growth in the number and size of bureaucratic entities has increased the locations of power and the tools for exclusion from power.[6]

The gradualist approach also neglects the politics of procreation. Reproduction power is, unlike money or status, distributed on equal terms among women. While infertility was formerly and, to an altered extent, still is a form of deviance from the performance of this function, many childless women used to have greater liberty for their 'advancement' (provided they had economic independence) even before they gained the privilege of the vote. While women have this one-dimensional power, they are allowed to shadow the structures of privilege or class as wives, but seldom participate in their own right, either in statistical or in real terms. When registered as 'economically active' they are, in the main, occupationally segregated and tagged with low status, consequent low pay and limited consultative access.[7] When not 'economically active', they do not exist other than as adjuncts to a 'head of household' or 'chief economic supporter',[8] even if, as international surveys indicate, they may work forty to eighty hours a week for no financial reward. 'What is invisible does not count', J. K. Galbraith has remarked in this context, also arguing that the 'household' or family as the unit of consumer choice again obscures the balance or imbalance in the function and role of married women, within both the choice-making and household activities.[9] The occlusion of women from participation in decision-making in their own right other than through the party political vote is simultaneously obscured.

Fertility, while a form of power, was and is still also an instrument of physical and social subordination: constant child-bearing and child-rearing limits life options and at the very same time is used to 'justify' this limitation. The widespread availability of contraception and abortion in recent years seemingly puts greater liberty within reach of many of the world's women. Conversely, it could be said to place the denial of physiological fulfilment and access to 'advancement' within reach of women, which may offend the present arbiters of national policy. While choice seems possible, the supply of contraceptives is determined by capital, medical care by state capital, and natalist policy is determined throughout the world by predominantly male legislatures (or by military governments). Choice and liberty are restricted by many other factors before women can even attempt to stretch out for the ladders of advancement.

Many of the trip-wires between women and participation in life decision-making are couched in the mind, if manifest in law, administration and custom. In an analysis of the anomaly that while 41 per cent of the British work-force is female only 3 per cent of parliamentary seats in the United Kingdom are occupied by women, David Marquand did not restrict the explanation to awkward hours, unshared domestic responsibilities and problems of patronage, which are all very real to women candidates.[10] By examining the attitudes expressed towards the pregnancy and motherhood of a young woman Member of Parliament, he concluded that the hostility manifest towards her was not based on the 'indecency' of a bulging womb or breast-feeding amid portraits of past parliamentarians, but on masculine fear of this demonstration of female power within the context of political power. The 'indecency' arose from the collision of the two.

It is very possible to recognize the symptoms of this fear in other institutions: the churches, clubs, financial institutions, and military services are conspicuous bastions of male seclusion and collusion in Britain and elsewhere.[11] The hierarchies of the civil, health and social services and most traditional industries have few women participating at levels higher than the clerical equivalent of NOCs.[12] 'Containment' is in the language of international politics,[13] but it may equally be applied to the purpose and process of curtailing access of the 'inner enemy' to the instruments of their self-determination. The law, religious 'truth', myths, language, attributed images, assumed expertise, derogatory jokes[14] and force may all be employed to restrict the equality of women.

In controlling both resources and authority, the male may also determine the priorities of and beneficiaries in the domestic, national and international family.[15] War, industry, education, health and food production lie in, or have been assumed into, his hands. If there is any doubt in his value system, he may invoke the metaphysical support of a male deity or prophet and his 'en-Bibled' interpreters. This is not to deny that many of these factors may be employed to restrict other men within society. Those who are themselves physiologically different by skin colour or disablement are subjects of similar subliminal fears[16] and overt discrimination and are with women the first to feel the touch of fascism.[17] Some men, who may have come to understand their own advantages and the official disadvantage of women, may be at the mercy of collective male ridicule or indeed of collective or individual female distrust.[18]

The United Nations Commission on the Status of Women

The United Nations Decade for Women originated within the UN Commission on the Status of Women (hereafter referred to as the Commission). To this body was granted the custodianship of women's rights in the period immediately succeeding World War II. It was established by the Economic and Social Council of the UN at first as a sub-commission of the Commission for Human Rights in 1946 and a year later as a full Commission.[19] The USA and the UK among others opposed its formation on the grounds that women's rights could be adequately cared for under 'human rights'. The vigour of several prominent Latin American social reformers like Bertha Lutz, who contributed to the drafting of the UN Charter and later with Eleanor Roosevelt the Universal Declaration of Human Rights, convinced other ECOSOC delegates that a special body was required.[20] Successive UK governments have on the whole continued to maintain a conservative attitude towards the functioning of the Commission.

The Commission's terms of reference were to prepare recommendations and reports 'promoting women's rights in political, economic, civil, social, and educational fields' and on urgent problems requiring immediate attention 'with the object of implementing the principle that men and women shall have equal rights'.[21] During the following decade the Commission developed the Convention on the Political Rights of Women, in response to the fact that only twenty-five countries had yielded political (voting) rights to women by 1945. (France, for example, only changed its Constitution to this object in 1945 — Switzerland eventually in 1971. India's 1948 Constitution granted full and equal rights to women in all fields well before equal opportunities legislation was enacted in the USA or UK.) With the co-operation of UNESCO and the other UN agencies, related Conventions were enacted.[22] In its 'Guidelines Principles' the Commission had no authority other than to make recommendations towards non-discrimination:

many of these are still largely ignored by member states. For instance, the participation of women in national delegations to other committees and principal organs of the UN is very low and nominations to appointments above General Service levels within the Secretariat and agencies are infrequent.[23]

The Commission had no authority to develop a constituency, but ties were formed with those agencies that could break its isolation, assist in the preparation of legal measures and to which the Commission could make recommendations evolving from its own work. The Human Rights Commission was assisted in the drafting of the International Covenants, and the Trusteeship Council was asked to report on the situation of women in trust territories. ECOSOC Resolution 1503 was to grant NGOs access to the Human Rights Commission and to begin to play 'a more active and influential role than in any other organ of the UN.[24]

The Commission has a limited membership, but has expanded from nine to thirty-two members, who are nominated by governments for election on a regional basis. The expansion in numbers was to reflect the increase in UN membership as more states gained independence in the 1960s. This, above all, combined with the re-development of the women's movement in the wake of the civil rights movement in the Americas, propelled the Commission well beyond its tentative first years.[25] The two stimulants for American women activists in the 1960s were, on the one hand, recognizing that the rights they struggled for on behalf of others were not available to them, while the 'civilization' their country was defending in SE Asia failed to recognize their contribution to it.[26] On the other, the new political nations were reproducing the 'Whitehall' or 'Paris' model of political administration, which occluded women except as dependants.

Women and Development

The arrival of development as a major issue in world politics had its impact on the Commission. The role of women in agriculture was debated as early as 1963 with FAO; contact over the 'population explosion' developed with UNICEF and UNFPA; and eventually a formal relationship with UNDP was established in 1972. The General Assembly's Proclamation of the First Development Decade brought about a revision in the Commission's principles and produced a Programme of Concerted Action in 1970, which set forth minimum targets for all UN member states to achieve in education, training, health, unemployment and maternity protection for women, but it was not equipped with monitoring machinery.[27]

In 1970 a landmark book was published that has become a textbook in the USA, but is now out of print in UK where it first appeared. *Women's Role in Economic Development*, by a dour Danish economist, Ester Boserup, tackled the 'serious omission' of the 'particular problems of women' in economic development then being espoused by 'Third World' governments. Dr Boserup analysed the differential impact of development on women and men. 'Economic and social development unavoidably entails the disintegration of the division of labour among the two sexes traditionally established in the village. With modernisation of agriculture and migration to the towns, a new sex pattern of productive work must emerge, for better or worse.' This 'danger' was diagnosed as also being dependent on the varying customs and other economic and social features of different societies in the developing world.[28]

Boserup's book and the fate of 'women in development' were to influence the Commission, NGOs, individuals within UN agencies and within 'donor' governments and philanthropic foundations, creating the climate for the International Women's Year which was recommended by the Commission to the General Assembly in 1972.[29] That 'modernization' is causing poverty by depriving women of traditional livelihoods, but not replacing them with alternative sources of income or economic authority, is a direct outcome of the models created by Western economic planning. The process results from a combination of Western traditional attitudes to womanhood, exported in the Whitehall or Parisian colonial administrative structures and indigenous traditional attitudes to women.

Since Boserup's first examination of this concern, there has been an increasing number of bibliographies, research reports, case-studies,[30] and pilot-schemes for small-scale alternative models of development carried out by small newer research institutes,[31] by the established NGOs and within the UN and its agencies, FAO and UNDP in particular.[32] The World Plan of Action adopted at the opening of the Decade in 1975 was primarily concerned with 'integrating women into development'. The US Congress added the Percy Amendment to its Foreign Relations Act which stated that US foreign assistance 'be administered so as to give particular attention to those projects, programmes and activities which tend to integrate women into the national economies of developing countries, thus improving their status and assisting the total development effort', and established a Women in Development Office in 1974.[33] The Canadian, Norwegian, Swedish and Danish governments have taken similar measures, developing specific units for 'Women in Development' within their foreign ministries. The UK Government appointed a part-time adviser.[34]

Many UN agencies appointed Women's Project Officers, and opened Centres for Women and Development in all the Economic Commissions except the one for Europe. The first was the Asian and Pacific Centre for Women in Development (APCWD) in Tehran, with the remarkable Austrialian, Elizabeth Reid, in charge. Dr Reid, formerly adviser on women's issues to the Whitlam administration, was subsequently to organize the Tribune in Mexico in 1975, and to become Principal Officer of the Copenhagen intergovernmental conference after a brief commission to advise on the establishment of a 'Women and Development' division in the Commonwealth Secretariat. The international careers of a handful of such women embody the official international effort on behalf of women.[35] Regional seminars, leadership training sessions, and rural women's programmes were developed.[36]

International Women's Year itself was marked by the Mexico Conference which adopted unanimously a *World Plan of Action* and established the UN Voluntary Fund for Women (funds from which do not have to be channelled through governments).[37] It was also agreed to develop the Declaration on the Elimination of All Forms of Discrimination[38] into a Convention,[39] and to establish an International Institute for Research and Training for the Advancement of Women.[40]

The impetus in the USA was not lost with the National Women's Conference taking place in Houston in 1977 which adopted several international resolutions.[41] Not to be outdone, the OECD held a Women and Development Conference in 1978, while the Council of Europe inaugurated an *ad hoc* group in advance of the Copenhagen Conference, and the EEC appointed an effective feminist information officer, who publishes single-handedly an informative journal, *Women in Europe*,[42] aimed at non-governmental organizations, voluntary agencies and active individuals throughout Europe. The European Parliament put together a women's rights committee in 1979.[43]

Before it is assumed that all this energy since 1975 has totally transformed the donation, direction or use of 'aid', bilateral or multilateral, or changed the patterns of social development, the evidence is in 1980 that 'the situation of women has worsened all over the world'.[44] The Review of Progress at the UN Conference in Copenhagen found that although 'the integration of women into development has been formally accepted by most Governments . . . the transfer of inappropriate technology has worsened the employment and health conditions of women; displacement of labour occurs, and foreign models of consumption accompany such transfers', 'new discriminatory labour practices have appeared' and 'the current world economic crisis has contributed to the worsening of the situation of women in general.'[45]

The accomplishments of the first half of the Decade are hedged with conditions too; they

include the sensitising planners and decision-makers to women's needs and problems, conducting research and building a data base on women, and promoting legislation safeguarding women's rights. However, with the general exception of the countries with advanced social services, serious problems, such as *inadequate allocation of financial resources*, lack of skilled personnel, and so on, continue to exist in many countries. This constraint is to a considerable extent — especially in developing countries — due to the general economic problems, such as scarcity of resources and/or under-utilisation of existing resources. *In many cases it reflects the priority Governments accord to issues concerning women.* Another major constraint facing such mechanisms is their *limited mandates.* Thus, several existing mechanisms do not have strong executive and implementing authority. Similarly, the terms of reference given to such mechanisms tend to *restrict them to welfare activities traditionally associated with women* and thereby *reinforcing stereotyping* of women's roles and attitudinal prejudices. The sensitising task of these special mechanisms has, as yet, *insufficiently resulted in an actual integration into policy planning* and implementation by Governments and international organisations of *the question of sharing all responsibilities between the sexes.*[46] [Author's emphasis.]

The constraints enumerated are overt examples of containment, and can be said as much of the USA and UK governments as of, for example, Thailand or Peru. Financial restraints, the appointment of 'safe' representatives to national or international women's commissions are 'discrimination in very subtle guise'.[47]

The proliferation of women's bureaux since 1975 has been great, but as one whose task it was to assess their powers remarked, 'it is difficult to tell whether they are a desk in a passage or a whole ministry without visiting them.'[48] Very often they will consist of the energy and fearlessness of one or two individuals. The APCWD, already dislodged from Tehran to Bangkok, and consisting of three people in an 'undecorated office', is to be absorbed into the new Development Research Centre in Kuala Lumpur just as it has gained grass-roots contact and confidence, and increased effectiveness.[49] Is it possible that effectiveness, particularly in exposing the degradation of women, is the danger? In her 1980 equivalent to Boserup, Barbara Rogers examined the continued failure to take women into account as agents and beneficiaries of development and, unlike much of the official documentation, questions the use of 'status' as a fixed criterion, but more importantly examines the statistical invisibility of women in international materials.[50] A former UNDP employee and British diplomat, she also pins much blame on the failure to increase the number of women in decision-making occupations in the UN. In addition, the few who are there are isolated personally and politically, and are subject to sexual harassment and overt discrimination, which limits their effectiveness.[51] Political containment has become a particular interest for Ms Rogers, because one effect of programmes run by the UN and bilateral assistance from governments, as well as from the voluntary aid agencies, can be the export of discrimination and of personal prejudices.

The Official Intergovernmental Conference at Copenhagen

Delegates to the Commission and to the Decade Conference have been nominated and briefed by their foreign ministries. For their nomination, national, political and personal standing will be strong recommendations. Such factors at the same time dictate against their having international experience or, in many cases against their being broadly representative of the women's movement. This has certainly pertained in UK nominations. However, the New Zealand delegation at Copenhagen for instance, included a number of young feminists, one a Member of Parliament.[52] The US delegation included black and Hispanic women, feminists and internationalists — but it was led by a man,[53] as were the Australian and Canadian delegations. Kenya had representatives from almost all tribal groups, but other delegations were headed by 'celebrities' rather than women of active concern for their sisters. Iceland, Bolivia (before the coup), Guinea, Costa Rica and some others fielded articulate and active feminist delegation members.

The briefing of delegations by foreign ministries has a dual effect. It places foreign policy issues and regional alliances above priorities arising from women's concerns — what has been termed 'extraneous politicalization' by those who do not recognize, or choose not to recognize, that they are either implicitly 'political' or tools of foreign policy makers. It also reflects the degree to which the dichotomy between foreign policy (and multilateral UN affairs) and domestic policy still pertains in the minds of those within governmental circles. This itself mirrors the separation of 'public' and 'private' ethics that influences much domestic social policy. Non-intervention into the domestic family unit remains the norm: thus, the saviour of human rights or leader of men may beat his wife with impunity. The intervention of the UN into the domestic realm has probably come to the bemusement of those governments that hold to or reinforce, this conventional dichotomy, and prefer the familiarity of external, state-to-state relations (even inimical ones) to the complexities of international social development. The International Convention on the Elimination of All Forms of Discrimination adopted in December 1979 by the General Assembly, may suffer from such patterns of thought.[54]

There was a perceptible assumption that 'consensus' would or should obtain when decisions were being taken at the intergovernmental conference.[55] While the majority of delegates were female, their relationships to each other were predetermined by their own government's position on 'imperialism, colonialism, neo-colonialism, zionism, racism, racial discrimination, apartheid, hegemonism, and foreign occupation, domination and oppression' as well as 'unjust economic relations'.[56] Therefore speeches could follow the current patterns of UN debates. The presence of two items on the agenda relating to the plight of women under apartheid and women under Israeli occupation enabled hours to be taken up with familiar divisive themes and established positions. The Palestinian question, raised and roused far beyond the terms of the Agenda by a large PLO observer delegation, took the Conference to depths of bitterness hardly reached in recent years, at the same time as the General Assembly was also debating it in New York. The US delegation led the opposition and ultimately voted against the 'Programme of Action', as did Australia, Canada and Israel, because of the condemnation of 'zionism'.[57] During consultations between the US delegation and NGOs prior to this vote, it was described by several black women within and without the US delegation as 'selling out' American black citizens for the Israelis. However, many of the previous amendments from the USA had been constructive and supported by a variety of countries.

The assumption that 'consensus' should have been possible must be based either on hopes for a unique superabundance of goodwill related to women or on an underestimation of the commitment to international and internal political change which is necessary to right the wrongs. The assumption ignores the reality of the dominant contemporary North–South and East–West issues and, in the same breath, 'the *de facto* discrimination on the grounds of sex', tailed in the Conference Report by a coy footnote 'which in a group of countries is called sexism'.[58]

. Although the *Historical Perspective on the Roots of Inequality of Women* adopted at the intergovernmental conference has the following to say (and is close to some of the arguments discussed at the beginning of the chapter), the assumption of welfare consensus induces immediate doubts on the intentions of governments to implement the Programme of Action:

> Throughout history and in many societies women have been sharing similar experiences. One of the basic factors causing the unequal share of women in development relates to the division of labour between the sexes. This division of labour has been justified on the basis of the childbearing function of women, which is inherent in womanhood. Consequently, the distribution of tasks and responsibilities of women and men in society has mainly restricted women to the domestic sphere and has unduly burdened them. As a result, women have often been regarded and treated as inferior and unequal in their activities outside the domestic sphere and have suffered violations of their human rights. They have been given only limited access to resources and participation in all spheres of life, notably in decision-making, and in many instances institutionalised inequality in the status of women and men has also resulted.
>
> The inequality of women in most countries stems to a very large extent from mass poverty and general backwardness of the majority of the world's population caused by underdevelopment which is a product of imperialism, colonialism, neo-colonialism and also of unjust international economic relations. The unfavourable status of women is aggravated in many countries, developed and underdeveloped, by *de facto* discrimination on the grounds of sex.
>
> It can be argued that the predominant economic analyses of labour and capital insufficiently trace the linkages between production systems in world economics and women's work as producers and reproducers; nor is the subjection, exploitation, oppression and domination of women by men sufficiently explained in history. Women are not simply discriminated against

by the productive systems, but are subject to the discrimination that arises by virtue of being the reproductive force.

While women's childbearing function and their traditional nurturing roles are respected, in many countries there has been little recognition of women's actual or potential contribution to economic activity. The role of women within the family, combined with a high level of unemployment and underemployment of the population in general, often results in priority being given to the employment of men in economic activities outside the family household.[59]

Of the 135 NGOs represented at the intergovernmental conference, twenty-four were specifically 'women's NGOs'.[60] The balance were international bodies initially established without any specific reference to women, but which have adopted or adapted programmes to include women, or which have generated specific action groups related to women.[61] Some, like the International Social Science Council and the International Peace Research Association have developed Research Committees related to the role, image and representation of women in their academic disciplines. Others were federations of trade unions, and professional associations, or welfare associations. A further 'concern' category would include those working in the fields of population,[62] education,[63] development[64] and religion.[65] The representatives of these NGOs came predominantly from Western Europe and North America, but Eastern Europe, Latin America and Asia were well represented.

The 'women's NGOs' accounted for far larger delegations, and the older, wealthier ones were represented by members from affiliates from several continents. The long-established international women's organizations can each trace their origin back to the turn of the century suffrage movement (International Council of Women, International Socialist Women's Federation, International Alliance of Women) and religious, welfare or propaganda movements (Women's World Christian Temperance Union, World Association of Girl Guides).[66] These are the constitutional bodies based in Western Europe and North America with affiliates around the world. They now maintain a gradualist approach to women's advancement and operate welfare programmes in co-operation with UN agencies, rather than engaging in conspicuous political pressure. The next generation of organizations was born out of the rise in professionally qualified women between the wars and again were largely European in origin, and maintained headquarters in Europe (International Federation of University Women, Soroptimist International, International Federation of Business and Professional Women, Zonta International). They are predominantly discipline-based and conservative.[67] All these organizations pre-dated the United Nations system and the Commission and their internationalism followed colonial footsteps. The YWCA, for instance, was founded in Sri Lanka in 1888 and the Women's Temperance Union only a few years later. They remain protective of their role as agents of welfare rather than change, and of their reputations with governments. Their average membership today, as represented at the Copenhagen intergovernmental conference, came from the post-World War I generation. Indeed, many government delegates were younger. Some maintain permanent 'watchdogs' at the UN in New York and it is these whose somewhat separate and unfettered existence have influenced the Commission in its work.[68] The isolation of these representatives from the bulk of their conservative national affiliates may explain the paradox of their relatively radical interaction with the Commission before it was transferred to Vienna in 1979.[69]

The NGOs founded after World War II fall into a pre-1975 mould and a post-1975 mould. The Women's International Democratic Federation is the most significant new foundation. Based in East Berlin, it vies for the new African and Latin American élites from the opposite end of the political spectrum to the professional associations. That Marxist Socialism contains a specific written prescription for the participation of women other than through education and welfare is undoubtedly in its favour, and the women's programmes adopted by the Angolan and Nicaraguan governments owe their origins to WIDF.[70]

The Unofficial NGO Forum at Copenhagen

The frustrations experienced by the NGOs at the intergovernmental conference sometimes ignored the potential for influence by lobbying delegations and presenting them with desired amendments. As a result of their frustration, most of the NGO representatives invited by the UN along with many members of governmental delegations, spent much of their time at the Forum. The abundance of people came from the networks, caucuses, federations and groups that have blossomed since 1975, and who do not have (or seek) official consultative status with the UN.[71]

Overall organization of the NGO Forum was the responsibility of the retired General Secretary to the World YWCA (Geneva) and a Decade Committee of thirty-four NGOs based in New York. Her assistant was a young British woman who had been President of the NGO Council in New York. The premises were booked, a consortium of international journalists (including many male Britons) were hired for the Forum newspaper, and a series of basic discussion panels were arranged by the Committee. Additional NGOs were invited to arrange 'workshops'. Many others applied to hold workshops during the ten days — indeed, any individual could book a room, attract an audience by adding to the swarms of fly-posters or daily listings and if the audience could find her, there was a workshop. The 8,000 participants and the diversity of their origins probably surprised the organizers, who had perhaps envisaged more order and less spontaneity.[72] The Forum was funded by private donations and one of the Scandinavian governments. There were three Forums within the Forum, funded separately by US philanthropic foundations. Two were consortia of celebrated

'Third World' women scholars (predominantly educated in the USA) and activists, aiming to form links with their uncommitted sisters. One, *Vivencia*, was staffed by the International Women's Tribune Centre, itself a product of the Mexico Tribune (the 1975 equivalent to the Forum, but far smaller), now based in New York with an international staff. The more recent, *Exchange*, was formed specifically for the Copenhagen Forum, and registered some 400 names, predominantly from the 'Third World' for future feminist 'networking'.[73] Both organized numerous workshops and in a neighbouring building the International Women's Studies Federation held a large number of scholarly inter-disciplinary seminars, predominantly attended by academics and administrators of equal opportunities in Western industrialized countries, who preferred the purposefulness and calm of this environment to the jostle and 'fun' of the central Forum.

The Forum organizers were responsible for arranging daily briefing sessions about the intergovernmental conference but, more significantly, a series of panels. These were based on the Decade themes, Equality, Development and Peace, Employment, Education and Health, to which were added the Family, Facism and Apartheid. The speakers were celebrated names, scholars and activists, appropriately balanced according to region and political system. While the intellectual level of the panels was high, their status between Forum and Conference and their relative formality drew speech-making rather than debate from its audience. Latin Americans, many in European exile, sought scope for the expresssion of political opinions persecuted at home and ignored in refuge. (Although inimical to their governments represented at the Conference, their speeches against imperialism were remarkably similar.) East Europeans chose the translation facilities (not available elsewhere at the Forum) and the size of the captive audience to extol the advancement of women in their communities. A contingent of the PLO brought their problem to predominate here, too, and to supersede other Middle Eastern discussion. It should be added that some non-governmental participation at the Forum had the appearance of heavy state subsidy: there were colourful displays in close proximity by Iraq who had a team of boy dancers, and Iran, the latter with a large portrait of Ayatollah Khomeini which was offensive to many.

The relative informality of the workshops made exchange of opinion and experience their means and their end. The spontaneous recurrent themes of the Forum reflected the sources of increasing alientation of women from their own societies. The average age of participants was 35–40 and two-thirds were probably married women with children. While the age range suggests financial status, it also indicates that the concerns, aspirations or demands of the global movement are not solely the passions of frivolous youth or deprived spinsters. It suggests, too, a degree of moral support from male spouses, who may recognize that women's alienation is less from themselves than from social institutions. While it is impossible to summarize every point made, it must be contended that the concern of most participants in the Forum was no less than the future of world society and their place within it.

The Issues Discussed at the NGO Forum

It was an Indian participant who suggested that the priorities of the Decade should be reversed to place Peace first.[74] While this may be a reflection of the circular problem — how to secure development in a warring country and will it in turn secure peace — it also bears consideration by and in the context of women. On the one hand, women and female children form seven out of ten refugees, a fact that emerged from UNHCR's preparatory work for the conference.[75] On the other hand, peace and war have become major preoccupations of the women's movement in many regions. The Nordic countries gathered half a million signatures in six months for a peace petition, and the link with the anti-nuclear lobby in Germany, Japan, Canada and the Pacific Islands is developing all the time.[76] Meanwhile, the entry of women into military forces as combat troops poses intrinsic moral problems for women, as well as immediate hostility from men.

Domestic violence has become the subject of research and legislation since it broke out of the hidden dynamics of the family, by the opening of the first Women's Refuge in Britain in 1971.[77] Refuges are now to be found all over the world and, while the Forum was in session, Copenhagen's second was opened. But violence against women is increasing, particularly against those whose consciousness of their own situation has been awakened. Asian feminists believe it to be the most global danger to women. The first feminist magazine in India, *Manushi*, was founded to provide an organ of protest against rape, violence against women, dowry murders or forced suicides.[78] The implicit threat of women's liberation to masculine ideals is recognized as being disturbing, by many women and men alike.

The image of women and their roles is of increasing global concern. The enterprise of an individual in, for instance, the Malaysian broadcasting service is to bring about the first 'Women in Media' conference in the East. Shortly before the Copenhagen conference, a 'Women in Media' seminar was held in New York of 'Third World' women under the auspices of UNITAR.[79] The expansion of marketing techniques of film and of television has allowed the efficacious housewife and the manipulated mannequin (and their converse, the 'true male', the voice of authority but inefficient at domesticity) to creep into the shanty huts and high-rise flats the world over during the past ten years.

The failure of governments to implement the 1975 World Plan of Action for the Decade for Women has left the running sore of unpaid household labour still open. In Africa 80 per cent of agricultural work is performed by women and consequently the survival of society depends on women. In Central America migration of rural men to urban centres for potential employment has left villages of women with children and the aged. Urban areas, and the males therein, receive priorities for such national resources, education and health as exist. Urban men collected together represent a greater threat to government, with their potential for armed expressions of discontent. National 'machismo' and transnational priorities determine the rest.[80] In the West the 'conversion of women into a crypto-servant class has been an achievement of the greatest magnitude.'[81] Housework, child-care and service to the disabled or elderly is the unremunerated duty of women.[82] Meanwhile the physical survival of an Indian family may rest on the collection of roots by its mother – male pride may prevent the father from such exercise – or in widowhood the woman may have no right to land cultivated by her over a lifetime.[83] In most parts of the world, the 'farmer' is the woman but statistically she is the 'farmer's wife' and owns nothing in her own right.[84] Everywhere she is responsible for the life and death of her children, but family administration is not regarded as a qualification for participation in societies' decision-making institutions.

The correlation of 'invisible work', that is non-monetary work, with the absence of rights is almost tangible. The dispossesion of women is increasing. Many of the Forum workshops were concerned with income-generation schemes for women. If poverty and status-deprivation are related to gender, so must be the solutions. Even the 'basic needs' policies now adopted by many aid agencies are still based on a persistence of the former 'trickle-down' theory: the trickling assumed to be going from the male spouse (head of household) to his dependants.[85] Even 'community development' or 'community caring' may disguise the difference, the division of labour and in earning power, between men and women. Western feminism, which looks to the woman as the object of study in order to become the subject of herself, is no longer regarded as irrelevant to the non-Western world. 'Integration into development' may itself be interpreted as 'how patronising do you like your tokenism?'[86] Research into ways and means of integrating women's uncounted work into the measurement of GNP is being undertaken, on a small scale, in India, the USA, the UK and France.[87]

The 'double burden' of employed women – those who run 'invisible' households and clock in for the assembly line as well – is also of global concern.[88] It is seen not merely as unfair, but inhibiting to active participation in trade unions, in formal political arenas and in other institutions. The 'double burden' is still carried by East European women, where it offsets to some extent the constitutional advances they have made.[89] Participation in the labour market is the Marxist key to equality, but unresearched cultural chauvinism (sexism is not recognized by communist regimes) and the failure to replace the nuclear family with 'socialized family labour' means that women have little domestic support from their husbands. International time-budget studies indicate that women work several hours more per day than their partners and consequently have less leisure.[90] Even in Sweden 70 per cent of men never undertake any shopping and 60 per cent of men never help with housework.[91]

The yielding by women by child-rearing responsibilites is not, however, wholly without dispute.[92] The example of the 'professionalization' of obstetrics, with the down-grading of female midwives and assumption of authority by a predominantly male medical profession, is fearful to many.[93] Childbirth has itself become a feminist issue to mothers and health workers alike. The experience of childbirth in the 'production line' of large hospitals is one that alienates many women from their own bodies and from the profession which takes over control. This has been recorded in both East and West and with the export of inapprorpriate technology it may be the experience elsewhere.[94]

The connection between employment policy and natalist policy is recognizable in Eastern Europe,[95] where the requirements of the labour market measure the access of women to abortion (the main method of contraception) and nursery care. The connection is far more insidious in other industrialized countries. While moral issues are presented as the determinant, the web is spun of more fibres: at one time or in one place reproduction is divine, in another it is anti-social, in another patriotic, in another 'natural', in another a service, in another it absorbs resources. Similarly, its negation is sinful, against women's nature, necessary for the survival of the nation, necessary for development, necessary for advancement. It is not often regarded as a woman's right to make an informed choice.[96]

Working conditions, as well as low pay, under transnational companies are also the topic of some international campaigning.[97] The microchip assembly plants and other industries of South East Asia make use of cheap, 'malleable', female labour, on short, tightly-controlled contracts. Low wages, blindness, post-contract unemployment and broken kinship patterns, all lead to destitution or prostitution. Local traditional attitudes towards women complete this twentieth-century 'fatal impact' — Buddhist spiritual hierarchy prevents women from reaching nirvana in their own right.[98] The degradation of women through prostitution enforced out of economic need, bodily sale and pretended marriage formed the subject of many other workshops.

Transnational companies' marketing practices are also the subject of criticism. Baby foods and drugs have been the major concern. The former have been the subject of an extended campaign. The discouragement of breast-feeding that increased in the 1960s was perceived by feminists as a commerical manipulation of women's natural function. Then the TNCs' response was to export baby foods to the developing countries. The expenditure of scarce resources to reach towards a marketed image of Western sophistication became a deadly moral issue. The impossibility of sterilizing equipment and the difficulties for illiterate purchasers to make up correctly the baby's milk led to infection and death. Today it is the contraceptive drugs that have been banned in the West as unsafe which form the topic of campaigning. The ethical relationship of Ministers of Health, TNCs, doctors and the individual is one where the rights of the patient, particularly if she is 'only a woman', loses out. Sedative drugs, predominantly advertised to the medical profession as treatment for women, are 'keeping the cork in the bottle of women's discontent with her socio-economic conditions.'[99]

The subject where there was least harmony was the question of 'female circumcision'. A variety of practices are still continued on the African continent and have recently attracted the interest of Western feminists,[100] an interest that is rejected by many articulate African women activists (particularly from the francophone West) as a form of neo-imperialism. While few support the practices on health grounds, they resent the Western emphasis on sexual reasons for their abolition, while ignoring the priorities of economic deprivation in Africa.[101] The most heated workshops were held on this subject and on prostitution, where the difference lies in choice and exploitation of prostitution.[102]

The Forum closed a week before the intergovernmental conference and most of the 8,000 opinions drifted out of Copenhagen. However, accredited non-governmental representatives who had divided themselves between different locations for ten days could now return single-minded to the PLO controversies at the Bella Centre. Before the Forum closed, groups of representatives drew up summary declarations of their views in an attempt to reach the delegates at the intergovernmental conference. A *17 July Plenary Committee* emphasized implementation of the World Plan of Action, the formation of an international tribunal on crimes against women, representation of women in delegations to the UN, nominations to the Secretariat of the UN and ratification of the Convention on the Elimination of all Forms of Discrimination against Women. In contrast, the *Third World Caucus of the 1980 NGO Forum* emphasized imperialism, racism, exploitation by multinational corporations, national liberation struggles, 'dumping' of drugs, 'attempts at forcing birth control' on developing nations, migrant workers, nuclear tests in the South Pacific, violence in the Lebanon, the plight of the Palestinians and the low status of women's agricultural work and housework.

Conclusions

Thus battered, it is surprising that women are not more bitter. Like Uncle Tom, many prefer not to risk recognizing the condition of their lives, or identifying the causes. Yet others retreat into isolationism, even suicide. Active feminism is the result of an experience or an accumulation of bruising experiences, within the social institution of modern life. It is a personal response (as is political affiliation) that is becoming more collective. Even Simone de Beauvoir, long regarded as the doyenne of post-war Western feminism, said that until the early 1970s 'I believed in social development' rather than feminism.[103] It is probable that the internationalism of the movement so far has been as much founded in the internationalist becoming feminist as the reverse. The experience of women in international institutions may be as catalysing as the back-street abortion or the loneliness of the divorce court: the context is different, but the problems are replicated universally. Whether priorities lead to confrontation politics, topic-related action groups, research committees, women's liberation networks, socialist feminism, rape crisis work, refuge building, professional caucuses, the essence of the women's movement is change.

In this process of change it is difficult to estimate the effect of the events in Copenhagen. For those who participated in the Forum, it was a stimulating and exhilarating experience: hope and strength was gained to return to the struggle at home with the knowledge that one was part of a global social movement.[104] The intergovernmental conference appeared to many to be physically and ideologically distant from the Forum, but official delegates did take part in some of the workshops and accredited NGOs were able to lobby at the Bella Centre. Perhaps the strongest link between the two arenas of debate was the conference newspaper, *Forum*. It reported on activity in both the official conference and the Forum. The delegates did not ignore this newspaper, despite its occasionally irreverent attitude to their work. They read it avidly. A more formal link was provided by the daily briefings arranged by the secretariat for the Forum participants about developments in the official proceedings. On a day-by-day basis at Copenhagen the Forum could not exert more than an informal influence on the intergovernmental discussions, but the long-term effect may be rather more pronounced. Many of the ideas from the 1975 NGO Tribune in Mexico had by 1980 made their way into the official documents. There were also personnel links, for example, Elizabeth Reid, one of the activists in 1975 for the Tribune, became in 1980 the Principal Officer in the conference secretariat assisting the Secretary-General, Lucille Mair (former Jamaican delegate to the UN General Assembly) in running the intergovernmental conference. In 1985 a third conference will be held to review progress by governments in implementation of the programme of the Decade for Women. When this convenes in Nairobi, it will be possible to assess the extent to which Copenhagen produced new pressures on governments to change or encouraged more extensive networking among today's women.

References

1 *Report of the World Conference of the International Women's Year, Mexico City, 19 June–2 July 1975* (New York, United Nations, 1976, publication No. E.76.IV.1).
2 *World Conference of the UN Decade for Women: Equality, Development and Peace. List of Participants*, UN document A/CONF.94/INF.3, 25 July 1980.
3 *List of Non-Governmental Organisations Participating at the World Conference of the UN Decade for Women 1980*, Ref. No. 80-46925.
4 Prepared by about thirty NGO representatives over the weekend 19–20 July. The author participated and her suggestion that newer NGOs were vulnerable and required particular protection from government 'obstruction, harassment and persecution' became part of the statement after some resistance from the older, more established NGOs.
5 UN General Assembly Resolution 3010(XXVII) of 18 December 1972.
6 The United Nations itself and all its agencies, the Commonwealth Secretariat and other regional organizations, etc. together form an international civil service. The massive expansion of multi-locational companies also provides examples. The communication

industry itself has expanded immeasurably, taking with it the ideology and perceptions of 'civilization' and 'progress', including the purveyor's personal perception of the role of women.

7 See *Equal Opportunities Commission Research Report No. 1* (Manchester, EOC, 1978) and *Equal Opportunities Commission Annual Report 1979* (Manchester, EOC, 1980).

8 An interesting account of this is in Muriel Nissel's paper, 'Women in Government Statistics: Basic Concepts and Assumptions', presented to the Equal Opportunities Commission/Social Science Research Council Conference on Women and Statistics, June 1980. To be published.

9 Galbraith, J. K., *Economics and the Public Purpose* (Boston, Houghton Mifflin, 1973 and Harmondsworth, Middx., Pelican Books, 1975), Chapter 4.

10 Broadcast, 'Women in Parliament', BBC Radio 4, June 1980, based on Elizabeth Vallance, *Women in the House* (London, Athlone Press, 1979). Essential reading on women in British society in the 1980s is Ann Oakley, *Subject Women* (Oxford, Martin Robertson, 1981); Elizabeth Wilson, *Women in the Welfare State* (London, Tavistock Press, 1977) and Elizabeth Wilson, *Half-Way to Paradise* (London, Tavistock Press, 1980)

11 In the Church of England no women have been admitted as priests, but the Episcopalian Church, the member of the Anglican Communion in the USA, has commenced ordination of women; the Australian Church has made a commitment to start training some women for the ministry. The Roman Catholic and Orthodox Churches do not allow any women as priests, which has become a controversial issue among nuns in the USA. Islam, Buddhism and Hinduism exclude women from some forms of public worship or the priesthood (with regional variations). Some liberal branches of Judaism have allowed women Rabbis.

    In 1979 a City of London livery dinner, attended by the author's husband, had one woman present — the harpist. In 1980 an Engineering Company reception list several hundred guests from among the 'Great'. One woman was noticed but did not appear on the list. Female guests at the Athenaeum, the sanctuary of the liberal 'Great' in London, enter a small separate dining room by an external side-staircase. See also 'Power' in *Participation of Women in Decision-Making. Some Guidelines* (Bangkok, Asian and Pacific Centre for Women and Development, 1980).

12 Any general reference book, such as *Whitaker's Almanac* for Britain, provides evidence. See also the EOC Research Report No. 1, op. cit., and *European Parliament Working Documents 1980–81, 29 January, Luxembourg*, document number PE67.021/fin, which surveys the position of women in all the Community member countries.

13 For example, D. Horowitz (ed.), *Containment and Revolution. Western Policy toward Social Revolution, 1917 to Vietnam* (London, Anthony Blond, 1967). Chile presents an overt example of this phenomenon, now being termed 'stabilization': see especially *Military Ideology and the Dissolution of Democracy: Women in Chile*, CHANGE International Reports, No. 4, 1981.

14 Spender, Dale, *Man Made Language* (London, Routledge and Kegan Paul, 1980), or *Identification of Basic Needs* (Tehran, Asian and Pacific Centre for Women and Development, 1977), or Bradford Morse's statement to the Copenhagen conference for UNDP.

15 Rendel, Margherita, with Georgina Ashworth (eds.), *Women, Power and Political Systems* (London, Croom Helm, 1981) and James P. Grant's thoughtful written statement for UNICEF, of which he was Director, to the 1980 Copenhagen conference, see UN document A/CONF.94/BP.12.

16 Tajfel, Henri, *The Social Psychology of Minorities*, Minority Rights Group, Report No. 38, 1979; B. Adam, *The Survival of Domination* (Amsterdam and New York, Elsevier, 1978) is also interesting although it evades sex.

17 Deutsch, Karl, *The Roots of Fascism* (Harmondsworth, Middx., Pelican Books, 1957) and Lewenhak, Shelia, *Women at Work* (London, Macmillan, 1980).

18 The former President of the Israeli Council for Civil Liberties, Israel Shahak, has mooted that persecution has become such a part of Jewish experience that its absence leaves the Israeli insecure, so he will provoke persecution to ensure 'normality' and national cohesion. A parallel with women is sometimes suggested.

19 Galey, Margaret E., 'Promoting Nondiscrimination Against Women. The UN Commission on the Status of Women' in *International Studies Quarterly*, Vol. 23, No. 2, June 1979, pp. 273–302.

20 Information from correspondence with the late Dame Margery Corbett-Ashby.

21 Galey, op. cit., p. 275.

22 See, for example, *ILO List of Major Instruments and Documents concerning Women Workers*, ILO/WI/1980; UNFPA, *Review of UNFPA's Assistance to Women, Population and Development Projects 1969–79* (New York, May 1980); UNESCO, *Half of the World. UNESCO Activities for the Advancement of Women* (Paris, 1980).

23 Menon, T., 'Equality of Women' in *The United Nations Secretariat. The Rules and Practice* (Lexington, Mass., Lexington Books, D. C. Heath and Co., 1977), and *Women's Participation — the UN 'Example'*, paper presented to the NGO Forum by active women UN employees at workshop resulting from a suggestion by this author.

24 Galey, op. cit., p. 284.

25 The origins of the civil rights movement itself lay in the realization among black and other minority Americans that African states were themselves fighting for and achieving independence and rights which were not available to black Americans.

26 The North American women's movement cannot be described here in the space available, but the influence of the English-language literature emanating from it has been strong in the UK.

27 Galey, op. cit., p. 278.

28 Boserup, E., *Women's Role in Economic Development* (London, Allen and Unwin, and New York, St. Martin's Press, 1970), Introduction.

29 The origin of the idea came some years earlier from a man working in FAO. It was taken up by the delegate of the USA to the Commission: conversation between the originator and the author. See also *International Women's Issues. Hearing and Briefing before the Subcommittees on International Organisations and on International Development of the Committee on International Relations*, House of Representatives, Ninety-fifth Congress, Second Session, 8 and 22 March 1978 (Washington, 1978).

30 See, for example, Buvinic, M., *An Annotated Bibliography* (Washington DC, Overseas Development Council, 1976) and Massiah, J., *Women in the Caribbean. An Annotated Bibliography* (Cave Hill, Barbados, Institute of Social and Economic Research, 1977).

31 For example, International Centre for Research on Women, Washington DC., and Wellesley College, *Women and National Development: The Complexity of Change* (Chicago, Ill., 1977).

32 For example, *Expert Consultation on the Integration of Rural Women in Development* (FAO ESHH/IRWD, 1976). The classic, *The Missing Half* (Rome, FAO, 1975), was prepared for the Mexico conference. There has also been a series of internal bibliographies and studies prepared by the FAO.

33 *International Women's Issues*, loc. cit.

34 See a useful discussion in *An International Women's Policy: a survey of thoughts and proposals from the Norwegian National Council of Women*, October 1979.

35 Others would include Dr Margaret Snyder, USA Women's Voluntary Fund; Marcella Martinez, Jamaica; Irma Garcia Chafardet, Venezuela, who worked on the Convention and is now with ECLA; Wassila Tamzali, Algeria and UNESCO; Elsa Chaney and Irene Tinker, both USA and ex-Peace Corps.

36 For example, UNDP, *Guidelines on the Integration of Women in Rural Development*, 25 February 1977, or IPPF, 'Women and Development' Programme.

37 *World Plan of Action*, UN document E/CONF.66/34, usefully summarized for the Commission Twenty-Sixth Session, October 1976 in E/CN.6/600. The Voluntary Fund has a consultative committee, the composition of which includes NGO representatives and others.

38 General Assembly Resolution 2263(XXII) of 7 November 1967. See also International Instruments Relating to the Status of Women, Twenty-Sixth Session of the Commission on the Status of Women 1976, UN document E/CN.6/592.

39 *International Convention on the Elimination of All Forms of Discrimination Against Women*, General Assembly Resolution 34/180, 18 December 1979. The draft papers in UN document E/CN.6/591 are interesting.

40 *UN International Research and Training Institute for the Advancement of Women — Board of Trustees Proposed Budget 1980–81. Memorandum of the Secretary-General*, INSTRAW/BT/1979/R.2 *Decade Note* (New York, UN Office of Public Information, October 1978); UN documents E/1979/11 and E/1979/37; and *Training for Women* (New York, INSTRAW, 1980).

41 *The Spriit of Huston. National Commission of the Observation of International Women's Year Report to the President, Congress and People of the United States* (Washington DC, NCOIW, 1978).

42 *Women of Europe*, Quarterly Information Bulletin for the Press, Women's Organizations and individuals, European Community, Brussels.

43 See *Women of Europe*, Supplement No. 4 (Brussels, EC, 1980), 'Women in the European Parliament'; the European Parliament *Ad Hoc* Group on Women's Rights report to a full session of the Parliament on 10–11 February 1981.

44 UN Division for Economic and Social Information, *Worsening Situation of Women will be Main Issue Confronting Commission on the Status of Women*, DPI/DESI NOTE IWD/22, 13 February 1980.

45 *Report of the World Conference of the UN Decade for Women — Equality, Development, Peace, 14–30 July 1980,* UN document A/CONF.94/35.

46 Ibid., p. 8.

47 Conversation and correspondence with several international civil servants, not all women, from Jamaica, Canada, Burma, Bangladesh, *et. al.* The person quoted was Indian.

48 Conversation with editor of a survey, conducted prior to Copenhagen conference by a large international NGO.

49 Correspondence between author and former employees of the Asian and Pacific Centre for Women and Development. See also *The Guardian*, London, 27 January 1981.

50 Rogers, Barbara, *The Domestication of Women. Discrimination in Developing Societies* (London, Kegan Page, 1980).

51 Conversation with many international civil servants and an internal journal, *UN Women's Caucus, New York, passim.*

52 Marilyn Waring was surprisingly a member for a conservative, rural constituency. She was personally responsible for the amendment that became item 13 of the Final Report; see p. 18 of A/CONF.94/35.

53 It also held pre-conference consultations with NGOs which were described variously as 'very useful' and 'not consultative, just letting the State Department have its say'. In the UK, the only consultation between delegates and NGOs was arranged by the author on her own initiative. This has now become a continuing, informal consultative grouping known as the DECADE NETWORK.

54 General Assembly Resolution 34/180 of 18 December 1979, opened for signature 1 March 1980.

55 Conversation with British delegates and reported conversation with Lucille Mair, Secretary-General of the conference and former Jamaican Ambassador to the UN.

56 *Report of the World Conference . . .*, loc. cit., p. 76.

57 Ibid., p. 196.

58 Ibid., p. 7.

59 Ibid.

60 This was an expression used by a British Foreign and Commonwealth Office delegate, but also at times used by the women's NGOs themselves, who have in New York coined the acronym 'WINGOs', See *List of NGOs . . .*, op. cit., for the variety of those present.

61 For example, World Council of Churches, Anti-Slavery Society, World Council of Credit Unions and International Co-operative Alliance.

62 For example, International Planned Parenthood Federation, The Population Crisis Committee and The Population Institute.

63 For example, Association for World Education, International Studies Association, International Union of Students and International Youth and Student Movement for the UN.

64 For example, Society for International Development, Oxfam and Pan-African Institute for Development.
65 For example, World Lutheran Federation, Centre for Concern (Washington), International Association for Religious Freedom and Caritas Internationalis.
66 Boulding, Elise, 'Female Alternatives to Heirarchical Systems, Past and Present — A Critique of Women's NGOs in the Light of History', *International Associations*, Brussels, 1975, pp. 340–46.
67 Annual Reports of International Alliance of Women, Women's International League for Peace and Freedom, International Federation of Business and Professional Women 'Golden Jubilee'; personal observation and conversations with Presidents' Secretaries and members. However, there are great regional variations.
68 This group also formed the nucleus of the Decade Committee of the Conference of NGOs and appointed the Forum organizers and the team of journalists for *Forum 80*. There are some very seasoned diplomats among them.
69 The move was brought about by General Assembly Resolution 31/194, 1976.
70 *Women of the Whole World*, WIDF for Copenhagen, 1980.
71 There are many names, but only a few of the most international can be mentioned here, e.g. MATCH International Center, which grew in Canada in order to relate to Third World Women as a result of the Mexico conference (source, Match Newsletters, conversation and correspondence with its founder); Women's Organization of Europe, Brussels; Equity Policy Centre (EPOC), Washington; New Transcentury Corporation, Women in Development Secretariat; ISIS International Bulletin, Geneva and Rome.
72 Many conversations and *Forum 80*, Copenhagen, 14–30 July 1980.
73 International Women's Tribune Centre Newsletters, New York, published since 1977 and their useful directories. *Exchange* circular issued after the conference in November 1980.
74 *Forum 80*, July 1980, and see also World Peace Council statement to the intergovernmental conference, A/CONF.94/NGO/42.
75 UN document A/CONF.94/PC.15.
76 Women for Peace was founded in January 1980 in preparation for the conference. An active feminist, Petra Karin Kelly, formerly employed by the European Community, became President of the 'Green Movement' in West Germany in 1980, after unsuccessfully standing for the European Parliament.
77 *A Refuge from Violence* (London, Chiswick Family Rescue Ltd., 1980). The representative in Copenhagen held several workshops. Both she and the doyenne of the American women's movement, Betty Friedan, surprised listeners by suggesting that the family must be rescued not from 'women's lib' but from modern life. The Centre for Women's Policy Studies, Washington DC, also focuses its programme on domestic violence.
78 *Manushi. A Journal About Women and Society*, New Delhi, Vol. 1, No. 2, and conversations with the editor and other Indian, Bangladeshi and South East Asian participants in Copenhagen and elsewhere.
79 UN Division for Economic and Social Information, *New International Media Networks Recommended by Seminar*, DPI/DESI NOTE IWD/25, 2 June 1980; UN document E/CN.6/627, *Report of Special Rapporteur*, 10 January 1980, to Commission Twenty-eighth Session 1980; and conversations at the Forum.
80 Elsa Chaney for USAID, *Women in International Migration*.
81 Galbraith, J. K., op. cit., Also Ilona Kickbush, 'A Hard Day's Night: Women, Reproduction and Service Society' in Rendel with Ashworth, op. cit.
82 Equal Opportunities Commission Press Release, 'Burden of caring for elderly and handicapped traps women at home' (Manchester, EOC, November 1980).
83 International Center for Research on Women abbreviated documentation for World Conference on Agricultural Reform and Rural Development 1979.
84 International Federation of Agricultural Producers, *Women Farmers: Action, No More Plans*, Copenhagen, July 1980; and Rogers, op. cit.
85 Palmer, Ingrid, 'Rural Women and the Basic Needs Approach to Development', *Development Digest*, Vol. XVII, No. 1, January 1979.

86 *Punch* cartoon, October 1980, and FAO economist at the conference.
87 At the Institute of Economic Studies, New Delhi; the Policy Studies Institute, London; the former Department of Health, Education and Welfare, Washington; and the Centre Européen Feminin de Recherches sur L'Evolution de la Société, (CEFRES), Paris. The International Centre for Research on Women has published *Keeping Women Out. A Structural Analysis of Women's Employment in Development Countries* for USAID, April 1980, which calculates GDP contributions in ten countries. The 'International Wages for Housework' campaign was particularly well organized and publicity conscious in the Forum, but it is worth adding that the UN Commission itself regards the question of the productivity of women as a major concern.
88 It appeared with comparative honesty in many governmental presentations to the conference, too.
89 CHANGE International Reports, No. 3, *The New Soviet Woman. Myth or Model?*; Sheila B. Kamerman, 'Work and Family in Industrialised Societies', *Signs. Journal of Women in Culture and Society*, Vol. 4, No. 4, Summer 1979, pp. 632–50; Sharon S. Wolchik, 'Demography, Political Reform and Women's Issues in Czechoslovakia', in Rendel with Ashworth, op. cit.; Eastern European delegates to the conference and participating in the Forum, particularly those from East Germany and Czechoslovakia, maintain there is absolute perfection in their countries.
90 Quoted without reference in *Mid-Decade Review and Evaluation of Progress 1980: Austria*, Vienna, 1980.
91 Figure quoted in Maria Begom Larsom, *Technology and Developed Societies*, UN Institute for Training and Research Technology Series, No. 8, 1980.
92 Workshop discussion, Betty Friedan *et. al.*
93 Workshop discussions; the Boston Women's Health Collective, 'Our Bodies Ourselves'; and Jean and Jon Davies, 'The Equal Crunch', unpublished paper, Newcastle, 1980; Ehrenreich and English, *Witches, Midwives and Nurses. A History of Women Healers*, (Westerbury, Mass., Feminist Press, 1975).
94 Rogers, op. cit.; appropriate technology workshops.
95 Wolchik, op. cit.; CHANGE International Reports, No. 3, op. cit.
96 International Contraception Abortion and Sterilization Campaign, *Information*, No. 3, 1980.
97 Workshops and Cynthia Enloe, *Sex and Levi's: The International Division of Labour* (published privately, Worcester, Mass., 1978); South-east Asian Newsletter, 1977; the Culture Learning Institute of the East–West Center in Hawii has started a three-year, ten-country study of Women and Multinational Corporations; and the American Friends Service Committee has a research group on Women and Global Corporatism.
98 CHANGE International Reports, No. 2, 1980, *Providence and Prostitution — Image and Reality for Women in Buddhist Thailand.*
99 Ian Kennedy, 1980 Reith Lectures on the BBC radio, lecture no. 1, reprinted in *The Listener*, London, 6 November 1980, pp. 600–4.
100 Particularly *WINews*, an international resulting from the 1975 Mexico conference, published from Lexington, Mass.
101 Conversations with African and other abolitionists.
102 'Female Sexual Slavery' and other workshops.
103 Interview with Alice Jardine in *Signs. Journal of Women in Culture and Society*, Vol. 5, No. 2, Autumn 1979, pp. 224–36.
104 A few sentences cannot do justice to the breadth of ideas, expression and wisdom of these workshops, which are without references since the discussions were not recorded. This paper has of necessity, being in an edited volume, been abbreviated.

8 A Governmental Response to Pressure Groups —
The Case of Sweden

OLLE DAHLÉN

Pressure Groups in Swedish Society

For someone who has been active in Swedish politics for a few decades, there is absolutely no doubt that the Swedish popular movements have played and still play a very important role in moulding public opinion and as pressure groups. These movements are part of the reality with which politicians are concerned. The religious revival movement with its roots in the free churches, the temperance organizations and the labour movement, in that chronological order, have played a substantial role on the political scene from the 1850s and in the following decades. *All these movements wanted to change society.*[1] The free churches wanted freedom from the repression exercised by the state and the official Lutheran church on their members. The members of the temperance organizations wanted to save people from the terrible torpidity which accompanied widespread alcoholism. The labour movement demanded political rights and the right to form trade unions.

The churches and the temperance movement were the first to get their members elected to the lower chamber of the Swedish parliament and to local government bodies. In the period before the First World War, two-thirds of the members of the lower chamber were teetotallers. Around the turn of the century between 15 and 20 per cent of members of the lower chamber belonged to free church congregations. It was not until after the First World War that more members of parliament represented the labour movement than the free churches. Such a pattern is well known in the Anglo-Saxon world. In Sweden, however, these movements were more broadly anchored in the population as a whole. The Swedish researcher, Dr Sven Lundkvist, has pointed out that in many parts of the country the rural population was more active than has been found in comparable studies on Britain.[2]

Lundkvist also underlines another difference. He says that it is often emphasized in the international literature that

> membership of (those) voluntary organizations, which are directly comparable to the Swedish popular movements, depends on social status: the higher that status, the greater is the propensity to join organizations in

modern society. But this hypothesis from organization theory does not, however, fully apply to conditions described in material from the industrialization period in Sweden.[3]

The active groups were primarily the upper working class and the lower middle class. Activity also spread to large parts of the rural areas, where of course many workers and middle class people were living in the numerous ironworking and forestry districts.

This widespread support among the Swedish population provided a firm foundation for massive political action. Another consequence was that when the free churches and the temperance movement became less important forces themselves, their members retained a strong hold over nominations to political posts both in local and central government. Today, the Swedish parliament has 349 members, about 100 of whom are active church members. The proportion of teetotallers among members of parliament is still much higher than in the population as a whole. These facts are not only of statistical and historical interest: they are also of significance in Swedish politics today.

In the last half-century, the sectional interest organizations have gained in importance among Swedish NGOs. This is particularly true of the associations of employees, which are more in the nature of interest organizations than they were to start with. But the confederation of employers has also grown stronger. The consumer co-operative movement is of long standing and has exercised considerable influence, rather more in the past than now. As economic difficulties have increased, its activity in the community as a whole has declined. Another group of consumers — tenants in apartments — has made itself increasingly felt. The farmers' organization has become a force to be reckoned with, but its political importance has diminished somewhat, in line with the reduction in the proportion of the population employed in agriculture and forestry.

According to Swedish tradition, and now also under the Swedish constitution, before the government presents a bill to parliament it is required to give central and local government authorities as well as other organizations (NGOs) the opportunity of stating their opinion on the bill. Co-operation is often established at the preparatory stage in governmental committees of inquiry. Here, too, it is possible for NGOs in general and especially for interest organizations and non-profit-making associations to influence the formulation of coming government proposals. The government is, of course, not bound to accept proposals made by these committees, but it is not easy for it to disregard strong opinion. Committee proposals are as a 'rule circulated to a large number of central and local government authorities and the NGOs concerned. When the government puts a bill before parliament it is required to give a detailed account of the views put forward in statements of opinion received from these sources.

Private bills and party group motions from the opposition often direct attention to the views of the bodies to which bills have been circulated, views which the movers regard as not having been taken sufficiently into account. The right to introduce private bills or propose amendments to government bills is practically unlimited, a practice which is very different from that in the British House of Commons. No matter which government is in power, it has to take this Swedish practice into account before presenting bills to parliament. The fact that so many members of the Swedish Riksdag belong to one or more organizations is of decisive importance. If the government disregards strong opinion in the NGOs, it must expect that amendments or counter-proposals will be put before the Riksdag.

Three Examples of NGOs Influencing Swedish Policy-Making

A knowledge of these aspects of conditions in Sweden — the role NGOs play in the nomination of candidates to political posts and the procedure for proposals put before the Riksdag — is necessary for a real understanding of Swedish society today. I would now like to illustrate the importance of the NGOs in spheres where the emphasis is on ideological influence but where interest organizations also have a certain need to make themselves heard. Three fairly obvious fields spring to mind for present purposes: international development co-operation, environment conservation and, thirdly, apartheid and Southern Africa. Where these matters are concerned, personal, idealistic involvement has predominated, even in the case of the interest organizations.

International development co-operation

There has been a strong desire to support and assist the poor countries of the world, particularly within churches and missionary societies. In many cases this commitment began as pure evangelization, but as more believers became increasingly aware of the needs of the countries concerned, greater efforts were put into schools, hospitals and health services. During the Second World War Sweden, as a non-belligerent power, obviously tried to find ways of helping while the war was still on. The end of the war was followed by a growing realization of the need for help and a growing determination to pursue on a more organized basis what is today known as international development co-operation. Developments during the period immediately after the war have been described by Ernst Michanek, former Director-General of the Swedish International Development (SIDA), as primarily a question of co-operation between NGOs and the state:

> There is no real dividing line between governmental and non-governmental efforts as described in these notes from the 'pre-aid' history. Government and NGOs worked hand in hand, supplementing each other. Over the years, an ideology developed, and it was applied when the post-war rehabilitation and reconstruction effort gave way to an international aid programme.[4]

A central committee for international development assistance was set up in 1952 by forty-four Swedish NGOs. The Ministry for Foreign Affairs provided secretarial personnel, but otherwise the whole venture was supported by private efforts. Development activities began in Ethiopia and Pakistan. For ten years this committee worked to disseminate information on development assistance needs and conducted large appeal campaigns. Rather less than half its total income was derived from governmental sources.

Thus Swedish international development assistance was started by the voluntary organizations, and it was only later on that the government gradually entered the arena. Co-operation with the Swedish NGOs has also continued and been expanded since 1962, when the Riksdag resolved on the launching of an official programme of international development co-operation. In 1980 government funds totalling Skr.50 million (approximately $8.9 million) were channelled through Swedish organizations, mainly through the churches and their foreign aid agencies. NGOs receive Skr.15 million (approximately $2.7 million) for public information work concerning assistance requirements and forms of assistance. Sometimes these funds are also used to criticize official assistance measures, criticism which is anything but welcome in some quarters. But such is the value attached to these information activities that the grants continue to be paid. It is no exaggeration to say that, without the strong popular support for Swedish international development assistance, Sweden could not have become one of the four countries in the world to have reached the proportion of its GNP required to meet the UN target for international assitance.

There is a certain degree of scepticism in Sweden concerning official assistance by the Swedish government and the development assistance activities of the United Nations. Many people say that too much money is wasted on administration. Voluntary organizations, on the other hand, have a very good reputation, and in most cases this is certainly well deserved. They can often reach the really poor, in a way official bodies find difficult. The costs for administration in NGOs are low.

Some NGOs have also been instrumental in making people aware of the need for assistance in areas where they are active. Democracy must be built up from below; individuals must feel involved. Michanek quotes this as a further argument in favour of the support given to NGOs by SIDA:

> One particular aim of supporting NGO field work is that the Swedish organizations may be instrumental in the build-up and strengthening of corresponding organizations and people's movements in the host countries, which is indeed often one of the purposes of the projects. This would, it is anticipated, help mobilize forces of development and contribute to development from below and a more democratic system. Organizations which have developed in the political, socio-economic and cultural circumstances of countries like Sweden may, in one form or another, be adapted to the

conditions of Third World countries. Positive experience has been gained from the development of national churches in the developing countries. Although political parties, trade unions and co-operatives of a European type have met greater difficulties, experiments seem to be welcomed by many developing countries.[5]

I know from my own experience how important it is for international NGOs to have strong national branches in the Third World. It gives those INGOs which have members from the developing countries more chance of being *world* organizations, and also of being regarded as such, in deliberations in the UN system. Generally speaking, religious organizations appear to have been most successful in obtaining a globally balanced representation, a status to which many NGOs nominally aspire but tend to fall short of in reality. Churches in the affluent countries are influenced by the powerful position occupied by Third World churches in their international organizations. Ideas have extensive spin-off effects, and palpable influence is exerted on the parliaments of many affluent countries. The attitude of Sweden's government and Riksdag towards conditions in South Africa was influenced by the Swedish religious deonominations, and this issue provides a second illustration of the way in which NGOs can influence government authorities.

South Africa and the system of apartheid

Ever since the close of the 1960s, the World Council of Churches (WCC) has been increasingly concerned with the situation in Southern Africa and with the system of apartheid. At its General Assembly in 1968 held in Uppsala in Sweden, the Council resolved 'to embark on a vigorous campaign against racism' and to launch a crash programme to guide the churches in their struggle against racism. This programme was drawn up in May 1969 at Notting Hill, London, in a consultation led by Senator George McGovern of the United States.

Two Swedish denominations are affiliated to the WCC, namely the Church of Sweden (the established Lutheran church) and the Covenant Church of Sweden (which belongs to the World Alliance of Reformed Churches, WARC). The Archbishop of the Church of Sweden and the Principal of the Swedish Covenant Church's Theological College served on the WCC Central Committee during the 1970s. The present Swedish Minister of Education Mr Wikström, is Vice-Chairman of the WCC Information Committee, and I myself have since 1971 been Chairman of the Committee of the Churches on International Affairs (CCIA), which amounts to the WCC 'Foreign Office'. It would not have been very creditable if this involvement had not had repercusssions at home.

The Swedish Ecumenical Council is a joint body representing practically all Protestant, Orthodox and Catholic denominations. The Council has a *Committee on International Affairs* which began in 1974 to investigate the economic commitments of Swedish companies in South Africa. At that time, Mr Wikström was chairman of the Committee. Bankers and industrialists were asked to attend hearings organized by the Committee. In response to a proposal made by the Committee, the Ecumenical Council later resolved to call on Swedish firms active in South Africa to make heavy reductions during the next two years in differences in pay and social benefits between black and white employees and to counteract apartheid. Meanwhile, extensive material on employment conditions in South Africa was collected and published, in part. The following year the Archbishop and the President of the Covenant Church caused quite a sensation by attending the AGMs of various big companies and demanding reports on what the companies had done. The Confederation of Swedish Industries later conducted a survey of its own. The Archbishop and I had a meeting with the Directors of the Confederation to discuss what progress could be made. The Confederation eventually issued a code of ethics for Swedish companies.

The Committee's evaluation report was presented to the Ecumenical Council on 10 May 1977. It was not very complimentary to Swedish companies. On the same day the Riksdag's Standing Committee on Foreign Affairs was to hold a final meeting to consider private members' bills from Social Democrats and Liberals concerning measures against South Africa. The Ecumenical Council recommended action by Sweden at the United Nations, to secure an embargo on the export of arms to South Africa and a ban on new investments in South Africa. It also called on the government to appoint a committeee to investigate the feasibility of introducing legislation to stop the export of capital to South Africa. In addition, companies were urged to refrain from expanding their commitments in South Africa. The Council's recommendations were immediately conveyed to the Standing Committee by messenger, and several members of the Standing Committee have told me that these recommendations played an important part in securing consensus within the Standing Committee in favour of a request to the Government to appoint a committee of inquiry to investigate the feasibility of stopping new investments in South Africa. This has since resulted in legislation on the subject.

One might add that other Swedish NGOs — such as those specializing in African affairs, the UN Association of Sweden, the Swedish Confederation of Trade Unions (LO) and the Swedish Central Organization of Salaried Employees (TCO) — also took action to the same end. It was not the intention to describe all the protagonists, merely to demonstrate the importance of contact between national NGOs and their joint international organizations. It is also worth mentioning that when LO and TCO sent a delegation to South Africa to investigate conditions there, the delegation, not having at that time conducted a similar survey of its own, was anxious to obtain a copy of the survey report produced by the Committee of the Ecumenical Council.

The connection between the ecumenical action and the handling of the issue by the government and the Riksdag is thrown into still sharper relief by the fact that the two experts who had worked on behalf of the Committee of the Ecumenical Council later were taken on, one as secretary and one as an adviser to the government's own committee of inquiry. Thus, the ramifications of this external issue raised by an external organization were felt throughout much of Swedish society and government. It would be wrong to deny the *personal, spontaneous* interest of those working in the ecumenical field in opposing the system of apartheid, but they would be the first to confirm the great importance of contacts with an INGO, i.e. the World Council of Churches.

Environmental questions

Environmental problems have now captured the interest of large numbers of people. Organizations set up to safeguard the environment are growing more powerful and exerting heavy pressure on public opinion, in Sweden as in most other parts of the world. Many people regard the 1972 UN Stockholm Conference on the Human Environment as signalling the breakthrough of the environmental approach. An interesting point is that when the proposal leading to this conference was first put forward on behalf of the Swedish government at the United Nations in 1968, no conspicuous part was played by the NGOs.

Mr Ingemund Bengtsson, now Speaker of the Riksdag but Minister of Agriculture in the late sixties and early seventies, has put the matter as follows:

> In Sweden, as in many other countries, interest in environmental questions is a long-standing tradition. At first people spoke in terms of nature conservancy, not environment conservation. The strength of this interest is reflected by the early formation of the Swedish Society for the Conservation of Nature, with the aim of stimulating public concern and influencing public opinion so as to bring about legislation for the protection of our natural environment.[6]

But it is very clear that the worldwide need for measures to safeguard the environment did not galvanize either Swedish or international NGOs into requesting UN action. Ambassador Sverker Åström, who at that time was the Permanent Swedish Representative to the United Nations, has given the following description of the situation:

> At the time when the Swedish initiative calling for the convening of a United Nations conference on the human environment was taken in 1968, there was a striking lack of awareness among politicians and administrators about the global significance of the environmental problems. Political parties and national bureaucracies, with some notable exceptions, largely ignored warnings from scientific, literary and other non-governmental circles that the threat to the environment caused by man's activity was of critical importance to mankind. These warnings were dramatized in books such as Rachel Carson's 'Silent Spring' and provided an important intellectual background for the Swedish initiative, although no particular pressure was exerted

from organized non-government groups on the Swedish Government when it took its initiative in the United Nations. Once the United Nations discussions on the environment got underway, they became in themselves an important means of political pressure and contributed undoubtedly to the triggering of the explosion of environmental consciousness in the world around 1970.[7]

Once the United Nations had resolved on a conference, extensive preparations started. Governments were asked to submit national reports on the environmental situation in their various countries. Ambassador Åström writes that this made it necessary for governments to consult their scientific institutions in order to be able to present exhaustive replies, which in turn frequently gave those institutions, for the first time ever, 'the opportunity to present effectively their views to those in power'.[8] Work on these reports also came to involve the relevant NGOs. Mr Bengtsson says that their influence cannot be quantified, but 'It is clear that the governments drew on the experience and knowledge of the environmental organizations in compiling the national reports required of them.' He continues: 'The Swedish national committee . . . included representatives of environmental organizations and of the trade union movement.'[9]

The general view would seem to be that the Stockholm Conference set a trend whereby NGOs were enabled to operate jointly with a UN conference. During the preparatory phase and in the course of the ensuing activities, the NGOs were stimulated by the experience, which had a permanent impact and was of great political significance. But that is another story.

The Establishment of a Swedish Ambassador to NGOs

The political environment in Sweden has already been outlined. The popular movements exert a great deal of political influence in certain matters, and they are also accepted as natural participants in questions concerning foreign affairs. I started thinking about the possibility of Sweden going beyond domestic NGOs and co-operating more with international NGOs. They were so influential in mobilizing public opinion. Better channels to them, stronger ties with them could be mutually beneficial. The Ministry for Foreign Affairs would get better information about their work and their understanding of the world. For NGOs it could be of importance to have direct access to a government. Common ground for joint efforts could be found. When pondering on this idea it became clear to me that there was a need to create a position in the Ministry in order to get something started. In short, that was what I suggested to the Prime Minister, Mr Olof Palme.

By Swedish standards, there was nothing very sensational about a proposal to appoint an ambassador to be specially responsible for contacts with national and international NGOs. But why was I offered the post? I had a fairly long political career behind me as Secretary-General of the Liberal Party, and MP, Vice-Chairman of the party, Vice-Chairman of the Standing Committee of the Riksdag on Foreign Affairs, delegate to the United Nations and, for some years, a member of the Swedish delegation at the Geneva disarmament negotiations. In addition, I belonged to various Swedish NGOs and one international NGO. In short, I was fairly much at home with both Swedish and international conditions. Whatever party a politician with a background like this may belong to, Swedish governments are often inclined to make use of such a person. Thus, when I suggested the need for such a post, my idea was accepted by Olof Palme. It is of interest to note that although I am a Liberal, I was appointed by a Social Democratic government. Parliament was not involved. The government could act on its own. (It would be less than honest were I to hide the fact that there were also party political considerations involved.) Several of my fellow MPs said that this must be the ideal job for me, and it was.

A press communiqué was issued about the appointment. In the UN the Permanent Representative of Sweden to the United Nations informed the UN Secretary-General:

> I hereby have the honour to inform you that Ambassador Olle Dahlén has by decision of the Government of Sweden been appointed Ambassador at large at the disposal of the Minister for Foreign Affairs to deal specifically with matters concerning Non-Governmental Organizations. His special fields of interest will be social and humanitarian items, human rights and disarmament. The post is a new creation and should be seen as a manifestation of the particular interest my Government takes in the work of the NGOs and an acknowledgement of the increasingly important role that these organizations play in international affairs. Ambassador Dahlén's task will be to keep in close liaison with the NGOs and to act as a two-way channel of information and views on matters within the respective fields of competence of these organizations. In his new capacity Ambassador Dahlén will follow and keep in contact with the work of the various United Nations organs in these fields. . . .
>
> I shall be grateful to have this notification brought to the attention of the Permanent Missions to the United Nations through the courtesy of the Secretariat.[10]

During my years in parliament I was always in opposition and I had had quite a few political skirmishes with the then Foreign Minister, Mr Sven Andersson. In Sweden this augurs well for co-operation on a personal level, especially if the party political element can be eliminated. It was eliminated upon my new appointment because I left the Riksdag and party politics and so got off to a very good start with the Foreign Minister. One advantage was that my earlier international assignments had acquainted me with most of the leading officials at the Ministry. The Under-Secretary of State for Foreign Affairs was the former UN Ambassador, Sverker Åström, a good friend with whom I had shared many sessions at the United Nations. During the seventies there have been five occasions when politicians have been given completely new appointments in the Foreign Service and such a decision always arouses a certain scepticism. No doubt this was also the mood among some officials at the Ministry for Foreign Affairs. But there is no telling what trouble a politician may cause when roused, and besides as diplomats they were trained to conceal any criticism they may have felt! Consequently, I encountered nothing but courtesy and benevolence, for which I am grateful. It is essential for an 'outsider' to avoid interfering with things that do not concern him or trying to gain influence by devious ways. After some months, Mr Åström told me that it was evident that I had avoided trying to do that, and that my attitude had been appreciated.

My own idea of the task was that it ought to be something like a liaison officer. The ambassador should be a link between the NGOs and the experts inside the Ministry. At all costs I must avoid being looked upon as some competing nucleus or as a government policy-maker. My duty should be to spell out the views of 'my NGOS'. If I thought they were sound, I must argue in favour of them, but not try to have experts of my own trying to influence the decisions of the Cabinet. That would have been wrong both as a matter of principle and of practice. So when I was offered two secretaries, I declared that one was enough. At whatever cost, I wanted to avoid being forced into having a staff around me. When necessary, I should rely on the assistance of the other divisions in the Ministry. My impression is that this attitude was of value in my relations with the Ministry as a whole.

My nomination caused some questions on the part of some Swedish NGOs. They wanted to know my exact duties. I got in touch with them immediately and tried to explain my appointment in greater detail to those NGOs directly concerned. I expressed the hope that we would succeed by concerted efforts in finding the appropriate forms of co-operation. I do not recall any negative criticism. On the other hand, the government received quite a few compliments on having made the appointment. The appointment aroused a great deal of attention among the international NGOs (INGOs), for this was the first time in history that a government had appointed an ambassador to INGOs. The INGOs clearly felt honoured, and invitations began to flow in. It has been a constant problem choosing from all the requests and invitations received for visits, lectures and so on. Four months a year has seemed a reasonable maximum limit for globetrotting.

Formal and informal inquiries have been received from other governments concerning the implications of the appointment. I have myself on many occasions tried to explain this matter to people in foreign offices and to diplomats. This has not been so difficult in countries where NGOs are influential, but it has been more of a problem in countries whose governments do not desire pressure from or co-operation with NGOs. Many INGOs and NGOs have asked for a description of my duties and have then approached various governments in the hope of their following suit. Many national NGOs have criticized the hesitation of their own governments to follow the same course as the Swedish government. To my knowledge, only the French and Norwegian governments have established similar appointments. The duties involved vary, however. The Norwegian Ministry for Foreign Affairs paid me two visits during 1979 before the decision was taken in January 1980. The French ambassador in Geneva asked to see me as far back as mid-1974 in order to be informed. He was later appointed to a similar post.

The Development of the Task

It goes without saying that the activities entailed by a completely new appointment will not develop exactly as envisaged, and there are a number of unexpected additions worth considering in detail in connection with the description of my duties. However, as envisaged, it has turned out to be an office with heavy stresses on *personal* contacts; being personally accessible, for small as well as large INGOs and NGOs, concerned with all sorts of issues; building up a personal relationship with representatives of national and international NGOs. As there are so many of them, this is possible only with a limited number. That is one reason why it has been of such importance to follow closely the work of the Conference of NGOs (CONGO) at the United Nations.

Diary of a year's work

Maybe my diary for 1980 could be a starting-point for giving an impression of the range of the work. During the year I travelled abroad for eighty days, which was less than other years. My visits to Geneva and New York included contacts at the UN as well as numerous meetings with INGOs, collectively and separately, and with diplomats dealing with NGO matters. One of the visits to Geneva included the Non-Proliferation Treaty Review Conference, part of which I attended, combining it with the Central Committee of the World Council of Churches. Other trips took me to Cyprus, Egypt, Finland, Federal Republic of Germany, Kenya, Spain and Tanzania. In most cases the meetings concerned human rights and/or the arms race. The reason for visiting Tanzania was that the Swedish ambassador had invited fifty persons working for Swedish churches in Tanzania to discuss common concerns. They included doctors, nurses, teachers, pastors, engineers, economists, etc. One of the days during the conference was devoted to discussions with high-level officials in both the Tanzanian government and in the national churches. The conference was the second of its kind. The first one had taken place in New Delhi in 1978. Both occasions were very inspiring in what was learnt about development at the grass roots.

There are sixty-one meetings with INGOs noted in my diary for 1980, some quite brief, others lengthy: one lasted twelve days. During the year I met thirty-eight times with Swedish NGOs. Even these meetings were not all of the same length or the same type. One full day was spent on a conference with NGOs, when a number of experts from the Ministry of Foreign Affairs gave information, under my chairmanship, about important issues on the agenda of the forthcoming UN General Assembly session. The Swedish United Nations Association arranged another forum, on the subject of the General Assembly, and I gave a lecture about the regional groupings among the UN's members. Special stress was laid on the Nordic group and their voting record on crucial issues. In connection with the UN Women's Conference in Copenhagen, several preparatory meetings were held with governmental agencies, both about NGO participation in the official conference and about grants to the 'unofficial' NGO Forum. I was able to arrange for one of the co-ordinators for the Forum to visit Sweden to meet with representatives of the Government's preparatory committee and with representatives of Swedish NGOs which were interested. The preparations for the UN Conference on New and Renewable Sources of Energy, which was held in Nairobi in August 1981, also started in 1980 and resulted in talks in Stockholm, Geneva, Nairobi and New York regarding NGO participation in the conference.

International NGOs

INGOs publish a great deal of information material, periodicals, resolutions, statements, research reports and so on. Another type of information emerges during attendance at the conferences, meetings and workshops to which I am invited. INGOs also make direct representations to the Swedish Government, and I usually have the task of replying to them. All information from these various channels is useful for notes, memoranda, etc., which I prepare and send to Ministry experts, to the ambassadors concerned and sometimes to the Minister for Foreign Affairs. The job is quite like that done by an ambassador to a foreign country. People back home have to be kept informed about the lie of the land, general trends and concerns. In addition, it is important to report about emerging ideas, which will influence the political scene in the future.

No one can report everything. One has to be something like a warehouse manager — able to deliver the goods when they are wanted: 'What do you know about these people?' or 'Do you know anyone who could give us the information we need?' These are questions which I am always being asked by colleagues at home or abroad at our embassies. Sometimes I know, sometimes I have to ask my friends among the INGOs and they usually come up with the answer.

Political surveys

In several cases my activities have also resulted in memoranda aimed at summarizing a whole group of problems. This is a role which was not foreseen when the post was originally established. For example, I produced a general memorandum on religious conflicts. When I took up my new appointment in January 1974, they were already becoming more and more a pronounced feature of world politics. Clashes between the adherents of different religions were taking place on an unprecedented scale. My contacts with the world religions, above all with Judaism, Christianity and Islam, had made it possible to augment the information reaching us through other channels. The personal links I have gradually been able to forge in various parts of the world have proved valuable and I have benefited from meetings and visits to some of the trouble spots. Quite a few surveys have been compiled, bringing together the results of this kind of fact-finding work. They are sent not only to the relevant departments at the Ministry, but also to our embassies in the countries concerned. Judging by the comments received, it seems as though they have also been read sometimes!

Information to others about Swedish initiatives

When the Swedish Government takes a new foreign policy initiative, it is my task to inform the INGOs, especially if the issue concerns disarmament, *détente* or human rights. In this way, important Swedish speeches and proposals in the United Nations and other fora reach a wider audience. One also finds that Swedish standpoints often coincide with those of many of the INGOs, a fact which perhaps is not very surprising in the light of our foreign policy of not having any bloc commitments. Many INGOs are endeavouring similarly to be independent and critical in relation to the great powers. It is often rewarding to compare notes, particularly with representatives one has come to know well and to regard as colleagues.

Sweden has a good position among the INGOs. Many of them closely monitor the record of governments on international development co-operation. As Sweden is one of only four countries which have reached the United Nations target for levels of assistance, we have gained the respect of the INGOs and this has a favourable effect on our contacts with them. We have found that INGOs are interested in receiving from us short surveys on such topics as the treatment of disarmament problems in the First Committee of the UN General Assembly and at the Conference of the Committee on Disarmament in Geneva. These surveys are written as objectively as possible, but I suppose that more scope is given to Swedish initiatives than would be the case had they been written in Moscow or Washington. Consequently, knowledge of action taken by little Sweden is probably more widespread than information about the actions of other similar countries.

One unexpected development in the work of the Ambassador to INGOs has been the invitations received from universities and colleges, to lecture and to participate in seminars on international affairs or Swedish foreign policy. Unfortunately, it has been impossible to accept more than a few of these invitations. This I regret, because I find the encounters very stimulating. But an overloaded work schedule rules out more lectures.

Financial grants to INGOs

Since 1977 it has been possible for INGOs to apply to the Swedish Ministry for Foreign Affairs for grants towards special projects of limited duration, particularly projects concerning disarmament and human rights. Grants are not available for the regular activities of INGOs, their secretariats or their annual congresses, because in our opinion this would imply too great a degree of financial dependence on a particular government. These grants were introduced at my suggestion; the government presented a bill which was passed by the Riksdag. The sums involved are not particularly large, totalling as they do Skr.300,000 per annum, which at the present rate of exchange is roughly £30,000. One reason for having these grants available is to be able to help people from the Third World to take part in INGO activities.

INGOs in the UN System

Article 71 of the United Nations Charter authorizes the Economic and Social Council to make special arrangements for consultation with NGOs. On the strength of this Article, arrangements have evolved, to the mutual satisfaction of both the United Nations and the INGOs. The system has spread to large sectors of the United Nations network, including UNICEF, UNDP, UNESCO, the Disarmament Centre and the Department of Public Information, for example.[11] ECOSOC's relations with INGOs are governed by Resolution 1296(XLIV), but the implementation of this resolution has not been without its problems. A committee of thirteen from the governments represented on the Council is appointed to attend to the details. Sweden was a member during the sixties and has now been a member since 1976. I chaired this committee from 1977 to 1979.

ECOSOC concedes INGO status at three distinct levels which in itself prompts rivalry between some of the INGOs (see Chapter 1). The member states sometimes have political viewpoints on applications from different NGOs. This applies above all to the permanent Security Council members which are always members of the committee, with the exception of China. Good intentions are mingled with suspicion, and this sometimes generates conflicts. For the greater part of its existence, the committee has based its decision-making on the consensus principle, and blockages have therefore occurred as a result of one or two committee members exercising their power of 'veto'. Usually these 'vetoes' are put forward by the major powers.

Governmental attitudes

My impression is that many governments are now keeping themselves more closely informed about the work of the NGOs than they used to. When talking now to colleagues from other delegations at the UN, I can see a change of attitude compared to when I started in this post in 1974. The change is clear, even if some governments try to give the opposite impression. It is impossible, however, to quantify the influence which is being exerted, especially as many governments, if taxed on the subject, would profess complete indifference to the signals given by NGOs and other opinion-moulding groups. There are several reasons for the increased attention given to INGOs. Generally speaking, they now obtain more publicity when they issue statements concerning disarmament, human rights, international assistance, the environment and other questions. The participation of INGOs in specialized UN conferences has attracted considerable public and media interest, as witness the 1972 Stockholm Conference on the Human Environment, the Food and Population Conferences, the 1975 Women's Conference in Mexico and the 1978 Special Session of the UN General Assembly on Disarmament. There is a distinct element of political rivalry involved. The INGOs linked with the World Peace Council and nearly all those whose names include the word 'democratic' have close ties with the Eastern bloc. During the 1970s abundant financial support enabled them to expand their activities substantially, and this inevitably gained the attention of the Western countries. Thus, for this reason, there has been a certain heightening of the interest taken in INGOs. Accordingly, no matter whether a government regards INGOs as allies or troublesome opponents, many governments tend to be less indifferent to their actions.

During the period in which I have been in a position to observe its work, the ECOSOC Committee on NGOs has come to take its duties increasingly seriously. Applications from INGOs for consultative status or to change their existing status, coupled with the review conducted in recent years of the INGOs' own quadrennial reports, have forced the committee members into greater activity. But in some cases interest has also increased independently of this kind of pressure. Third World committee members are now often more favourably disposed towards INGOs. They have realized that INGOs and NGOs are their best friends in promoting bigger international development assistance and a new international economic order. In some cases when an Eastern State has criticized an INGO for not being 'sufficiently international', i.e. having too many Western members in its directorate, the INGO concerned has been vigorously defended by some Third World representatives, often with the result that the Eastern state has had to climb down. Exceptions apply, above all if an NGO can be suspected of not having a clearcut stand against apartheid. Another particular difficulty occurs with NGOs which devote great attention to the violation of human rights in certain member countries. In recent years, for example, Argentina, which is not a member of the Committee, has often requested observer status and has taken this opportunity of sharply criticizing such INGOs as the International Commission of Jurists.

The Soviet Union sometimes displays some irritation towards certain NGOs. The Soviet delegates have said on several occasions that it is the 'duty' of NGOs to work for the resolutions passed by the United Nations. I have had reason to remark that this is very 'generous' of the Soviet Union, because in many disarmament votes, for example, the Soviet Union — and the United States — feel unable to vote in favour of a resolution. Thus the Soviet view implies that an NGO is duty bound to pursue an aim which the Soviet Union feels unable to support. But this observation, when made, is not appreciated.

The working relationship

Most of the NGOs originated in the Western world, a fact which influences their policies. Some INGOs have changed drastically and have become truly international as regards both the composition of their directorates and the numbers of countries which they represent. In the latter respect, however, there is a clear difference between NGOs with extensive grassroot contacts in their countries — the religious NGOs, for example — and the INGOs which, formally speaking, have many national ramifications but in many cases are really confined to a small national committee without popular support.

INGOs naturally vary in their attitudes towards co-operation with the United Nations. Those which are truly influential do not need the UN as a sounding board; instead the UN needs them, and some of them know it. Others entertain what might almost be termed an unrequited love for the UN. They are immensely honoured by being able to print 'Consultative status with ECOSOC' on their letter heads, but that is more or less the sum total of their dealings with the United Nations. Their resources and aims are rather limited. Being there is enough for them.

Where the powerful NGOs are concerned, the present situation at the UN is not satisfactory. One problem is what facilities are to be accorded NGOs in connection with the many special conferences and meetings arranged by the UN. A constantly recurring question is that of which NGOs are to be allowed to participate in, or be invited to, these events. Often one has to start from scratch every time a special UN event is being planned. Are NGOs with ECOSOC status to be invited regardless of category? Or just NGOs which have displayed concern for the subject of the meeting? If the number of participants has to be limited, who is to make the selection? In recent years some of the secretariats of the various UN meetings have tended to claim for themselves the power of deciding these questions. Sometimes the results have been acceptable, sometimes the most representative NGOs have been kept outside. If the various secretariats alone were to select from among the NGOs, neither the NGOs themselves nor the member states would have any chance of influencing the selection. There can be no question of selecting NGOs according to whether one endorses their views or not. There must be objective criteria of selection. One such criterion, for example, is that NGOs must have displayed genuine interest in the problem concerned — *before* there was any talk of a conference.

It is all to the good that INGOs should establish contacts with members of the ECOSOC NGO Committee, that they should attend sessions of the General Assembly and that they should take part in the special UN conferences to which they are invited. Activities of this kind ought in fact to be expanded. It is only by keeping close track of UN activities that INGOs can effectively bring pressure to bear, put forward proposals and mobilize opinion. Knowledge is power, but knowledge does not come down like manna from Heaven; it is to be acquired. On the other hand, it is regrettable that the majority of INGOs with national associations in many countries so conspicuously neglect the mobilization of opinion and lobbying activities in the various national capitals. Decisions about the guidelines for major political issues are made by governments and parliaments, not as a rule by national UN delegations. Opinion mobilized at home must be taken far more seriously by any impressionable government than statements made by INGOs at the international level. There are certain exceptions to this latter rule, such as statements concerning the violation of human rights by a regime, which also have a great impact when made by INGOs.

Needless to say, the Swedish government and Riksdag are sensitive to the powerful opinions voiced by the Swedish popular movements. I attempted by way of introduction to describe the part played by Swedish NGOs in moulding public opinion. Sweden is hardly an exception among democracies in this respect, even though conditions are never quite identical in different countries and cultural environments. One depressing observation is that many national NGOs are not very well informed about the activities of the INGOs to which they belong. Closer contacts and interchanges between national NGOs and their international organizations would in many cases lend added weight to the pressure they can exert on Governments.

Swedish proposals at the UN

Thus co-operation between the member states, the UN Secretariat and INGOs is by no means without its problems. There is little that outsiders can do about political antipathies, but there is a great deal that can be done about the actual technique of co-operation. Rules must be framed to facilitate co-operation. Problems also arise in a number of concrete situations, for example, when deciding which NGOs are to be invited to attend a UN meeting. Since, so far, I have been practically the only ambassador to NGOs, I am often contacted regarding problems of this kind, and it may be appropriate that somebody should always be available for consultations. I have no objection to being regarded as a kind of ombudsman for INGOs — not as an advocate of all their ideas and proposals but as an advocate of their right to put forward those ideas and proposals. Whether I have scored any success on this count is for others to decide.

At the ECOSOC NGO Committee in February 1981, I made a statement on behalf of the Swedish government from which the following is an excerpt:

Proposal regarding co-operation with NGOs

The fields where the UN is co-operating with the NGOs are growing constantly. That is a fact. However, certain anomalies are left to be remedied. The Swedish delegation would like to highlight some specific issues.

a) *The General Assembly*

The General Assembly committees are gradually opening themselves up to participation in different forms from the NGOs. We can today speak about an emerging praxis in this regard. This process should be welcomed and further strengthened.

b) *Ad Hoc conferences*

A standard formula ought to be set up for the NGO participation in *Ad Hoc* conferences. The formula used for the UN Conference on Desertification seems to be acceptable. (GA resolution 31/108, paras 3 and 4): The Secretary-General should be requested to invite 'interested non-governmental organizations in consultative status with the Economic and Social Council to be represented by observers . . .' and, in addition, he should be authorized to invite '. . . other interested non-governmental organizations that might have a specific contribution to make to the work of the Conference to be represented by observers.'

In order to avoid any biased selectivity when inviting NGOs, the Secretariat of a conference should inform the organizations about the conference and then it is up to them to request to be invited.

A useful formula for inclusion in the Rules of Procedure for the conferences regarding the arrangements for the participation of the organizations was offered by the First Vice-President of the Conference of NGOs, Ms Alba Zizzamia, in her statement to the UN Committee on Conferences, 23 April 1980.

1. Non-Governmental organizations invited to the Conference may designate representatives to sit as observers at public meetings of the Conference and its main committees.

2. Upon the invitation of the presiding officer of the body concerned and subject to the approval of that body, such observers may make oral statements on questions in which they have special competence.

3. Written statements submitted by such non-governmental organizations on subjects in which they have a special competence which are related to the work of the Conference, shall be circulated by the Secretariat in the quantities and in the languages in which the statements are made available to the Secretariat for distribution.

A formula like this will not solve the problem if there will not be a careful implementation. The bureau, as well as the Secretariats of the conferences, have to *plan* for the right kind of involvement from the NGOs. There have been some unfortunate mistakes in the past. We propose that this committee proposes to the General Assembly, through ECOSOC, that such a formula is accepted.

Staffing problems

The expanding co-operation between the UN system and the NGOs has not been accompanied by adequate increases in staffing. We are privileged in the ECOSOC to have a hard-working staff in the Department of International Economic and Social Affairs (DIESA). We are very grateful to them for the assistance we receive. But it is obvious that the ever-increasing bulk of matters makes it necessary to have additional staff in DIESA.

The first Vice President of the Conference of NGOs suggested that this secretariat should be consulted by other units when dealing with the NGOs. We certainly agree on that.

Even on another point we find ourselves in agreement with Ms Zizzamia when she suggested that there ought to be made clear what kind of distinction there is between the NGOs which have consultative status with the ECOSOC and those on the list of the Department of Public Information. There is a lot of confusion in this regard. We would be grateful if the Secretary-General could find ways to clarify the situation.

In Geneva at the UN there is a Liaison Office serving in relation to the NGOs, which has turned out to be of great value for both parts.

In view of this, I wrote in November 1979 on behalf of the Swedish government to the Assistant Secretary-General for Social Development and Humanitarian Affairs and proposed that a similar post had to be created in Vienna. The co-operation we all need cannot be achieved without someone having the responsibility, on a full-time basis, to carry this work through. It is not enough that a member of the different bureaus in Vienna, in addition to other responsibilities, are trying to have contacts with the NGOs.

In this connection I would like to express our concern that in UNEP in Nairobi the position of NGO Liaison Officer has been abolished.

In May 1981, ECOSOC decided that the NGO Committee should undertake a review of the relationship between the NGOs and the UN system and that the Secretary-General should propose a set of standardized procedures for inviting NGOs to UN conferences.

Relations with Swedish NGOs

As was made clear in the introduction, the Swedish NGOs are an inseparable part of contemporary Swedish society. Consequently, the channels leading to policy-making bodies, the government, the Riksdag and the national administrative boards are well known. This is not to say that they cannot be improved, and some attempts have been made in this direction in recent years. The Ministry for Foreign Affairs now holds regular briefings for Swedish NGOs, covering international development assistance, disarmament, apartheid and UN affairs generally. As a result, the inquiries received by us at the Ministry have been growing. The Ministry's Information Department produces several publications aimed at voluntary organizations, the mass media, schools and members of the general public wishing to keep abreast of international affairs.

In connection with particular Swedish initiatives at the United Nations and in other international fora, I supply the Swedish NGOs with more detailed information, providing a necessary supplement to that conveyed by the news media. Ministry officials are invited to visit NGOs to keep them informed, and occasions of this kind are also taken as an opportunity for NGOs to express their own attitude to current problems. For some years now I have been supplying about eighty national and local NGOs in Sweden with the Blue Book, published annually by the Ministry for Foreign Affairs, containing a summary of UN General Assembly proceedings. This also outlines a large number of topics which are likely to be raised at the next session of the General Assembly and about which the government is keen to hear views as to the position which ought to be taken by Sweden. This information, then, is both retrospective and forward-looking. Response frequencies vary. Not all NGOs respond every year. But over a period of three years most NGOs have reacted. All the answers received are summarized and put into the dossier of background material for the UN delegation.

At the instance of the government, the Riksdag makes annual grants to Swedish organizations providing information on international affairs. Similar grants are made by SIDA in the context of international development policy. Some years ago — at my suggestion — the Minister for Foreign Affairs introduced the practice of inviting two representatives of Swedish NGOs to spend four weeks observing the work of the Swedish delegation during the regular sessions of the UN General Assembly. All travel and living expenses are paid by the government, and the NGO representatives are included in the delegation as observers.

Contacts within the Ministry for Foreign Affairs

I have already shown how the various kinds of information reaching me are passed on to appropriate departments at the Ministry. Information is passed on both by word of mouth and in writing to the many experts and, in some cases, to the Minister personally. I get in touch with ambassadors who are concerned with a particular issue. Sometimes it has also proved useful to inform other Ministries and the Standing Committee of the Riksdag on Foreign Affairs. Memoranda and notes are sometimes transmitted to the relevant Swedish

NGOs, and this can also include classified documents. It has proved generally appropriate to classify some of the information which I receive in confidence from international personal contacts within NGOs concerning, for example the violation of human rights in a particular country. Sometimes too, of course, information is directly supplied to me from the people affected in the country concerned.

During my official visits abroad, I sometimes have special reason, when talking to members of governments or to diplomats, to emphasize Swedish standpoints relevant to the country concerned — Sweden opposes capital punishment, Sweden takes the question of political prisoners seriously — it was not foreseen that matters of this kind would form part of my duties.

It is becoming increasingly common for the political departments in the Ministry to get in touch with me concerning particular cases or the general situation in a country. It is always a pleasure to be consulted as though one knew something which nobody else does. Sometimes I do know the answer, and sometimes I promise to find out. While writing these words, I have been telephoned by a colleague who wants to know what is behind the desire expressed by an influential group of NGOs in a communist country for a visit by the King and Queen of Sweden! I knew the answer, partly because of my familiarity with the organizations. But this is an unusual example. Most of the questions I receive are of a down-to-earth political nature. It is important for ambassadors to have good contacts outside the official network. Judging by the kind remarks passed by my colleagues at a number of embassies, it would seem that I have been able to put them in touch with interesting personalities and organizations.

What I have to do is to supply the Ministry with something that is not already fully available there. One dimension of this kind is knowledge of the currents of opinion outside those traditionally observed by people concerned with international policy. Ideological, cultural and religious opinions have not always been given high priority. It has been correspondingly easier for the immediate political and economic causes of conflict to attract attention. It is unrealistic to forecast conceivable future alternatives without including factors of this other kind in the equations, which are hard enough to solve in any case, considering the many unknown variables they contain. Foreign policy forecasters have a traditional tendency to overlook this. I have made it my business to bring out these other forms of pressure exerted by opinion, of which attitudes in national NGOs and INGOs are often good indicators.

Naturally, both Swedish and international NGOs at times have specific problems which they want to have solved or elucidated. These problems are not always of a clearly political nature. On such occasions — and they are many — one's task is to try to provide service, to be of assistance even if this requires highly unconventional methods measured by diplomatic standards. It is not very difficult for a person with experience of party politics to cut red tape, especially if he avoids publicizing the fact.

Summary

What is the significance of an appointment like this at a foreign ministry?

- Providing constant reminders to diplomats of the existence of NGOs.
- Promoting their justified demands for a hearing, for participation both at home and abroad, at the United Nations and elsewhere.
- Engaging in reciprocal dealings with NGOs: seeing what they are doing and hearing what they want.
- Informing others what the Swedish Government is doing and what its views are concerning important points on the international agenda.
- Providing intervention and information in particular situations.
- Contributing to a long-term debate involving the flow of ideas in Sweden and in the world at large.
- Establishing good personal relations with the leaders of influential NGOs (there are many such organizations, sometimes in places where one would least expect to find them).
- Providing a rallying point for Swedish and international NGOs which have international issues on their agenda and often maintain activities of their own in different parts of the world: trying here to be something of a trouble-shooter.

Impressive action — which can hardly be very frequent — is not the most important thing. Instead, anyone with a job like mine should try to channel influence like water seeping through the various strata of opinion and power — anywhere and everywhere.

References

1 There is a problem in defining Swedish NGOs. The free churches, the temperance organizations and the labour movements came to be known early on as *popular movements* (folkrörelser). Further organizations were later added to the list: consumer and producer co-operatives, sports organizations, *voluntary agencies* like the Red Cross and the Save the Children Fund and a number of others. However, the co-operative organizations and the labour unions and other associations of similar kind are gradually developing in the direction of becoming *interest* organizations. I endorse the distinction made by the Swedish researcher in this field, Dr Sven Lundkvist, between popular movements, i.e. those still founded on 'voluntary support and the dynamic element' on the one hand, and all other organizations on the other. In this paper there is no need to deal with these two types separately. They are all NGOs influencing our society and are of importance in understanding the Swedish background. Sven Lundkvist: 'The Popular Movements in Today's Society' (Stockholm, the Swedish Institute, No. 218, May 1979), p. 2.
2 Lundkvist: *Folkrörelserna i det svenska samhället, 1850–1920* (Stockholm, Acta Universitatis Upsaliensis, 1977), p. 218. Lundkvist refers, for example, to the image conveyed by Harold Perkin in *The Origins of Modern English Society*, London, 1969.
3 Lundkvist, op. cit., p. 219.
4 Ernst Michanek: 'The Role of Swedish Non-Governmental Organizations in International Development Co-operation', paper written for UNITAR (Stockholm, SIDA, April 1977), p. 8.

5 Michanek, op. cit., pp. 18–19.

6 Ingemund Bengtsson, Swedish Minister of Agriculture, 1969–73, letter to the author, July 1980.

7 Sverker Åström, Swedish Ambassador to the UN, 1964–70, letter to the author, 19 August 1980.

8 Ibid.

9 Bengtsson, loc. cit.

10 United Nations document NV/374, 21 May 1974.

11 Marianne Huggard, NY, former Vice President of the Conference of NGOs in Consultative Status with ECOSOC (CONGO), is engaged on a review of the various forms of partnership between the UN agencies and NGOs. This study is being financed with grants from the Swedish Ministry for Foreign Affairs.

9 Participation of Non-Governmental Organizations in the Activities of the United Nations High Commissioner for Refugees

GILBERT JAEGER

Introduction

It would not be enough to say that the role of the non-governmental organization in the matter of refugees is important: it is vital. The Office of the United Nations High Commissioner for Refugees (UNHCR) was established in its present form as a subsidiary body of the General Assembly of the United Nations by Resolution 319(IV) adopted by the Assembly on 3 December 1949; it became operational on 1 January 1951. The UNHCR is, however, the direct heir to a series of successive bodies, starting with the High Commissioner for Russian Refugees, whom the League of Nations appointed on 20 August 1921 in the person of Dr Fridtjof Nansen, the Norwegian scholar, explorer and philanthropist, whose name is indissolubly linked to international activities on behalf of refugees.

The important point to be noted here is that the question had been brought to the attention of the Council of the League of Nations by a conference of non-governmental organizations which were directly concerned, convened by the International Committee of the Red Cross and the League of Red Cross Societies, and that it was in response to the invitation of that conference that the Council had set up an office of High Commissioner for Refugees. The Red Cross Societies and other charitable organizations, as well as a number of governments, had in fact initiated international work on behalf of refugees as soon as the problem had arisen, that is, already during the First World War (1914 to 1918). These organizations were in the best position to realize the need for the international co-ordination of those efforts and for the performance of certain functions — notably legal functions — for which non-governmental organizations are not qualified. This episode of 1921 summarizes, as it were, the fundamental role of the non-governmental organizations both with respect to the problem of refugees and with respect to the inter-governmental organization qualified to deal with it.

The Status of Non-Governmental Organizations with UNHCR

As an integral part of the United Nations, placed under the direct authority of the General Assembly of the United Nations and reporting also — if and when required — to the Economic and Social Council, the UNHCR naturally grants to the non-governmental organizations the status which each of them has with the latter Council, whether as organizations in categories I or II or on the 'Roster'. At the same time, however, the UNHCR, whose attitude is essentially pragmatic, co-operates with any organization if it considers that such co-operation is beneficial to refugees and provided that the co-operation is carried on for humanitarian and social, not for political, purposes.[1] The formal status of the non-governmental organization is therefore a matter of secondary interest for the UNHCR.

This comment is all the more important as quite a number of non-governmental organizations which enjoy a specific status with the United Nations are scarcely concerned with refugees and displaced persons or take only an occasional interest in them.[2] On the other hand, many non-governmental organizations that are concerned with refugees and displaced persons (either as a principal activity or as a part of other activities) do not even appear on the Roster. This is particularly true of non-governmental organizations which have a national status, but the remark applies also to some international or transnational associations.

While it is hardly possible to draw up a complete list of the national and international non-governmental organizations which deal with refugees and displaced persons and which co-operate in that capacity with the UNHCR, an attempt may, however, be made to estimate the number of strictly transnational and international organizations. In these two categories about a hundred such organizations can readily be identified with which the UNHCR has established relations of varying degrees of closeness. If non-governmental organizations having national status are added, the total figure rises to several hundred.

The Role of Non-Governmental Organizations with Respect to UNHCR

From the point of view of the UNHCR, the functions of the non-governmental organizations can be differentiated according to whether they are consultative, complementary or supplementing, or executive. Before these various functions are analysed, a succinct description is needed of the *functions of UNHCR*. According to the Statute of UNHCR, 'the United Nations High Commissioner for Refugees . . . shall assume the function of providing international protection . . . and of seeking permanent solutions for the problems of refugees. . . .

The objectives of international protection are:
To enable refugees to obtain durable asylum;

To make provision for the special position of the refugee as a resident alien who cannot enjoy the diplomatic and consular protection of the country of his nationality;

To grant to the refugee, in the country of asylum, a juridical status as close as possible to that of nationals resident in that country, particularly as regards civil, economic, social and cultural matters.

A distinction is drawn between general protection activities (development of the international and national juridical framework, implementation of laws and conventions, etc.) and direct protection activities (action on behalf of specific persons or groups).

The expression 'permanent solutions' covers voluntary repatriation (which may, particularly where large groups are involved, be associated with economic and social integration in the country of origin) and, in the more frequent cases where repatriation is not possible, the economic and social integration of refugees in the country of permanent settlement. This may be either the country of first asylum or a third country; in the latter case, integration is preceded by a phase of resettlement from one country to another.

The search for the furtherance and the application of permanent solutions form part, chiefly, in UNHCR terminology, of the material assistance programmes. They also include emergency relief, which is a phase preceding the permanent solutions. To an outside observer, the material assistance programmes are the most conspicuous, or even spectacular, of the activities of UNHCR. They have, moreover, expanded considerably in recent years and may involve an expenditure of over 500 million dollars in 1980.

The Consultative Role of the Non-Governmental Organizations

For the UNHCR the non-governmental organizations represent the organized expression of public opinion — and above all of interested public opinion — on refugees and displaced persons. Although the UNHCR is also in direct contact with refugees and displaced persons, and with the general public, in particular through the UNHCR branch offices which are established in a great many countries spread over the five continents, and even though the non-governmental organizations keep in constant touch with the authorities, the fact remains that the UNHCR is essentially intergovernmental, whereas the non-governmental organizations are private organizations which have the advantage of making closer contact, free of all formality, with the individual refugee and his family. This is particularly true of 'field work', that is, the local services of these organizations, which are obviously much more in touch with the public than are the executive committees or governing bodies at the international level.

The consultative role of the non-governmental organizations takes various forms:

Through the participation of non-governmental organizations in sessions of the Executive Committee of the High Commissioner's Programme and in *ad hoc* consultative meetings convened by the UNHCR;

Through the participation of UNHCR in congresses of a federal type (International Council of Voluntary Agencies, International Red Cross, World Federation of United Nations Associations, etc.), or in national meetings, or else in annual meetings of a particular non-governmental organization (e.g. Amnesty International);

Through the participation of the UNHCR in symposia, study sessions or seminars organized by one or more of the non-governmental organizations.

These modes of consultation and co-operation are familiar and need little or no further description. Rather, what should be noted is that the consultative role of the non-governmental organizations is in no way confined to such formal occasions. What are just as important — and probably even more important — are the daily contacts between the services of these organizations and those of UNHCR, at both central and local levels. It is in the course of these contacts, when the subjects discussed are about essentially specific problems, whether of a general nature or relating to particular situations (and one discovers affinities between persons motivated by the same concerns), that a genuine symbiosis develops and is maintained between the intergovernmental organization and the non-governmental society.

The Supplementary Role of the Non-Governmental Organizations

The problem of refugees and displaced persons has become so universal and omnipresent that its ramifications permeate the whole of the social fabric. It is of concern to the Red Cross Society of this or that African country which is called upon to organize an emergency medical service in some frontier area where there is an influx of refugees; to the captain at some port in South-East Asia who asks for permission to put ashore a group of 'boat people' rescued on the high seas; to the lecturer at an American university who is preparing a lecture on the 1951 Convention and 1967 Protocol relating to the status of refugees; or to the social services department of some city in Europe which is asked to prepare, with the assistance of local charities, for the reception and housing of twenty families due to arrive in two weeks' time.

The UNHCR is, so to speak, at the centre of a network of public and private, national and international bodies, for the purpose of performing promotional and co-ordinating functions. It is a kind of general staff headquarters which sends out into the field liaison officers on various missions. The protection of the millions of refugees throughout the world[3] and the provision of material assistance to a far greater number, if displaced persons are added, inevitably involve the mobilization — on a permanent footing — of the authorities and charitable organizations concerned. In the final analysis it is these authorities and bodies which are responsible for the immediate field work — the authorities ex officio and the non-governmental organizations by virtue of their vocation.

The supplementing role of the non-governmental organizations is most evident in the field of material assistance. Most frequently it is these organizations which distribute food, clothing and blankets, which organize health and sanitation services and which initiate — in so far as they do not assume full responsibility for — the process of integration.

The international protection of the refugee is the primary and most specific function of UNHCR and for this reason the High Commissioner does not, save in special circumstances, delegate this function to others. Yet, also in connection with the protection of refugees, the non-governmental organizations play an important supplementary part. In the first place, there is in actual practice a close connection between the protection of refugees and the function of providing material assistance to refugees. Economic and social integration involves the deployment of a whole series of material resources, necessarily within a legal framework (access to educational facilities, right to work, etc.).

Some non-governmental organizations do not carry on any material assistance activities, but concentrate on helping the individual to obtain asylum, a work permit, etc. Others, which are concerned with the more general problems of human rights, arrange seminars, draw attention to gaps in legislation or to administrative malpractices at the national or international level.

UNHCR is obviously called upon to publicize the problems of refugees, as well as the activities undertaken on their behalf. In this respect, too, the non-governmental organizations play an essential supplementary role. The publications, films, etc. of the UNHCR are written or spoken in only few of the world's better known languages and reach directly only a small fraction of world opinion. Material published by the non-governmental organizations, on the other hand, particularly that published at the national level, reaches the public in depth in its own language and in appropriate specific ways.

Lastly, the hundreds of millions of dollars which the UNHCR has to spend ($162 million in 1978, $350 million in 1979) require a corresponding fund-raising effort. Appeals for funds are addressed mainly to governments. However, the non-governmental organizations obtain very substantial sums for the UNHCR ($9.5 million in 1978, $17.6 million in 1979), which they collect by organizing fund-raising drives that can be quite spectacular, both as to the methods employed and as to their results. In most cases they entrust a large part of the funds so collected to the UNHCR, keeping for themselves resources which in any case are used to support and supplement the international work on behalf of refugees.

In some cases the supplementary role of the non-governmental organizations might better be described as a primary role, for in the first place, these organizations existed long before UNHCR and, secondly, they often act independently in situations where the UNHCR cannot intervene. There have in fact been, and there still are, refugee situations where the government concerned does not wish to 'internationalize' the problem by appealing to official organizations. In such cases, the scope for action by the non-governmental organizations, which by definition do not have an official mandate, is far more flexible, and even broader. This remark applies also to situations where the status of the persons in need is ill-defined and where the UNHCR, although it has been authorized for some years now to deal with displaced persons who do not have refugee status, is not in a position to intervene.

This 'primary' role of the non-governmental organizations does not, strictly speaking, come within the scope of the co-operation between them and the UNHCR. In the final analysis, however, and if one looks at the matter in a broader setting, it is, in effect a division of labour in the international work for refugees.

The Executive Role of the Non-Governmental Organizations

Governments frequently apply to the UNHCR for help in dealing in a concrete fashion with the problems arising out of the presence of refugees — especially of large groups of refugees and displaced persons — in the territory of the state concerned. The help requested may take several forms:

Emergency relief for refugees arriving from neighbouring countries;

Measures for the economic and social integration of refugees and displaced persons likely to take up permanent residence in the country of first asylum or in the country of resettlement (establishment of new farming communities for rural groups, employment and housing projects for refugees from urban areas, etc.);

Reintegration measures — in rural and urban areas — for former refugees repatriated to their country of origin.

The UNHCR entrusts the carrying out of these programmes to 'operational partners' or to 'executing agencies' which are, very often, non-governmental organizations possessing the necessary experience and facilities. Contractual relationships are thus established between the UNHCR and these organizations, the provisions of which vary according to the situation. As regards finance, for example, some contracts are financed wholly by the UNHCR, while in other cases, the non-governmental organization concerned makes a substantial contribution in personnel, relief supplies (medicaments, foodstuffs, etc.) or in cash.

Limits of Participation

Yet, on occasion, the interpenetration of the activities of the non-governmental organizations and of the UNHCR, the 'genuine symbiosis' mentioned earlier, is obstructed by circumstances which highlight the specificity of the inter-governmental organization and of the non-governmental organization respectively.

By the terms of the Statute, it is the function of the UNHCR to protect and assist refugees 'by assisting Governments'. So far as international protection is concerned, the High Commissioner very often acts on his own initiative, but as far as material assistance for refugees and displaced persons is concerned — which is pre-eminently the field set aside for collaboration between the non-governmental organizations and the UNHCR — it is inconceivable that the High Commissioner should operate in the territory of a state without the agreement, or at least the consent, of the government concerned. The agreement is bound to cover the principle of the assistance as well as its modalities, including the choice of the agencies which are to implement the assistance programme.

The truth is, however, that the governments of some countries do not readily agree that the implementation of programmes for the benefit of refugees should be entrusted to non-governmental organizations. Such countries are generally Third World countries where the existence and activities of private organizations of the non-governmental type do not correspond to any local tradition. This prejudice, which is even more pronounced *vis-à-vis* branches of foreign non-governmental organizations — transnational or international — is accounted for by a number of mutually corroborating reasons.

Most, if not all, refugee situations are the consequence of political events and represent delicate aspects of the foreign relations of the country in which the refugees are located. It would be rash, so it is felt, to introduce into such a situation a relatively unknown organization which may be suspected, rightly or wrongly, to be wanting in political and diplomatic experience and whose foreign connection might be misinterpreted.

Admittedly, while the non-governmental organizations which take an interest in refugees are present or represented in all, or nearly all, countries, they partake of a social structure that is peculiar to the industrialized countries. In the Third World, non-governmental organizations of local origin are relatively uncommon or those that do exist are associations very different from those referred to in the context of this paper.

The reluctant attitude sometimes displayed towards non-governmental organizations is not always insurmountable, and several examples can be cited of cases where the need for non-official assistance in the performance of an essentially humanitarian task was so manifest that the initial difficulties were overcome.

Conclusions

Assistance to refugees and displaced persons is, like other missions of a humanitarian character, *par excellence* a field of action for the non-governmental organizations. The international dimension of the problem of refugees and displaced persons, however, calls for the presence of a duly authorized inter-governmental body — and such a body was in fact brought into existence through the initiative of the non-governmental organizations.

For some sixty years, international action on behalf of refugees and displaced persons has been characterized by close collaboration between the non-governmental organizations and the intergovernmental organization — since 1951, the UNHCR. Such co-operation assumes various forms, according to the specific nature of the organizations concerned.

References

1 The Statute of the UNHCR provides that 'The work of the High Commissioner shall be of an entirely non-political character; it shall be humanitarian and social . . . .'
2 For some years the High Commissioner has been empowered — under resolutions of the Economic and Social Council and of the General Assembly of the United Nations — to deal also with displaced persons, in cases where they have been displaced in consequence of a 'man-made disaster'.
3 It is difficult for both practical and legal reasons to state with more accuracy how many refugees there are in the world. The number of refugees within the juridical meaning of the international instruments was, however, estimated at over five million at the beginning of 1980. The figure is of the order of seven million if the refugees from Palestine are added (who are not within the competence of UNHCR, but within that of the United Nations Relief and Works Agency for Palestine Refugees in the Near East). With the addition of the various groups of displaced persons (a loosely-defined category) in various continents, the figure is probably somewhere between ten and fifteen million persons.

10 The Impact of Promotional Pressure Groups on Global Politics

PETER WILLETTS

In the first chapter we began to consider how pressure groups fit into the structure of global politics. In the following six chapters we have looked at the organizational growth and the political strategy of groups which are active on some of the major contemporary global issues: self-determination in Southern Africa and the Middle East, human rights, development, conservation and liberation from sexism. The groups were not chosen to fit into any type of pattern. On the contrary, there was a deliberate attempt to obtain a diversity of groups engaged in global politics, so the similarities between the groups, which emerged from the various chapters and from the discussions among the authors, are quite striking. The remaining two chapters confirmed most of the general points from two quite different perspectives, those of a government and of an intergovernmental organization.

Formation of Groups as a Transnational Process

As all the issues, except liberation from sexism, are intrinsically international, it is not surprising that all the issues arose and became important to individual people as part of a transnational process. What will be surprising to some is that the establishment of the pressure groups was a transnational process. The groups did not result from a small number of individuals coming together in order to put pressure on their own government and then later deciding to engage in transnational contacts bypassing the government. They were transnational from the beginning.

The Anti-Apartheid Movement started in Britain because of four quite different external factors: Huddleston, a British priest who worked for twelve years in Johannesburg, was politicized by that experience and on his return campaigned in Britain; Nyerere, a foreign leader, who had been to university in Britain, while in London made an appeal to the British public; Luthuli, President of the African National Congress of South Africa, called for an international boycott of South African goods; and a major event, transmitted by the news media, the shooting of peaceful demonstrators at Sharpeville, affected attitudes in Britain.

The Palestine Liberation Organization was initiated and sponsored by the Arab League; the Algerian War of Independence inspired the Palestinian guerrillas; the 1967 Arab–Israeli War changed the Palestinians' perception of themselves and led to Fatah's takeover of the PLO.

Amnesty was launched in Britain by Benenson because his work as a lawyer had taken him to political trials in Hungary, Cyprus, South Africa and Spain and he was moved to act when he read of the arrest of two students in Portugal.[1] Amnesty was not aiming to work via the British government, because Beneson thought that government campaigns 'often achieve nothing but an intensification of persecution'.[2] The whole conception was transnational, with the launch covering six political prisoners from widely differing countries, newspaper coverage throughout the world and inside two months a meeting in Luxembourg with representatives from seven countries forming 'a permanent international movement'.[3]

World Refugee Year, sponsored by the United Nations, brought Oxfam for the first time into raising substantial sums of cash,[4] while participation in the Freedom from Hunger Campaign, sponsored by the Food and Agricultural Organization of the UN, brought Oxfam into development work.[5]

Friends of the Earth was formed in America six months after the United Nations, on a Swedish initiative, had decided to convene the UN Conference on the Human Environment.[6] Although the major aim was to mobilize pressure on the American government, it was, like Amnesty, conceived from the beginning as a transnational group. The methods of operation, the publicity and the organizational structure were not as deliberately transnational for FOE as for Amnesty, but globally attitudes were changing rapidly. The British group, for example, was established under the direct influence of the American FOE and within two years an international organization with six member countries had been set up.

Comparisons with the women's movement are more difficult to make, as there are not centrally organized groups in most countries and even less are there formal transnational structures. However, like the environment issue, the ferment of ideas has been transnational, with the contribution from the United States being strong. The modern American women's movement grew, at least partly, as a side-effect of the civil rights movement, which itself was inspired by the decolonization of Africa.[7] The impact of women's groups from many countries upon each other at the Mexico Tribune and the Copenhagen Forum came from an intergovernmental decision in the UN General Assembly, but this originated from the Commission on the Status of Women, itself a product of NGO activity in 1945–46.

While on all six issues there were many transnational interactions taking place when the groups were formed, the combination of significant processes varied from issue to issue. There appear to be four main types of process which can have an impact. Firstly, events which do not directly affect the people concerned can change their perception of the world and even of themselves. Sometimes there can be single dramatic events, as in the case of the Sharpeville shooting which changed British attitudes to South Africa, or there may be a longer sequence of events, as with the eight-year Algerian War which had a demonstration effect for the Palestinians of what they might achieve.[8] Secondly, repeated events which do directly affect an individual can bring about a political socialization, as with Huddleston, Benenson or many in the women's movement.[9] Thirdly, a direct initiative from another political actor can lead to recruitment. This process may depend upon governments, NGOs or intergovernmental organizations, as with the formation of Anti-Apartheid and the PLO and with Oxfam's move into development work. Lastly, there can be a steady change in the 'climate of the times'. This is a highly nebulous and unsatisfactory concept, but it does convey something which seems to have been important for the growth of Friends of the Earth. Perhaps general and widespread changes in attitudes occur when among ordinary people the other three processes — perceptions responding to events, socialization and recruitment — are occurring together at a slow rate for a long time.

The Targets of Pressure Group Actions

All six groups do operate to influence all three levels of the global system: international organizations, governments and the societies within countries. The primary targets for pressure vary according to the issues. Amnesty and the PLO aim at intergovernmental organizations and at governments; Anti-Apartheid and Friends of the Earth want to change both governmental policy and practice within society; Oxfam and the women's movement are concerned predominantly with the life of ordinary people 'at the grass roots'. However, the political strategies of the groups produce less contrast in their day-to-day work. At one end of the scale, as a means of bringing pressure to bear on governments, local Amnesty groups work closely with local religious and trade union groups in their own country and overseas. On the other hand, Oxfam, in order to assist ordinary people, helped to launch the International Baby Food Action Network, to campaign for governments and the World Health Organization to encourage breast feeding and to regulate commercial promotion of milk powders.

The differences between the primary targets for the pressure groups are related to the distinction made in chapter 1 between politics as the exercise of authority and politics as the mobilization of legitimacy. Amnesty and the PLO are challenging existing patterns of governmental authority, while Oxfam and the women's movement are challenging the allocation of economic and moral values which determine legitimacy in society at large. Anti-Apartheid and Friends of the Earth are offering both types of challenge. Because all those who exercise authority would prefer to be regarded as legitimate and ideas which achieve legitimacy often require the exercise of authority for them to be implemented, the distinction between influencing governments and affecting public attitudes becomes rather blurred in practice. The choice of what strategy to adopt is made pragmatically on an estimate of what is more likely to be successful. The choice varies from group to group according to the issue and it varies from time to time for the same group according to the details of the current specific question being pursued: a Welsh town council was persuaded to block the visit of a Welsh choir to South Africa; the New Zealand government was the target of pressure over the Springbok rugby team's tour of New Zealand; oil companies and the UN Security Council are the focus of attempts to impose economic sanctions on South Africa.

The finding that totally different types of strategy are complementary rather than alternatives to each other and that the choice is made pragmatically runs directly counter to conventional assumptions. Professor Finer has suggested that sectional interest groups in Britain aim to influence (a) the executive, both government and civil service, (b) the legislature, (c) parties and (d) the public, in that order of priority. Promotional groups are supposed to operate in the reverse order.[10] All the groups in this study are promotional groups, yet neither at the domestic level within countries nor at the international level do they conform to the predicted pattern. Inasmuch as there is a heirarchy in the ultimate targets which are the *ends* of pressure, the order is not the same for the different groups and with regard to the means of achieving results there is no preferred route for applying pressure.

In academic international relations theory of the Realist school, there is a presumption that only the decisions of governments have an impact and so they will be the focus of pressure,

> when private associations feel that their interests are seriously involved in a decision being taken within an international governmental organization, unless they have full rights of participation, and perhaps even then, they tend to give more emphasis to their efforts to influence decisions taken in national capitals than to those taken at the headquarters.[11]

Such an argument rests heavily on the fact that governmental delegates are supposed to be obeying instructions from their home foreign ministries. In practice instructions are not necessarily very detailed; it is the delegates who themselves have to decide whether to ask for further instructions as the debate progresses; and instructions may be reinterpreted or even on occasions disobeyed. At any rate, on all the six issues which we have examined there are a substantial number of delegates at the United Nations who will support a proposal from the pressure groups. The PLO, as an Observer, is virtually a UN member, able to participate in the majority of the work, except for voting on resolutions and taking part in elections. In all the other five cases, 'consultative status' has been obtained. This gives access both to the delegates and to the UN Secretariat. Furthermore, on each issue there is a specialized section of the Secretariat which is specifically concerned to promote change in the direction desired by the pressure groups.[12] The forums and the procedures vary greatly, but in each case the UN involvement in the issues has been intense and sustained over many years. The Anti-Apartheid Movement and the PLO have been influential in the Security Council, while Amnesty and women's organizations have worked unnoticed behind the scenes in the Commission on Human Rights and the Commission on the Status of Women, both of which report to the Economic and Social Council. Friends of the Earth can work with a major subsidiary body, the United Nations Environment Programme. Oxfam has very little contact with headquarters, but participates in specialist conferences on development and co-operates in field work.[13] Pressure groups are typically understaffed, overworked, short of finance and faced with more questions they would like to tackle than they can cope with. Yet the activists, who are usually shrewd about politics, choose to devote some of their scarce resources to work with the United Nations.[14] This fact alone suggests that traditional assumptions about the unimportance of the United Nations and the weakness of the relationship between domestic and international politics should be revised.

We saw in chapter 1 that there are connections between the six issues which we have examined and that the pressure groups have at times engaged in direct co-operation with each other. We should also note that there are strong connections with other groups in society. The churches in Britain, for example, are committed on human rights, apartheid and development, while feminist theology and the priesthood of women are important questions for debate. Similarly, the trade unions are committed on human rights and apartheid, while conservation and employment conditions for women vitally affect them. It is somewhat surprising that organizational connections do not exist to the same extent between groups active on these issues at the global level. Within societies non-governmental organizations (NGOs) relate to each other, but in global politics international non-governmental organizations (INGOs, the federations of NGOs) do not in a systematic manner try to involve each other in their campaigns. It is relatively rare that a group actively seeks to change the policy of an INGO.

Part of the explanation is that INGOs are usually considerably weaker, in terms of their financial resources and the number of staff, than the constituent organizations which sponsor them. They often do little more than provide facilities for the exchange of information. In addition, the overwhelming majority of INGOs are highly specialized. These factors mean that they can be highly useful for their constituent members, while at the same time very difficult for outsiders to influence. Because the INGOs have little formal authority they rarely take decisions which extend or change their original mandate and so do not provide a focus for pressure from outside. Most have a commitment to the idea that they are 'non-political', which makes them highly resistant to taking up questions that lie outside their specialist area of concern. However, there is one field in which all INGOs have full authority, that is, in deciding their own membership. This means that the Anti-Apartheid Movement's campaign to isolate from the global society those who help to maintain apartheid in South Africa can effect very many of the INGOs. For example, the behaviour of the doctors in the Steve Biko case made membership by the Medical Association of South Africa highly salient to the World Medical Association in 1981.

A minority of the INGOs, such as the World Council of Churches, the International Confederation of Free Trade Unions, the International Red Cross or Amnesty International, are much stronger organizations. They have constituent organizations with a large active membership in many countries, more financial resources and international secretariats with a significant number of staff. On the whole these too are highly unlikely to come into conflict with each other or even to seek deliberately to influence each other. Amnesty International is particularly unusual as an example of a strongly centralized INGO, but it also is so concerned to be seen as an independent organization that as a matter of policy it does not have formal links with any other organization.

Although political conflict among INGOs is rare, political co-operation occurs through a variety of mechanisms. Oxfam frequently initiates or joins *ad hoc* consortia to work on emergency relief programmes when a disaster arises. Umbrella organizations bring together for specific purposes INGOs, which would not otherwise work with each other. The Union of International Associations provides common information services, while the International Baby Food Action Network links for campaign purposes medical, church, development and consumer groups which have no other interest in common. Umbrella organizations can also bring together groups which are specialists with a common broader area of concern. For example, four Friends of the Earth country groups are among the thirty-nine members of the European Environmental Bureau, which exists to influence legislation by the European Community.[15] Co-operation occurs for a unique purpose at the United Nations, where a Conference of Non-Governmental Organizations (CONGO) exists in both New York and Geneva to safeguard the NGOs' rights of participation. But CONGO also serves as a rather more important organ for communication and co-operation than this limited UN function would suggest. In particular, the meetings of CONGO's sub-committees on human rights, on women, on development or on Southern Africa can be important in influencing political strategy, for the respective NGO members, both within and outside the United Nations. Not infrequently, the right to present written statements to ECOSOC is exercised jointly, usually by ten to twenty organizations but sometimes by more than a hundred endorsing a common policy position.[16] The rapid growth of activity on some issues has also produced problems of communication, which are being tackled by newsletters. The *Human Rights Internet Newsletter* based on Washington has been publishing nine times a year since 1976, while *ISIS International Bulletin*, a feminist newsletter, based on Geneva and Rome has been publishing quarterly since 1976 and works with 5,000 contact sources in 130 countries. The *ICSA Bulletin*, published every two months by the International Committee against Apartheid, Racism and Colonialism in Southern Africa, only started in August 1978, but in the field of development newsletters have been in circulation much longer. The *International Council of Voluntary Agencies News*, now a quarterly, started in 1962, while *Development Forum* has been published with ten issues a year by the United Nations Development Programme since 1973. The combination of operation consortia, umbrella INGOs, joint lobbying at the UN and information exchange networks means that the potential, still largely underutilized, for global mobilization is substantial.

The Resources Upon Which Pressure Groups Can Draw

What are the sources of strength that contribute to the success of pressure groups? Firstly, there is an intense personal commitment on the part of their members. This produces a dedication to hard work: the local groups of Amnesty who with persistence and ingenuity obtain information on and give support to 'their' three Prisoners of Conscience; the workers in Oxfam shops, who raise such large sums of money by selling secondhand clothes, books and bric-à-brac. This commitment also is shown by the loyalty of individuals to the cause, a loyalty which usually will be much stronger than the loyalty to political parties or to governments.[17] One result of this is that broadly-based pressure groups are infiltrated throughout the structure of government. It may be possible for Western governments to have a security apparatus which can locate and immobilize people working directly for foreign governments, but they cannot be secure against those who leak confidential documents to the pressure groups and the media.

The second resource of pressure groups is the fact that their leaders become specialists. They gain specialist knowledge of their subject, they learn how information can be obtained quickly and they gain skills in presenting their cause to the public and to the media. Again in these respects pressure groups can often be in a stronger position than governments, particularly in Britain where civil servants are generalists who never spend more than a few years in the same job or in America where political patronage produces a high turnover at the top of the administration.

A third resource of pressure groups, paradoxically, is their lack of a well-structured bureaucracy. This means that in periods of emergency or crisis they can respond with greater speed and greater flexibility than governments. It is not always necessary to obtain the approval of the Minister before action can be taken, nor is there an obligation to use routine procedures even when they are inappropriate. Thus in emergency relief operations aid from groups such as Oxfam often arrives at the scene of disaster some days in advance of that from governments. The problems caused by bureaucratic constraints are frequently more severe for intergovernmental organizations than they are for governments, so NGOs can be of assistance to the United Nations and its agencies. This is illustrated at the practical level when Oxfam recruits staff for UN field programmes, in order to bypass the delays and political restrictions upon recruitment to the UN Secretariat. A standard rule of conduct for governments and international secretariats is that there are very strict inhibitions upon criticizing other governments explicitly by name for specific acts.[18] The freedom of NGOs from such restrictions means that Amnesty and Anti-Apartheid have become important instruments for monitoring and implementing UN work on human rights and on the application of sanctions against South Africa. NGOs are also often more efficient than other larger bureaucracies in having relatively low administrative costs. Recognition of their flexibility, their efficiency and their superior contacts at the grass roots is shown by the way governments channel money through the NGOs. In the chapter on Sweden we saw that nearly half the income of the Swedish 'umbrella' committee, for development NGOs, came from government sources. Similarly in Britain the government operates a Joint Funding Scheme under which it will pay 50 per cent of the costs of approved small scale, grass roots NGO development projects. In the financial year 1980–81 Oxfam received approximately £1 million and Christian Aid £250,000, while some thirty other NGOs received smaller sums under this scheme. In addition, the government has donated a million pounds to each of the recent British NGO disaster emergency appeals. (Conversation with those who are active in development work indicates that the phenomenon occurs at the global level too, with United Nations programmes working at times through NGOs, but detailed and reliable data seem difficult to obtain.)

The first three factors mentioned all contribute to and reinforce the most important factor in giving strength to pressure groups: the personnel, particularly at the leadership level, become professionals in the use of information. Generally, promotional groups have very limited financial resources; when like Oxfam they do handle significant sums of money this is rapidly disbursed and has to be continually replenished. They also have a very limited ability to apply physical coercion. The PLO's use of force is significant for its political and not its military impact. The ability of NGOs to apply pressure is through the mobilization of legitimacy for their cause. Winning support by changing people's perception of the issues is done by presenting arguments and information. An argument that there must be sanctions against South Africa because the regime is oppressive, or that nuclear power cannot be used because it is dangerous, depends upon convincing people that South Africa is oppressive or nuclear power is dangerous. Both topics may seem very remote from the everyday lives of those who are not immediately involved. Anti-Apartheid and Friends of the Earth, respectively, have to find and transmit relevent information and once such propositions are established they have to continue to provide information which reinforces the propositions. It was emphasized in the previous chapters that for this work to be effective the information must be absolutely reliable.

Governments generally have a relatively high status by virtue of being in office and are generally assumed to be competent, including being in the possession of accurate information. Pressure groups, on the other hand, appear not to have the resources to be able to match those of governments. If they are arguing a controversial case, many people will assume that they are 'biased' and therefore they are not to be trusted. In this unequal contest pressure groups cannot afford to make mistakes, because thereafter their statements will not so readily be given credibility and references to the mistakes will continually be thrown back at them. (Here we have a contrast with journalists, who supposedly have a professional interest in providing accurate information. But they are not in practice forced to correct their frequent factual errors, because the media generally do not publicize their own mistakes.) After some time many pressure groups do get accepted as being trustworthy on information.[19] This can then give them privileged access to governments and enable the groups to persuade sympathetic governments to take diplomatic initiatives. Such 'insider status' can immensely increase the influence of a pressure group, but it is totally dependent upon the maintenance of reliability.[20] The relationship is not a symmetrical one. Governments can give false information to the public or to pressure groups without necessarily damaging their overall credibility.[21] Thus, contrary to popular assumptions, pressure group activists should often be regarded as being more reliable in presenting information than either journalists or government officials. Processing of information is always a major activity of pressure groups and often it is overwhelmingly the most important activity. Such skills and standards are required of their full-time personnel that they have in modern times become professionals in processing of political information.[22]

The weaknesses of pressure groups are generally the opposite side of the coin to their strengths. The dependence upon personal commitment and specialist skills means that the performance of the groups in a particular country or within a country at the grass roots varies in line with the particular individuals in the locality. At the local level, a chairperson or secretary who is partially motivated by self-importance or who is poor at communicating may alienate those who wish to work for the cause. Generational differences can prevent the acceptance of new, potentially fruitful ideas. When problems of personal relationships occur at the centre of the organization, they can have a more serious impact on the pressure group and generate damaging publicity. New groups and new ideas are often promoted by charismatic people, who attract and inspire others to work with them. But such leaders are frequently somewhat authoritarian and develop a possessiveness towards the organization they have built up. Clashes between pressure group leaders and their staff, which result in the leader being ousted, are common enough that the phenomenon requires detailed investigation.[23] An example occurred with the British section of Amnesty, when divisions at the headquarters were resolved by the Annual General Meeting narrowly voting in March 1981 to confirm the dismissal of the director, Cosmas Desmond, less than two years after his appointment. The fact that the individuals involved in such disputes have a strong personal commitment to the cause helps to increase the intensity of the disputes and produces an unfavourable contrast with the organization's professed idealism, in the eyes of those not directly involved.

Once a promotional pressure group becomes well established with a large membership, it is likely to consist of a coalition, ranging from impatient radicals wanting to see immediate progress through a spectrum to cautious conservatives who have never before been political activists. If the group does not appear to be sufficiently successful or if new challenges arise, there can be a split about the methods of political action. Not infrequently the result can be the formation of a new more radical group. One of the most spectacular examples was the split in the Campaign for Nuclear Disarmament, at the point when it was at the height of its influence and when it was the largest political organization in Britain. In October 1960 Bertrand Russell resigned as President of CND in order to form the Committee of 100, which briefly ran a mass civil disobedience campaign in favour of 'unilateralism' by Britain.[24] A different type of problem about methods arose at Oxfam in 1970, when Nicholas Stacey argued for the allocation of a quarter of Oxfam's income to educational work and political lobbying. Stacey failed to get sufficient support and the dispute ended with his resignation from the post of Deputy Director.[25] We saw in chapter 6 that a similar dispute within the Sierra Club led to the formation of the first national section of the Friends of the Earth. Not surprisingly the group which has seen the least progress on the substance of its goals, the Palestine Liberation Organization, has faced continual factional disputes over major questions of strategy. The lack of a strong bureaucratic structure for most groups and the fact that they are voluntary associations means that there is no central authority. There will usually be some central decision-making body, but it has little ability to enforce decisions. So the leadership of pressure groups has to try to maintain a consensus within the group. Breakdown in the consensus can be more damaging to promotional groups than to other groups such as companies, trade unions or governments, which have economic interests to help hold them together.

The Boundaries of the Group's Domain

Deciding what is the proper domain of action is never an easy or an obvious choice for pressure groups. It may be true that idiosyncratic, spur-of-the-moment decisions have led Friends of the Earth into new campaigns or Oxfam has evolved slowly without self-conscious formal policy making, but none the less the effect is still to give character and direction to the group. Three of the groups have significantly expanded their domain since they were founded. Anti-Apartheid started as a simple boycott movement, quickly took on the whole question of apartheid and then somewhat later became concerned with the Portuguese colonies and Southern Rhodesia. Amnesty started work in order to obtain the release of Prisoners of Conscience and then later took on the Campaign against Torture and opposition to all use of the death penalty. Oxfam started specifically to provide assistance to Greece, soon moved into emergency relief wherever it was necessary and much later provided development assistance and a limited amount of development education. While in each case there are clear logical reasons for the expansion of domain to have occurred, it was not just an automatic response to the tide of events. Certain equally logical extensions could have occurred. Anti-Apartheid could have become a general movement either against oppressive governments or against racism; Amnesty could have become a campaign for all civil and political rights; Oxfam could have become an expert group on the prevention of disasters or moved into an overriding concern with refugees; yet in each case these developments did *not* take place. The constraints which helped to shape the political domain of each group came both from the concerns and capabilities of the group's members and from the need to find an unoccupied, tenable niche in the global political system. Expansion will be limited by the existence of other groups in the same field and/or the need to avoid working on such a broad front that the challenge to any one target is diluted or discredited.

Friends of the Earth and the women's movement face quite different problems. Instead of starting with specific goals they start with specific moral principles. But conservation and sexual equality can be translated into an enormous number of specific campaign goals. For Friends of the Earth the problem is partly solved by the manner in which intergovernmental organizations and governments set the political agenda. Proposals for new legislation will often have significant implications for the environment, which the government has either failed to consider or deliberately ignored. Other campaign initiatives can then be taken on the basis of the extent to which they are likely to invoke a public response. For the women's movement there are divisions between those with a socialist concept of equality and those who seek a liberal–capitalist equality of opportunity and between those who want autonomy for women, leading some feminists to reject any contact with men, and those who want an end to any sex-role differentiation, leading to their co-operation with anti-sexist men. Such divisions both help to explain why there is no united anti-sexist movement with a single national organization in any country and why there are often differences on fundamental questions of policy.[26] Again, formal legislative questions have usually provided the most coherent focus, as with the campaign for an Equal Rights Amendment to the United States constitution or with campaigns in very many countries for the right to abortion and contra-ception facilities.

The PLO has faced a third type of problem. It is absolutely clear to out-siders that the PLO has no foreseeable prospect of achieving its original goal, the establishment of a secular, democratic state for Arabs and Jews within the whole of the former mandated territory of Palestine. Acceptance of this fact would require the PLO to narrow its domain of action to a more limited, achievable goal. However, no alternative has been both sufficiently attractive and more obviously attainable in the near future for such a transition yet to have been made.[27] On the other hand, the success of the PLO in obtaining diplomatic recognition has greatly expanded its domain of action. It must now have an official policy on all global issues and send its delegations to many international conferences. For any pressure group deciding the correct balance, between expanding its domain of action to cover all goals which might be theoretically desirable, and being limited to those goals which will sustain the unity of the group and remain within its capabilities, is an important task. The ability to strike an appropriate balance will be one of the hallmarks of a successful pressure group. Amnesty International is an outstanding example of a group which has explicitly and in specific detail defined its domain.[28] The clarity of Amnesty's definition of itself is undoubtedly one factor which ex-plains Amnesty's ability to challenge simultaneously the majority of the govern-ments in the world. The evolution of Amnesty shows that a successful formula is not necessarily a static one.

One of the ways in which governments seek to resist pressure upon them-selves, coming from other countries, is by assertion of the doctrine of sover-eignty. In its extreme form this becomes 'the principle of non-intervention and non-interference in the internal and external affairs of States'.[29] Taken literally the principle is nonsense, because it would prohibit virtually all inter-state diplomacy, by which governments do attempt to influence each other's policy. Even a more limited assertion by any government that there should be non-intervention in the internal affairs of states is humbug, because all govern-ments welcome both foreign support for themselves and foreign opposition to their internal and external opponents. Nevertheless, the doctrine of sovereignty does serve to fend off unwelcome criticism.

What is curious is the existence of a non-governmental mirror image of this practice. Pressure groups operating in global politics try to protect themselves from attack by governments by asserting that they are 'non-political'. For Oxfam and other charities in Britain and America, this is a direct necessity because there is a legal requirement that they remain 'non-political' in order to retain their tax-free status. The trouble is that no lawyer has tried or could possibly produce a workable definition of 'politics', which would permit educational work and the propagation of religious beliefs as charitable activities while excluding the propagation of so-called, political beliefs. The result is that control is exercised by the arbitrary decisions of officials, Charity Commissioners in Britain and the Internal Revenue Service in the United States. Not surprisingly anomalies arise, as in Britain when the Minority Rights Group is recognized as being 'politically impartial', while Amnesty lost a court case appealing for charitable status.[30] Even groups for which the question of charitable status does not arise endeavour in some sense to remain 'non-political'. The conservation goals of Friends of the Earth appeal to a range of people with widely differing political ideologies, so identification with a particular ideology would alienate other sections of the membership. But some groups, such as the anti-apartheid groups in Western societies, are strongly identified with, in this case, left-wing attitudes. Even so, the British Anti-Apartheid Movement has never sought to ally itself with the Labour Party and carefully includes a balance of both Labour and Liberal MPs among its Vice-Presidents and Sponsors.

Pressure groups are, of course, using a very narrow meaning to the word 'politics' when they claim to be 'non-political'. They are in practice simply refusing to become formally linked by organization or by finance with any one political party within a country or with any one government within the global system. On the other hand, the creation of informal links or non-exclusive formal links with several parties and/or governments are welcomed by all pressure groups, including the charities.[31] Any claim that a promotional group is 'non-political' is as bogus as a claim by any government that they believe in 'non-interference' in other countries.[32] What both governments and nongovernmental organizations share is a desire to maintain the maximum possible freedom of action to pursue their own objectives. For both it is useful to support the conspiracy of confusion that distinguishes between governments, dealing with the 'high politics' of security and 'national interest', and societies consisting of non-governmental groups engaged in 'low politics' or 'non-political' activity of an economic, cultural or moral nature. In reality the connections and feedback between the exercise of authority by governments and the mobilization of legitimacy within society at large are too great for governmental politics to be seen as an isolated realm. Many issues and possibly all issues to be decided by governments directly affect the aims and objectives of domestic 'non-political' groups, of INGOs, of other 'sovereign' governments and of intergovernmental organizations.

The Success of Pressure Groups

If there was one clear, but unconscious, bias in the original choice of the groups to be included in this study, it was that the groups have all been remarkably successful in gaining support in most Western societies and in helping to change the policies of Western governments. This is not to say that the groups have been anywhere near to being as successful as they would wish. Nor has there been an uninterrupted pattern of progress. When Margaret Thatcher became Prime Minister of Britain in May 1979, significant changes were threatened in Britain's policy on Southern Africa, on development and on some conservation questions. Despite a Conservative Party commitment to recognize the Muzorewa–Smith regime, domestic and global pressures quickly produced a reversal in the policy, averting a major crisis and leading to a negotiated settlement bringing Zimbabwe to independence. Similarly, the Brandt Report appeared in February 1980 and was followed by a government memorandum in July 1980 which was dismissive towards its approach to development issues.[33] Yet, the impression of Foreign Office opposition to the idea of a special North–South summit in Mexico was met with such hostility that within one month the government was committed to taking part. After two years in office unemployment was at record levels and the Prime Minister had lost the support of the majority of her Cabinet because of her economic policies. At this point parliament 'witnessed its largest mass lobby for years', in support of the Brandt Report.[34] Thus, at a markedly unpropitious moment to expect the British public to be concerned about the economic fate of others, the British government found the international pressures against its policy being expressed and reinforced through the domestic political system. In January 1981 the assumption of office as President of the United States by Ronald Reagan represented a direct setback for the groups on each of the six issues covered in this study. Indication of the extent to which we now have a global political system, from which no society can remain isolated, will be given by the extent to which the Reagan administration, like the Thatcher government, becomes subject to both global and domestic pressures on these six issues and the extent to which the policies being pursued at the end of the administration match the original expectations and intentions in early 1981.

In saying that we expect pressure groups such as these to have successes even in dealing with governments which are hostile to them, we must be careful not to attribute too much influence directly to the pressure groups. They do help to mould attitudes within society, but at the same time they are a reflection of society. If a cause is totally at variance with the prevailing social norms, it would be unlikely that any group could be formed or that it could obtain much publicity.[35] If, nevertheless, a group is formed which cannot evoke a response in the wider society, even if by pressure group standards it achieves a large membership, then governments and other targets will usually be able to afford to ignore it. So the size of a group is no measure of its representativeness or the impact it will have. The influence of the Anti-Apartheid Movement in Britain is out of all proportion to its tiny membership. In recent years, while there have been more than 300 organizations affiliating as members, only around 2,500 individuals are members. This figure does not even match the number of people who turn up on the group's own demonstrations, nor compare with the circulation of the group's own newspaper, *Anti-Apartheid News*, which has a regular print of 7,000 copies. Even less does this involvement correspond with the 44 per cent of the public who in May 1961 thought Britain should oppose apartheid in the United Nations or the 50 per cent who in 1970 thought Britain should not supply arms to South Africa.[36] Furthermore, *The Guardian* newspaper is positively sympathetic to the cause and *The Times* is not hostile, while a sizeable number of MPs will act on behalf of the Movement. A further complication is the extent to which there are overlapping memberships between different non-governmental organizations, with the result that they give each other support. Thus, a pressure group, such as the Anti-Apartheid Movement, can have an impact because it has far wider support than is indicated by the small number of its members and active supporters.

Pressure groups rarely find themselves to be the only group active on political issues. The Anti-Apartheid Movement may not be faced with any group, other than the South African embassy and a few fellow-travellers, which positively advocates apartheid, but there are significant interest groups, such as companies and sporting associations which are opposed to the policy of isolating South African society. If British politics (or American, French, German, Australian or New Zealand politics) were taking place in isolation from the rest of global politics, then one would not have expected so great a change from the 1950s to the 1980s in government policy towards apartheid. Major economic interests often have the ability to influence foreign policy, and in the case of relations with South Africa there is every reason to suppose that they could have successfully countered the anti-apartheid groups. But individual countries are not isolated and external support can be significant in sustaining pressure groups.

The inadequacies involved in trying to evaluate the effectiveness of pressure groups, while ignoring the global system, are mirrored in the inadequacies of trying to evaluate global actors, while ignoring the domestic political systems of countries. The traditional view is that governments are in control of all external relations and that they can, if only they are sufficiently determined, resist any external pressures to change, unless the pressure is backed up by the threat of the use of military force. Therefore, it is typical of the Realist approach that intergovernmental organizations are not seen as being of importance.

The state has not been displaced by the international institution as the main centre of initiative in the international system. The effectiveness of the

United Nations . . . does not rest upon any intrinsic power within that organization to affect events on its own account.[37]

Such assumptions contrast strongly with the attention that governments actually give to intergovernmental organizations. More countries are represented at the UN headquarters in New York, with a higher average number of diplomats in their missions, than at Washington, Moscow or any capital city.[38] The United Nations and other such organizations matter, because as we have frequently seen in this study governments cannot ignore them or isolate them from their domestic political systems. There are direct contacts with the various United Nations Associations and other pressure groups, notably those which have 'consultative status'.[39]

Governments may be able to resist the demands made by pressure groups, particularly if they do not have widespread support or if there are other countervailing groups. Governments may be able to resist demands made by other governments and by intergovernmental organizations, particularly if the government has a strong domestic base. What is highly unlikely is that a government can resist the same demand being made simultaneously by both internal and external actors, unless it too can obtain external support. Pressure groups are liable to face the charge by governments that they are abandoning the so-called 'national interest', or disrupting 'national unity', or putting their special concerns above the 'common good'. External support enables pressure groups to counter-attack that it is the government which is damaging the nation's prestige, by failing to conform to generally accepted standards of behaviour, performance or attitudes. If support for a pressure group comes from governments which are normally considered to be friendly, then this can be used as evidence that the government at home has failed to understand what is the 'true national interest'. Whether the arguments are put explicitly in the above terms or are only implicitly of such a form, it is now commonplace for political debate to be littered with references to external norms. Pressure groups are greatly strengthened if they have such references readily available. Support from United Nations resolutions, especially when they are adopted with little or no opposition, is one of the most useful types of external reference that can be made, because it can be presented as a global norm which it is deviant to reject. Conversely, the United Nations and other external actors are greatly strengthened if pressure groups take up and publicize their decisions. For all the countries in which they operate, the pressure groups on all the six issues in this study receive support from the UN, from other intergovernmental organizations, from INGOs and from many governments. Thus, these relatively successful groups are a reflection not just of individual societies but of the global society as a whole. Rarely, if ever, will even the more impressive successes of these groups be solely attributable to just the activities of the one group. Equally, it will frequently be the case that had the group not been active events would have followed a quite different course.

On all the issues in this study there have been spectacular successes for the pressure groups. On racism in Southern Africa, the Heath government in 1970 was prevented from resuming the supply of arms by Britain to South Africa; in 1977 the UN Security Council imposed a mandatory arms embargo; and in 1979 the British government was prevented from accepting the Muzorewa–Smith regime in Rhodesia. The PLO in 1974 obtained at the UN General Assembly both recognition of their 'right to self-determination' and a permanent observer status for themselves, while the European Community peace initiative in 1980 was greatly to their benefit. Amnesty International has obtained the release of very many Prisoners of Conscience and successfully promoted the adoption of international codes of conduct. Oxfam has greatly expanded its income and seen its emphasis on development 'at the grass roots' recognized by the World Bank, and other much larger agencies than itself, in their adoption of a 'basic needs' philosophy. The Friends of the Earth has seen governments starting to promote re-cycling and conservation, while some governments have abandoned or reduced their nuclear energy programmes. Women have obtained basic civil and political rights in virtually all countries of the world, while in many countries they have obtained formal legal rights to equal conditions of employment and have slowly begun to be able to exercise some of those rights. Many intergovernmental organizations have their programmes for the advancement of women. On none of the six issues would an activist be satisfied with the progress which has been made. Indeed, some might deny that any concept of there having been significant successes is at all appropriate, when consideration is given to how much more remains to be achieved.[40] However, on all the six issues, over a period of ten years comparing the beginning of the 1980s with the beginning of the 1970s, there has been a substantial shift in the balance of arguments and the way in which outcomes are decided. How much one can directly attribute these changes to the work of the pressure groups is problematic. At times they have been creating and leading opinion. At times they have been responding to and following the opinion of others. What cannot be doubted is the complexity of the processes of change and the involvement of pressure groups on a transnational basis.

At the beginning of this chapter it was suggested that three transnational processes, changing perceptions, socialization and recruitment, often contributed to the formation of pressure groups. Once they are established, pressure groups then act as agents of these same processes. All the groups in this study have proceeded to do this on a transnational basis themselves. The chapter on Sweden illustrated these processes from a different perspective, that of the impact on a particular country. Details were given of the socialization and recruitment initiated by an INGO, the World Council of Churches, upon the Swedish churches and hence the legislature, the Riksdag. However, the Swedish initative in 1968 to convene a UN Conference on the Human Environment also shows that the processes can easily operate in reverse, with one government having a great impact on the non-governmental world.[41]

To quite an extent the operation of politics within a global system is a new phenomenon. It is only in the last two decades or thereabouts that ordinary people have had global communications by airlines, by telephone and by television conveniently available to them. Such communication facilities were essential before pressure groups could become highly transnational. Many of the actual day-to-day activities, joint campaigns in more than one country, international newsletters, NGO forums at UN conferences, only became transnational from the early 1970s. Now it is possible for ideas to develop in one part of the world and to be transmitted quite rapidly throughout the world. This is perhaps the unique power of pressure groups. They may not have great military or economic resources but they can communicate political ideas. They may not be able to obtain the decisions for which they are working so hard, but they can frequently put issues on the political agenda, so that others are forced to respond. Increasingly, it is becoming a global political agenda rather than a set of separate agendas for each country and increasingly the responses to issues are global in origin rather than being contained within each country. Not only are the activities of sectional interest groups producing economic interdependence, but promotional pressure groups are also producing political interdependence within the global system.

References

1 Information from *Amnesty International 1961–1976. A Chronology* (London, Amnesty International Publications, 1976), p. 1.
2 'The Forgotten Prisoners', *The Observer*, London, 28 May 1961. This was the article by Peter Benenson which launched Amnesty.
3 *Amnesty . . .* (source in note 1), p. 3.
4 'In the early years, as much as four-fifths of the "money" raised by Oxfam was in fact the value of clothing, and the cash donations were spent largely on transporting the clothing. 1959 was the first year in which Oxfam raised more in cash than in kind.' M. Jones, *Two Ears of Corn. Oxfam in Action* (London, Hodder and Stoughton, 1965), p. 35.
5 Oxfam in its original work is an exception to the transnational model. The Oxford Committee for Famine Relief, set up in October 1942, was initially a domestic British pressure group, campaigning for the British government to lift the blockade on Greece. It was soon decided that the government was not going to respond. In March 1943 the Committee registered as a charity and launched an appeal for funds, to send supplies direct to Greece. From then on Oxfam did function as a transnational actor. See Jones, op. cit., chapter 3.
6 It is not suggested that the convening of the UN conference caused FOE–USA to be set up. Both were products of a changing climate of opinion. However, the four years of preparations for the conference did affect the politics of the environment throughout the world. As an illustration, one may note that the influential book, *Only One Earth. The Care and Maintenance of a Small Planet*, by Barbara Ward and René Dubos (London, André Deutsch, and Harmondsworth, Penguin Books, 1972), was an unofficial report commissioned by the Secretary-General of the UN Conference on the Human Environment and was prepared with the assistance of a 152-member Committee of Corresponding Consultants from fifty-eight countries.
7 It is difficult to substantiate such a general assertion without engaging in a major research

project. One many note several indicators that such issue linkages are made. Georgina Ashworth, the author of chapter 7 and a British woman, was affected by her work for the Minority Rights Group and the realization that reports came from a traditional male perspective. She proceeded to produce a report on Arab women and later left to establish Change International Reports. Davidson Nicol, the Executive Director of UNITAR, introduces a special issue of *UNITAR News* (Vol. 7, No. 1, 1975) on 'Women and the UN', with an extended comparison of the attitudes surrounding the replacement of Europeans by indigenous people in colonial regimes and the promotion of women in large organizations today. *The Times* (London, 1 August 1978), reporting on the debate on the ordination of women as priests at the 1978 Lambeth Conference of all the world's churches in the Anglican Communion, said 'Bishop Desmond Tutu, secretary of the South African Council of Churches, drew a parallel with the experience of apartheid. "Those of us who have been victims of a system of injustice and oppression known how women feel in this matter", he said.'

8 This does not imply that the author considers the Algerian and the Palestinian situations to have been similar, simply that many Palestinians believed this to be so.

9 The concept of socialization is normally used to describe the way individuals are educated to accept the existing system, but it seems just as valid to think of *negative* socialization. This occurs when an individual repeatedly experiences acts which are intended to promote conformity, but which actually provoke rebellion or rejection of the dominant values. There are many analytical problems in trying to use socialization in this way, but events in Czechoslovakia in 1968 or in Poland in 1980 suggest that there is an important phenomenon which needs to be analysed. The rapidity of political change throughout both these societies was only possible because the official government and party attempts at political socialization not only had failed to produce the intended result but also had politicized people with negative attitudes.

10 Finer, S., 'Interest Groups and the Political Process in Britain', in H. W. Ehrmann (ed.), *Interest Groups on Four Continents* (Pittsburgh, University of Pittsburgh Press, 1958), p. 130.

11 Jacobson, H. K., *Networks of Interdependence. International Organisations and the Global Political System* (New York, A. A. Knopf, 1979), p. 127. This work is one of the most sophisticated analytical studies of international organizations to have appeared for many years. Despite the fact that many behavioural questions about the processes within the institutions are asked, Jacobson still tends to fall back to the Realist assumptions.

12 The women's movement is an exception to the pattern as there is not a substantial body of delegates backing this cause. Resolutions are passed largely on the initiative of the Commission on the Status of Women. Within the Secretariat there is a Branch for the Advancement of Women in the Centre for Social Development and Humanitarian Affairs. Also there are two unofficial groups promoting sexual equality. The *Ad Hoc* Group on Equal Rights for Women is a pressure group with members from departments within the Secretariat, while the staff of UNITAR, both male and female, are committed and work on the issue.

13 The latter contact is so important that in July 1980, when Oxfam criticized the temporary suspension of famine relief operations in Karamoja, to their astonishment, the UN Secretary-General personally telephoned Oxfam to discuss the problem. Although the UNDP Resident Representative was appointed as the Secretary-General's Special Re-representative for Emergency Relief Operations in Uganda, the day-to-day work of the Special Operation for Humanitarian Assistance to Uganda was put under the UNHCR.

14 While working on this book, the editor tried to call a meeting of the contributors in October 1980. This proved to be impossible because Martin Ennals (Amnesty), Abdul S. Minty (Anti-Apartheid Movement), Georgina Ashworth (women's movement) and Olle Dahlen (NGO Ambassador) were all in New York for the start of the UN General Assembly session.

15 As the European Environment Bureau does not include Friends of the Earth International but some of its constituent members, and the same is true for other INGOs,

the Bureau is not really an example of co-operation among INGOs. It was used as the illustration to avoid referring solely to Oxfam each time.

16 Joint statements by groups of INGOs occur on a variety of issues: for example, on 14 July 1971, twelve youth and student INGOs put their views on the Second Development Decade (UN document E/C.2/739); on 17 May 1972, nineteen human rights and religious INGOs protested at the slow rate at which the Commission on Human Rights was dealing with its work (E/C.2/747); on 4 July 1972, eighteen women's INGOs put their views on women in development and women's rights to education (E/C.2/750); and on 6 October 1972, a mixed group of twenty-four INGOs, mainly women's and religious INGOs, called for the implementation of the recommendations of the Stockholm Conference on the Human Environment (E/C.2/760).

17 In the 1960s the Campaign for Nuclear Disarmament in Britain had an offshoot, the Committee of One Hundred, whose members went to prison, some for several years, as a result of symbolic anti-nuclear, civil disobedience. In the United States the campaign for civil rights in the southern states also led to activists spending time in prison and in a few cases they lost their lives in work for the cause.

18 This diplomatic practice derives from the principle of international law that there is a 'duty on the part of states to refrain from intervention in the internal or external affairs of other states' in I. Brownlie, *Principles of Public International Law* (Oxford, Clarendon Press, third edn., 1979), p. 291. If taken seriously, this principle would virtually bring to an end all diplomacy and it is clearly breached every day by every government, but it does still act as a constraint upon style and procedure in diplomacy.

19 It is difficult to specify what leads to a pressure group being accepted as trustworthy on information. Partly it must be a question of the organization being established over some time, working within a clearly specified domain; partly that the nature of its contacts and procedures becomes known and respected; partly that the leaders gain a personal reputation; and partly that there has been no successful challenge to its information. Probably the relevant factors vary from group to group. In addition, the objective reliability of a group will not be the only factor affecting its reputation. An evaluation of its goals also affects an evaluation of its actions. Amnesty International would appear to have a higher status as an authorative source than the Anti-Apartheid Movement in Western societies, but in Third World societies the situation would often be reversed.

20 The term 'insider groups' has been coined by Wyn Grant in 'Insider Groups, Outsider Groups and Interest Group Strategies in Britain' (University of Warwick, Department of Politics Working Paper No. 19, May 1978).

21 Some very clear examples exist of governments putting out highly inaccurate information. The Gulf of Tonkin incidents in August 1964 were initially portrayed as unprovoked surprise attacks by North Vietnamese torpedo boats on US ships. Now it is known that South Vietnamese and American forces had already been active and the balance of probability is that no North Vietnamese boats were present during the second incident. When after several years the facts were established, much damage was done to the government's case. In contrast to this, the joint invasion of Egypt by Israel, Britain and France in 1956, when Britain and France claimed to be peacekeeping between Egypt and Israel, never became a matter of general public debate when the true facts were known and the original arguments were shown to be deliberate lies.

22 Martin Ennals pointed out to the author that there is not yet much professionalism in the technology of information processing. The communications among the myriad of groups concerned with human rights do not match, for example, the computer networks used by the world's airlines to control passenger bookings. (Such a criticism would still apply with great force to many governments and businesses.) For the time being at least, powerful computer technology would seem to be beyond the financial reach of most promotional pressure groups.

23 Significant clashes of personality and/or policy, which seriously divided the group's leadership, have occurred in Amnesty, the Campaign for Nuclear Disarmament, Oxfam,

the Royal Society for the Prevention of Cruelty to Animals, Shelter, Task Force, the United Nations Association and Voluntary Service Overseas. Even deeper divisions producing splits, new groups and regrouping, have occurred in both the Trotskyist and other Marxist parties and the fascist parties in Britain.

24 See particularly *The Times*, London, 29 and 30 September and 10, 20 and 25 October 1960.
25 See P. Gill, *Drops in the Ocean. The work of Oxfam 1960–1970* (London, Macdonald Unit 75, 1970), pp. 156–7.
26 There is, for example, no agreement within the women's movement on the place of women in the economy. Some have campaigned for wages for housework, others argue that housework should not be regarded as important and others want men to share responsibility. With respect to child-care, some advocate replacing marriage with communal living, some want child-care facilities at places of work, some concentrate on generous provision of maternity rights, while some think the main changes should be in men's employment patterns, to allow them to participate.
27 David Gilmore has discussed in chapter 3 how in June 1974 the Palestine National Council declared its policy was 'to liberate Palestinian soil and to set up on any part of it which is liberated' a new state. Thus the PLO has begun to move towards having a more limited, achievable goal. But the 1974 decision still leaves a state based on part of the Israeli-occupied territories as a short-term expedient on the road towards control of the whole of the former mandated territory of Palestine. Recognition of Israel's right to exist, even if only in a circumspect manner by acceptance of the 'Fahd plan' announced in August 1981, would be an even more significant change for the PLO.
28 See the quote from Amnesty International's Statutes given at the beginning of the section on structure in chapter 4.
29 Quote from the opening sentence of the section on 'Interference and Intervention in the Internal Affairs of States' in the Political Declaration of the Sixth Non-Aligned Summit, Havana, September 1979. The text of the section appears in P. Willetts, *The Non-Aligned in Havana. Documents of the Sixth Summit Conference and an Analysis of their Significance for the Global Political System* (London, Frances Pinter, and New York, St Martin's Press, 1981), pp. 125–7.
30 The Minority Rights Group have produced a leaflet, *Aims, Work, Reports*, describing the group. It contains the statement that 'in choosing priorities MRG aims . . . to remain politically impartial.' It also says 'MRG is registered as an educational charity (No. 282305).' The Amnesty court case was reported in *The Times*, London, 19 March 1981. In the judgement it was said that 'a trust to procure an alteration of United Kingdom law could not be charitable.'
31 It would hardly be possible to better the political status of the Royal Institute of International Affairs, which has as its Patron Queen Elizabeth, as its Presidents Lord Noel-Baker (Labour Party), Rt. Hon. Jo Grimond (former Liberal Party leader) and Lord Home (fomer Conservative Prime Minister) and as its Honorary Presidents the 'Presidents and Prime Ministers of the United Kingdom and the other Commonwealth governments'. *Report of the Council 1980–81* (London, RIIA, 1981), p. 2.
32 The sectional interest groups may at times be 'non-political' with respect to society at large. Economic groups, professional associations and recreational clubs can hypothetically be restricted to activities which only affect significantly their own members. In practice they do have an impact on the wider society and are only politically inactive when their interests are in harmony with the prevailing status quo.
33 The Brandt Report is dated 20 December 1979 and was published in Britain on 13 February 1980. *North–South: A Programme for Survival. The Report of the Independent Commission on International Development Issues under the Chairmanship of Willy Brandt* (London and Sydney, Pan Books, 1980). On 26 July 1980, *The Guardian*, London, reported 'so far the book has had five printings of 10,000 each.' This represents an exceptionally high level of public interest in such a specialist and complex subject. The British government memorandum was published on 16 July 1980. *The Brandt Commission Report. Memorandum prepared by the Foreign and Commonwealth*

Office for the Overseas Development Sub-Committee of the Foreign Affairs Committee (Foreign and Commonwealth Office, Foreign Policy Document No. 51, London, 1980, available on microfiche no. 80.1003 of ISBN 085964 113 9 from Chadwyck-Healey, Cambridge, UK and Teaneck, USA, 1981).

34 *The Times*, London, 6 May 1981, 'Mass Lobby for Third World'. Around the same time there was also a mass demonstration on unemployment, 'The People's March for Jobs', see *The Times*, London, 1 June 1981.

35 Furthermore, it is possible that success in obtaining publicity can increas opposition to a group and its cause. There has been, for example, some sympathy to EXIT's belief that individuals should have the right to take their own life, but recent detailed argument of EXIT's case has alienated some who were previously sympathetic.

36 In May 1961 the Gallup Poll in Britain asked 'When questions about apartheid (racial segregation) come up in the United Nations should Britain support South Africa, join with other countries like India and Canada in opposing apartheid, or be neutral?' The results were:

	%
Oppose apartheid	44
Be neutral	27
Support South Africa	12
Don't know	17

In 1964 and 1970–71 the Gallup Poll asked on several occasions 'Do you think the British government should or should not supply arms to South Africa? The results were:

	Nov. 1964 %	June–July 1970 %	Oct. 1970 %	Nov. 1970 %	Jan. 1971 %	May 1971 %
Should	25	25	25	30	31	29
Should not	45	50	55	51	50	48
Don't know	30	25	20	19	19	23

The questions and the results are given in Gallup, G. H., *The Gallup International Public Opinion Polls. Great Britain 1937–1975* (New York, Random House, 1976), pp. 587, 781, 1102, 1111, 1115, 1124 and 1133.

37 Northedge, F. S., *The International Political System* (London, Faber and Faber, 1976), p. 138.

38 Willetts, P., *The Non-Aligned Movement. The Origins of a Third World Alliance* (London, Frances Pinter, and New York, Nichols, 1978), p. 65.

39 For an interpretation of the United Nations, which is consistent with the Global Politics paradigm, see P. Willetts, 'The United Nations and the Transformation of the Inter-State System', chapter 6 of B. Buzan and R. J. B. Jones (eds.), *Change and the Study of International Relations: The Evaded Dimension* (London, Frances Pinter, and New York, St Martins Press, 1981).

40 A further complicating factor is that the issues are cross-cutting. Success along one dimension will not necessarily produce success on the other dimensions: it might even produce set-backs, as when 'progress' in economic development sometimes results in women being relatively or absolutely worse off. The status of women in society is the most extensive of the issues, as it is an aspect of virtually all other issues.

41 A second example of this process was the Libyan initiative which led to the International Year for Disabled Persons.

Appendix 1
The Legal Relationship between the United Nations and Non-Governmental Organizations

Charter of the United Nations

Article 71. The Economic and Social Council may make suitable arrangements for consultation with non-governmental organizations which are concerned with matters within its competence. Such arrangements may be made with international organizations and, where appropriate, with national organizations after consultations with the Member of the United Nations concerned.

ECOSOC Resolution 1296(XLIV)

Adopted unanimously on 23 May 1968.
The Economic and Social Council,
Having regard to Article 71 of the Charter of the United Nations,
Recognizing that arrangements for consultation with non-governmental organizations provide an important means of furthering the purposes and principles of the United Nations.
Considering that consultations between the Council and its subsidiary organs and the non-governmental organizations should be developed to the fullest practicable extent,
Approves the following arrangements, which supersede those set out in its resolution 288 B (X) of 27 February 1950:

ARRANGEMENTS FOR CONSULTATION
WITH NON-GOVERNMENTAL ORGANIZATIONS
Part I
PRINCIPLES TO BE APPLIED IN THE ESTABLISHMENT
OF CONSULTATIVE RELATIONS

The following principles shall be applied in establishing consultative relations with non-governmental organizations:

1. The organization shall be concerned with matters falling within the competence of the Economic and Social Council with respect to international economic, social, cultural, educational, health, scientific, technological and related matters and to questions of human rights.

2. The aims and purposes of the organization shall be in conformity with the spirit, purposes and principles of the Charter of the United Nations.

3. The organization shall undertake to support the work of the United Nations and to promote knowledge of its principles and activities, in accordance with its own aims and purposes and the nature and scope of its competence and activities.

4. The organization shall be of representative character and of recognized international standing; it shall represent a substantial proportion, and express the views of major sections, of the population or of the organized persons within the particular field of its competence, covering, where possible, a substantial number of countries in different regions of the world. Where there exist a number of organizations with similar objectives, interests and basic views in a given field, they shall, for the purposes of consultation with the Council, form a joint committee or other body authorized to carry on such consultation for the group as a whole. It is understood that when a minority opinion develops on a particular point within such a committee, it shall be presented along with the opinion of the majority.

5. The organization shall have an established headquarters, with an executive officer. It shall have a democratically adopted constitution, a copy of which shall be deposited with the Secretary-General of the United Nations, and which shall provide for the determination of policy by a conference, congress or other representative body, and for an executive organ responsible to the policy-making body.

6. The organization shall have authority to speak for its members through its authorized representatives. Evidence of this authority shall be presented, if requested.

7. Subject to paragraph 9 below, the organization shall be international in its structure, with members who exercise voting rights in relation to the policies or action of the international organization. Any international organization which is not established by inter-governmental agreement shall be considered as a non-governmental organization for the purpose of these arrangements, including organizations which accept members designated by governmental authorities, provided that such membership does not interfere with the free expression of views of the organization.

8. The basic resources of the international organization shall be derived in the main part from contributions of the national affiliates or other components or from individual members. Where voluntary contributions have been received, their amounts and donors shall be faithfully revealed to the Council Committee on Non-Governmental Organizations. Where, however, the above criterion is not fulfilled and an organization is financed from other sources, it must explain to the satisfaction of the Committee its reasons for not meeting the requirements laid down in this paragraph. Any financial contribution or other support, direct or indirect, from a Government to the international organization shall

be openly declared to the Committee through the Secretary-General and fully recorded in the financial and other records of the organization and shall be devoted to purposes in accordance with the aims of the United Nations.

9. National organizations shall normally present their views through international non-governmental organizations to which they belong. It would not, save in exceptional cases, be appropriate to admit national organizations which are affiliated to an international non-governmental organization covering the same subjects on an international basis. National organizations, however, may be admitted after consultation with the Member State concerned in order to help achieve a balanced and effective representation of non-governmental organizations reflecting major interests of all regions and areas of the world, or where they have special experience upon which the Council may wish to draw.

10. Consultative arrangements shall not normally be made with an international organization which is a member of a committee or group composed of international organizations with which consultative arrangements have been made.

11; In considering the establishment of consultative relations with a non-governmental organization, the Council will take into account whether the field of activity of the organization is wholly or mainly within the field of a specialized agency, and whether or not it could be admitted when it has, or may have, a consultative arrangement with a specialized agency.

Part II
PRINCIPLES GOVERNING THE NATURE OF THE
CONSULTATIVE ARRANGEMENTS

12. A clear distinction is drawn in the Charter of the United Nations between participation without vote in the deliberations of the Council and the arrangements for consultation. Under Articles 69 and 70, participation is provided for only in the case of States not members of the Council, and of specialized agencies. Article 71, applying to non-governmental organizations, provides for suitable arrangements for consultation. This distinction, deliberately made in the Charter, is fundamental and the arrangements for consultation should not be such as to accord to non-governmental organizations the same rights of participation as are accorded to States not members of the Council and to the specialized agencies brought into relationship with the United Nations.

13. The arrangements should not be such as to overburden the Council or transform it from a body for co-ordination of policy and action, as contemplated in the Charter, into a general forum for discussion.

14. Decisions on arrangements for consultation should be guided by the principle that consultative arrangements are to be made, on the one hand, for the purpose of enabling the Council or one of its bodies to secure expert information or advice from organizations having special competence in the subjects for which consultative arrangements are made, and, on the other hand, to enable organizations which represent important elements of public opinion in

a large number of countries to express their views. Therefore, the arrangements for consultation made with each organization should involve only the subjects for which that organization has a special competence or in which it has a special interest. The organizations given consultative status should be limited to those whose international activities in fields set out in paragraph 1 above qualify them to make a significant contribution to the work of the Council and should, in sum, as far as possible reflect in a balanced way the major viewpoints or interests in these fields in all areas and regions of the world.

Part III
ESTABLISHMENT OF CONSULTATIVE RELATIONSHIPS

15. In establishing consultative relationships with each organization, regard shall be had to the nature and scope of its activities and to the assistance it may be expected to give to the Council or its subsidiary bodies in carrying out the functions set out in Chapters IX and X of the Charter of the United Nations.

16. In establishing consultative relations with organizations, the Council will distinguish between:

(*a*) Organizations which are concerned with most of the activities of the Council and can demonstrate to the satisfaction of the Council that they have marked and sustained contributions to make to the achievement of the objectives of the United Nations in the fields set out in paragraph 1 above, and are closely involved with the economic and social life of the peoples of the areas they represent and whose membership, which should be considerable, is broadly representative of major segments of population in a large number of countries (to be known as organizations in general consultative status, Category I);

(*b*) Organizations which have a special competence in, and are concerned specifically with, only a few of the fields of activity covered by the Council, and which are known internationally within the fields for which they have or seek consultative status (to be known as organizations in special consultative status, Category II).

17. Organizations accorded consultative status in Category II because of their interest in the field of human rights should have a general international concern with this matter, not restricted to the interests of a particular group of persons, a single nationality or the situation in a single State or restricted group of States. Special consideration shall be given to the applications of organizations in this field whose aims place stress on combating colonialism, *apartheid*, racial intolerance and other gross violations of human rights and fundamental freedoms.

18. Major organizations one of whose primary purposes is to promote the aims, objectives and purposes of the United Nations and a furtherance of the understanding of its work may be accorded consultative status in Category II.

19. Other organizations which do not have general or special consultative status but which the Council, or the Secretary-General of the United Nations,

in consultation with the Council or its Committee on Non-Governmental Organizations, considers can make occasional and useful contributions to the work of the Council or its subsidiary bodies or other United Nations bodies within their competence shall be included in a list (to be known as the Roster). This list may also include organizations in consultative status or similar relationship with a specialized agency or a United Nations body. These organizations shall be available for consultation at the request of the Council or its subsidiary bodies. The fact that an organization is on the Roster shall not in itself be regarded as a qualification for general or special consultative status should an organization seek such status.

Part IV
CONSULTATION WITH THE COUNCIL
Provisional Agenda

20. The provisional agenda of the Council shall be communicated to organizations in Categories I and II and to those on the Roster.

21. Organizations in Category I may propose to the Council Committee on Non-Governmental Organizations that the Committee request the Secretary-General to place items of special interest to the organizations on the provisional agenda of the Council.

Attendance at Meetings

22. Organizations in Categories I and II may designate authorized representatives to sit as observers at public meetings of the Council and its subsidiary bodies. Those on the Roster may have representatives present at such meetings concerned with matters within their field of competence.

Written Statements

23. Written statements relevant to the work of the Council may be submitted by organizations in Categories I and II on subjects in which these organizations have a special competence. Such statements shall be circulated by the Secretary-General of the United Nations to the members of the Council, except those statements which have become obsolete, for example, those dealing with matters already disposed of and those which had already been circulated in some other form.

24. The following conditions shall be observed regarding the submission and circulation of such statements:

(*a*) The written statement shall be submitted in one of the official languages.

(*b*) It shall be submitted in sufficient time for appropriate consultation to take place between the Secretary-General and the organization before circulation.

(*c*) The organization shall give due consideration to any comments which the Secretary-General may make in the course of such consultation before transmitting the statement in final form.

(*d*) A written statement submitted by an organization in Category I will be circulated in full if it does not exceed 2,000 words, Where a statement is in excess of 2,000 words, the organization shall submit a summary which will be circulated or shall supply sufficient copies of the full text in the working languages for distribution. A statement will also be circulated in full, however, upon a specific request of the Council or its Committee on Non-Governmental Organizations.

(*e*) A written statement submitted by an organization in Category II or on the Roster will be circulated in full if it does not exceed 500 words. Where a statement is in excess of 500 words, the organization shall submit a summary which will be circulated; such statements will be circulated in full, however, upon a specific request of the Council or its Committee on Non-Governmental Organizations.

(*f*) The Secretary-General, in consultation with the President of the Council, or the Council or its Committee on Non-Governmental Organizations, may invite organizations on the Roster to submit written statements. The provisions of sub-paragraphs (*a*), (*b*), (*c*) and (*e*) above shall apply to such statements.

(*g*) A written statement or summary, as the case may be, will be circulated by the Secretary-General in the working languages, and, upon the request of a member of the Council, in any of the official languages.

Hearings

25. (*a*) The Council Committee on Non-Governmental Organizations shall make recommendations to the Council as to which organizations in Category I should be heard by the Council or by its sessional committees and on which items they should be heard. Such organizations shall be entitled to make one statement to the Council or the appropriate sessional committee, subject to the approval of the Council or of the sessional committee concerned. In the absence of a subsidiary body of the Council with jurisdiction in a major field of interest to the Council and to an organization in Category II, the Committee may recommend that an organization in Category II be heard by the Council on the subject in its field of interest.

(*b*) Whenever the Council discusses the substance of an item proposed by a non-governmental organization in Category I and included in the agenda of the Council, such an organization shall be entitled to present orally to the Council or a sessional committee of the Council, as appropriate, an introductory statement of an expository nature. Such an organization may be invited by the President of the Council or the Chairman of the committee, with the consent of the relevant body, to make, in the course of the discussion of the item before the Council or before the committee, an additional statement for purposes of clarification.

Part V

CONSULTATION WITH COMMISSIONS AND OTHER
SUBSIDIARY ORGANS OF THE COUNCIL

Provisional Agenda

26. The provisional agenda of sessions of commissions and other subsidiary organs of the Council shall be communicated to organizations in Categories I and II and those on the Roster.

27. Organizations in Category I may propose items for the provisional agenda of commissions, subject to the following conditions:

(*a*) An organization which intends to propose such an item shall inform the Secretary-General of the United Nations at least sixty-three days before the commencement of the session and before formally proposing an item shall give due consideration to any comments the Secretary-General may make.

(*b*) The proposal shall be formally submitted with the relevant basic documentation not later than forty-nine days before the commencement of the session. The item shall be included in the agenda of the commission if it is adopted by a two-thirds majority of those present and voting.

Attendance at Meetings

28. Organizations in Categories I and II may designate authorized representatives to sit as observers at public meetings of the commissions and other subsidiary organs of the Council. Organizations on the Roster may have representatives present at such meetings which are concerned with matters within their field of competence.

Written Statements

29. Written statements relevant to the work of the commissions or other subsidiary organs may be submitted by organizations in Categories I and II on subjects for which these organizations have a special competence. Such statements shall be circulated by the Secretary-General to members of the commission or other subsidiary organs, except those statements which have become obsolete, for example those dealing with matters already disposed of and those which have already been circulated in some other form to members of the commission or other subsidiary organs.

30. The following conditions shall be observed regarding the submission and circulation of such written statements:

(*a*) The written statement shall be submitted in one of the official languages.

(*b*) It shall be submitted in sufficient time for appropriate consultation to take place between the Secretary-General and the organization before circulation.

(*c*) The organization shall give due consideration to any comments which the Secretary-General may make in the course of such consultation before transmitting the statement in final form.

(*d*) A written statement submitted by an organization in Category I will be circulated in full if it does not exceed 2,000 words. Where a statement is in excess of 2,000 words, the organization shall submit a summary, which will be circulated, or shall supply sufficient copies of the full text in the working languages for distribution. A statement will also be circulated in full, however, upon the specific request of the commission or other subsidiary organs.

(*e*) A written statement submitted by an organization in Category II will be circulated in full if it does not exceed 1,500 words. Where a statement is in excess of 1,500 words, the organization shall submit a summary which will be circulated, or shall supply sufficient copies of the full text in the working languages for distribution. A statement will also be circulated in full, however, upon the specific request of the commission or other subsidiary organs.

(*f*) The Secretary-General, in consultation with the Chairman of the relevant commission or other subsidiary organ, or the commission or other subsidiary organ itself, may invite organizations on the Roster to submit writtent statements. The provisions in sub-paragraphs (*a*), (*b*), (*c*) and (*e*) above shall apply to such statements.

(*g*) A written statement or summary, as the case may be, will be circulated by the Secretary-General in the working languages and, upon the request of a member of the commission or other subsidiary organ, in any of the official languages.

Hearings

31. (*a*) The commission or other subsidiary organs may consult with organizations in Categories I and II either directly or through a committee or committees established for the purpose. In all cases, such consultations may be arranged on the request of the organization.

(*b*) On the recommendation of the Secretary-General and at the request of the commission or other subsidiary organs, organizations on the Roster may also be heard by the commission or other subsidiary organs.

Special Studies

32. Subject to the relevant rules of procedure on financial implications, a commission may recommend that an organization which has special competence in a particular field should undertake specific studies or investigations or prepare specific papers for the commission. The limitations of paragraph 30 (*d*) and (*e*) above shall not apply in this case.

Part VI

CONSULTATIONS WITH *AD HOC* COMMITTEES
OF THE COUNCIL

33. The arrangements for consultation between *ad hoc* committees of the Council authorized to meet between sessions of the Council and organizations in Categories I and II and on the Roster shall follow those approved for commissions of the Council, unless the Council or the committee decides otherwise.

Part VII

CONSULTATION WITH INTERNATIONAL CONFERENCES
CALLED BY THE COUNCIL

34. The Council may invite non-governmental organizations in Categories
I and II and on the Roster to take part in conferences called by the Council
under Article 62, paragraph 4, of the Charter of the United Nations. The organizations shall be entitled to the same rights and privileges and shall undertake
the same responsibilities as at sessions of the Council itself, unless the Council
decides otherwise.

Part VIII

SUSPENSION AND WITHDRAWAL OF
CONSULTATIVE STATUS

35. Organizations granted consultative status by the Council and those on
the Roster shall conform at all times to the principles governing the establishment and nature of their consultative relations with the Council. In periodically
reviewing the activities of the non-governmental organizations on the basis of
reports submitted under paragraph 40 (*b*) below and other relevant information,
the Council Committee on Non-Governmental Organizations shall determine
the extent to which the organizations have complied with the principles
governing consultative status and have contributed to the work of the Council,
and may recommend to the Council suspension or exclusion from consultative
status of organizations which have not met the requirements for consultative
status as set forth in the present resolution.

36. The consultative status of non-governmental organizations with the
Economic and Social Council and the listing of those on the Roster shall be
suspended up to three years or withdrawn in the following cases:

(*a*) If there exists substantiated evidence of secret governmental financial
influence to induce an organization to undertake acts contrary to the purposes
and principles of the Charter of the United Nations;

(*b*) If the organization clearly abuses its consultative status by systematically
engaging in unsubstantiated or politically motivated acts against States Members
of the United Nations contrary to and incompatible with the principles of the
Charter;

(*c*) If, within the preceding three years, an organization had not made any
positive or effective contribution to the work of the Council or its commissions
or other subsidiary organs.

37. The consultative status of organizations in Categories I and II and the
listing of those on the Roster will be suspended or withdrawn by the decision
of the Economic and Social Council on the recommendation of its Committee
on Non-Governmental Organizations.

38. An organization whose consultative status or whose listing on the Roster
is withdrawn may be entitled to reapply for consultative status or for inclusion

on the Roster not sooner than three years after the effective date of such withdrawal.

Part IX
COUNCIL COMMITTEE ON NON-GOVERNMENTAL ORGANIZATIONS

39. The members of the Council Committee on Non-Governmental Organizations shall be elected at the first session of the Council each year, on the basis of equitable geographical representation, in accordance with Council resolution 1099(XL) of 4 March 1966 and rule 82 of the rules of procedure of the Council. The Committee shall elect its Chairman and other officers as necessary. A member shall serve until the next election unless it ceases to be a member of the Council.

40. The functions of the Committee shall include the following:

(*a*) The Committee shall hold a session before the first session of the Council each year to consider applications for consultative status in Categories I and II and for listing on the Roster made by non-governmental organizations and requests for changes in status, and to make recommendations thereon to the Council. Organizations shall give due consideration to any comments on technical matters which the Secretary-General of the United Nations may make in receiving such applications for the Committee. The Committee shall consider at each such session applications received by the Secretary-General not later than 1 June of the preceding year, on which sufficient data have been distributed to the members of the Committee not later than six weeks before the applications are to be considered. Reapplication by an organization for status, or a request for a change in status, shall be considered by the Committee at the earliest at its first session in the second year following the session at which the substance of the previous application or request was considered, unless at the time of such consideration it was decided otherwise.

(*b*) Organizations in consultative status in Categories I and II shall submit to the Council Committee on Non-Governmental Organizations through the Secretary-General every fourth year a brief report of their activities, specifically as regards the support they have given to the work of the United Nations. Based on findings of the Committee's examination of the report and other relevant information, the Committee may recommend to the Council any reclassification in status of the organization concerned as it deems appropriate. However, under exceptional circumstances, the Committee may ask for such a report from an individual organization in Category I or II or on the Roster, between the regular report dates.

(*c*) The Committee may consult, in connexion with sessions of the Council or at such other times as it may decide, with organizations in Categories I and II on matters within their competence, other than items on the agenda of the Council, on which the Council or the Committee or the organization requests consultation. The Committee shall report to the Council on such consultations.

(*d*) The Committee may consult, in connexion with any particular session of the Council, with organizations in Categories I and II on matters within the competence of the organizations concerning specific items already on the provisional agenda of the Council on which the Council or the Committee or the organization requests consultation, and shall make recommendations as to which organizations, subject to the provisions of paragraph 25 (*a*) above, should be heard by the Council or the appropriate committee and regarding which subjects should be heard. The Committee shall report to the Council on such consultations.

(*e*) The Committee shall consider matters concerning non-governmental organizations which may be referred to it by the Council or by commissions.

(*f*) The Committee shall consult with the Secretary-General, as appropriate, on matters affecting the consultative arrangements under Article 71 of the Charter, and arising therefrom.

41. The Committee, in considering a request from a non-governmental organization in Category I that an item be placed on the agenda of the Council, shall take into account, among other things:

(*a*) The adequacy of the documentation submitted by the organization;

(*b*) The extent to which it is considered that the item lends itself to early and constructive action by the Council;

(*c*) The possibility that the item might be more appropriately dealt with elsewhere than in the Council.

42. Any decision by the Council Committee on Non-Governmental Organizations not to grant a request submitted by a non-governmental organization in Category I that an item be placed on the provisional agenda of the Council shall be considered as final unless the Council decides otherwise.

Part X
CONSULTATION WITH THE SECRETARIAT

43. The Secretariat should be so organized as to enable it to carry out the duties assigned to it concerning the consultative arrangements as set forth in the present resolution.

44. All organizations in consultative relationship shall be able to consult with officers of the appropriate sections of the Secretariat on matters in which there is a mutual interest or a mutal concern. Such consultation shall be upon the request of the non-governmental organization or upon the request of the Secretary-General of the United Nations.

45. The Secretary-General may request organizations in Categories I and II and those on the Roster to carry out specific studies or prepare specific papers, subject to the relevant financial regulations.

46. The Secretary-General shall be authorized, within the means at his disposal, to offer to non-governmental organizations in consultative relationship facilities which include:

(*a*) Prompt and efficient distribution of such documents of the Council and its subsidiary bodies as shall in the judgement of the Secretary-General be appropriate;

(*b*) Access to the press documentation services provided by the United Nations;

(*c*) Arrangement of informal discussions on matters of special interest to groups or organizations;

(*d*) Use of the libraries of the United Nations;

(*e*) Provision of accommodation for conferences or smaller meetings of consultative organizations on the work of the Economic and Social Council.

(*f*) Appropriate seating arrangements and facilities for obtaining documents during public meetings of the General Assembly dealing with matters in the economic and social fields.

ECOSOC Resolution 1919(LVIII)

Adopted without a vote on 5 May 1975

The Economic and Social Council,

Considering that in its resolution 454 (XIV) of 28 July 1952 it decided that all communications emanating from non-governmental organizations in consultative status containing complaints of alleged violations of human rights should be dealt with not under the rules of consultative relationship but under the decisions for the inclusion of such material in confidential lists of communications prepared for the Commission on Human Rights, as further set out in paragraph 2 (*b*) of Council resolution 728 F (XXVIII) of 30 July 1959,

Considering further that it had been clearly laid down in paragraph 8 of its resolution 1503 (XLVIII) of 27 May 1970 that all actions envisaged in the implementation of that resolution by the Sub-Commission on Prevention of Discrimination and Protection of Minorities of the Commission on Human Rights should remain confidential until such time as the Commission might decide to make recommendations to the Council,

Recognizing that non-governmental organizations have an important role to play in the promotion and protection of human rights,

Having been made aware by the Commission on Human Rights that some non-governmental organizations have occasionally failed to observe the requirements of confidentiality stated in paragraph 8 of Council resolution 1503 (XLVIII),

Having also been made aware by the Commission on Human Rights that, in their oral interventions, some non-governmental organizations have occasionally failed to observe fully the terms of paragraph 36 (*b*) of Council resolution 1296 (XLIV) of 23 May 1968,

1. *Appeals urgently* for the strict observance of the requirements of confidentiality stated in paragraph 8 of Council resoltuion 1503 (XLVIII);

2. *Confirms* that communications from non-governmental organizations containing complaints of alleged violations of human rights shall be handled according to the provisions of Council resolutions 454 (XIV) and 728 F (XXVIII), paragraph 2 (*b*);

3. *Decides* that in future non-governmental organizations in consultative status:

(*a*) Must comply without exception as regards their submissions both in written and oral form, in so far as they relate to allegations or complaints on human rights, with the provisions of paragraph 36 (*b*) of Council resolution 1296 (XLIV);

(*b*) Must also observe strictly the provisions of paragraph 8 of Council resolution 1503 (XLVIII);

4. *Decides* that any non-governmental organization failing to observer the provisions of paragraph 36 (*b*) of Council resolution 1296 (XLIV) may render its consultative status subject to suspension or withdrawal under the terms of that resolution;

5. *Reminds* the Sub-Commission on Prevention of Discrimination and Protection of Minorities of the conditions of admissibility of communications approved in its resolution 1 (XXIV) and requests it to apply these criteria strictly;

6. *Decides* that the Council Committee on Non-Governmental Organizations should continue to examine carefully the activities of non-governmental organizations, bearing in mind the provisions of the present resolution.

Appendix 2
Non-Governmental Organizations in Consultative Status with the Economic and Social Council of the United Nations

There are currently 640 NGOs which have been granted consultative status, under the provisions detailed in Appendix 1. Of these, 31 are in Category I and are all listed below, 215 are in Category II, while 394 are on the Roster. There are three ways of gaining a place on the Roster: 152 NGOs have been approved by ECOSOC; 28 have been recommended by the UN Secretary-General; and 214 are on the list by virtue of having consultative status with specialized agencies or other UN bodies.

While the 31 NGOs in Category I are all major organizations, with members in a large number of countries, there are also some very important NGOs which are in Category II. Among the most prominent are the International Air Transport Association, the International Commission of Jurists, the International Committee of the Red Cross, the International Union for the Conservation of Nature and Natural Resources, the Christian Democratic World Union and the Socialist International. In addition most of the world Christian federations are in Category II, including the Commission of the Churches on International Affairs of the World Council of Churches, the Baptist World Alliance, the Friends World Committee for Consultation, the Lutheran World Federation and the Salvation Army. The overwhelming majority of the 394 NGOs on the Roster are highly specialized, although this can still mean that they are important within their particular field. They vary from the International Association for Suicide Prevention to the International Association of Fish Meal Manufacturers or the International Association of Lighthouse Authorities.

Of the groups chosen for this study, the PLO does not have consultative status with ECOSOC, but can address ECOSOC in its capacity of an Observer to the UN and it even has full membership of the subsidiary Economic Commission for West Asia. Amnesty International, the Anti-Apartheid Movement and Oxfam are all in Category II and Friends of the Earth is on the Roster. The international women's organizations are in all three categories. The status with ECOSOC of other NGOs which have been mentioned in this book is given in the Index of Non-Governmental Organizations.

NGOs in ECOSOC Category I

International Alliance of Women — Equal Rights, Equal Responsibilities
International Association of French-Speaking Parliamentarians
International Chamber of Commerce
International Confederation of Free Trade Unions
International Co-operative Alliance
International Council of Voluntary Agencies (ICVA)
International Council of Women
International Council on Social Welfare
International Federation of Agricultural Producers
International Federation of Business and Professional Women
International Organization for Standardization (ISO)
International Organization of Consumers Unions (IOCU)
International Organization of Employers
International Planned Parenthood Federation
International Social Security Association (ISSA)
International Union of Local Authorities
International Youth and Student Movement for the United Nations
Inter-Parliamentary Union
League of Red Cross Societies
Muslim World League
Organization of African Trade Union Unity (OATUU)
Society for International Development (SID)
United Towns Organization
Women's International Democratic Federation
World Assembly of Youth (WAY)
World Confederation of Labour
World Federation of Democratic Youth (WFDY)
World Federation of Trade Unions (WFTU)
World Federation of United Nations Associations (WFUNA)
World Muslim Congress
World Veterans Federation

The information for this appendix is taken from United Nations documents E/1981/INF/2 of 3 February 1981, E/1981/INF.2/Corr. 1 of 23 July 1981 and E/1981/INF.2/Add. 1 of 8 July 1981.

Index of Non-Governmental Organizations

If the NGO has consultative status with the UN ECOSOC (see Appendix 2), this is indicated after the index entry, with (I) for Category I status, (II) for Category II and (R) for the Roster.

General Index

Abbreviations used in the Indexes

Assoc.	Association	Confed.	Confederation	Int.	International
Co.	Council	Dev.	Development	Nat.	National
Comm.	Committee	Fed.	Federation	Org.	Organization
Commiss.	Commission	Inst.	Institute	Soc.	Society
Conf.	Conference				

DATE DUE

DEC 1 3 1991			
NOV 1 9 2000			
DEC 0 1 2001			
FEB 0 5 2004			